FREE Study Skills DVD Offer

Dear Customer,

Thank you for your purchase from Mometrix! We consider it an honor and a privilege that you have purchased our product and we want to ensure your satisfaction.

As a way of showing our appreciation and to help us better serve you, we have developed a Study Skills DVD that we would like to give you for <u>FREE</u>. This DVD covers our *best practices* for getting ready for your exam, from how to use our study materials to how to best prepare for the day of the test.

All that we ask is that you email us with feedback that would describe your experience so far with our product. Good, bad, or indifferent, we want to know what you think!

To get your FREE Study Skills DVD, email <u>freedvd@mometrix.com</u> with *FREE STUDY SKILLS DVD* in the subject line and the following information in the body of the email:

- The name of the product you purchased.
- Your product rating on a scale of 1-5, with 5 being the highest rating.
- Your feedback. It can be long, short, or anything in between. We just want to know your impressions and experience so far with our product. (Good feedback might include how our study material met your needs and ways we might be able to make it even better. You could highlight features that you found helpful or features that you think we should add.)
- Your full name and shipping address where you would like us to send your free DVD.

If you have any questions or concerns, please don't hesitate to contact me directly.

Thanks again!

Sincerely,

Jay Willis
Vice President
<u>jay.willis@mometrix.com</u>
1-800-673-8175

SAT

Prep 2020 & 2021

SAT Secrets Test Prep Book
for the Math, Reading, &
Writing and Language Sections

Full-Length
Practice Test

Detailed Answer
Explanations

Includes
Step-by-Step
Review Video
Tutorials

Written and edited by the Mometrix College Admissions Test Team

Printed in the United States of America

This paper meets the requirements of ANSI/NISO Z39.48-1992 (Permanence of Paper).

Mometrix offers volume discount pricing to institutions. For more information or a price quote, please contact our sales department at sales@mometrix.com or 888-248-1219.

Mometrix Media LLC is not affiliated with or endorsed by any official testing organization. All organizational and test names are trademarks of their respective owners.

Paperback
ISBN 13: 978-1-5167-1241-0
ISBN 10: 1-5167-1241-2

DEAR FUTURE EXAM SUCCESS STORY

First of all, **THANK YOU** for purchasing Mometrix study materials!

Second, congratulations! You are one of the few determined test-takers who are committed to doing whatever it takes to excel on your exam. **You have come to the right place.** We developed these study materials with one goal in mind: to deliver you the information you need in a format that's concise and easy to use.

In addition to optimizing your guide for the content of the test, we've outlined our recommended steps for breaking down the preparation process into small, attainable goals so you can make sure you stay on track.

We've also analyzed the entire test-taking process, identifying the most common pitfalls and showing how you can overcome them and be ready for any curveball the test throws you.

Standardized testing is one of the biggest obstacles on your road to success, which only increases the importance of doing well in the high-pressure, high-stakes environment of test day. Your results on this test could have a significant impact on your future, and this guide provides the information and practical advice to help you achieve your full potential on test day.

Your success is our success

We would love to hear from you! If you would like to share the story of your exam success or if you have any questions or comments in regard to our products, please contact us at **800-673-8175** or **support@mometrix.com**.

Thanks again for your business and we wish you continued success!

Sincerely,
The Mometrix Test Preparation Team

TABLE OF CONTENTS

Introduction

Thank you for purchasing this resource! You have made the choice to prepare yourself for a test that could have a huge impact on your future, and this guide is designed to help you be fully ready for test day. Obviously, it's important to have a solid understanding of the test material, but you also need to be prepared for the unique environment and stressors of the test, so that you can perform to the best of your abilities.

For this purpose, the first section that appears in this guide is the **Secret Keys**. We've devoted countless hours to meticulously researching what works and what doesn't, and we've boiled down our findings to the five most impactful steps you can take to improve your performance on the test. We start at the beginning with study planning and move through the preparation process, all the way to the testing strategies that will help you get the most out of what you know when you're finally sitting in front of the test.

We recommend that you start preparing for your test as far in advance as possible. However, if you've bought this guide as a last-minute study resource and only have a few days before your test, we recommend that you skip over the first two Secret Keys since they address a long-term study plan.

If you struggle with **test anxiety**, we strongly encourage you to check out our recommendations for how you can overcome it. Test anxiety is a formidable foe, but it can be beaten, and we want to make sure you have the tools you need to defeat it.

Secret Key #1 – Plan Big, Study Small

There's a lot riding on your performance. If you want to ace this test, you're going to need to keep your skills sharp and the material fresh in your mind. You need a plan that lets you review everything you need to know while still fitting in your schedule. We'll break this strategy down into three categories.

Information Organization

Start with the information you already have: the official test outline. From this, you can make a complete list of all the concepts you need to cover before the test. Organize these concepts into groups that can be studied together, and create a list of any related vocabulary you need to learn so you can brush up on any difficult terms. You'll want to keep this vocabulary list handy once you actually start studying since you may need to add to it along the way.

Time Management

Once you have your set of study concepts, decide how to spread them out over the time you have left before the test. Break your study plan into small, clear goals so you have a manageable task for each day and know exactly what you're doing. Then just focus on one small step at a time. When you manage your time this way, you don't need to spend hours at a time studying. Studying a small block of content for a short period each day helps you retain information better and avoid stressing over how much you have left to do. You can relax knowing that you have a plan to cover everything in time. In order for this strategy to be effective though, you have to start studying early and stick to your schedule. Avoid the exhaustion and futility that comes from last-minute cramming!

Study Environment

The environment you study in has a big impact on your learning. Studying in a coffee shop, while probably more enjoyable, is not likely to be as fruitful as studying in a quiet room. It's important to keep distractions to a minimum. You're only planning to study for a short block of time, so make the most of it. Don't pause to check your phone or get up to find a snack. It's also important to **avoid multitasking**. Research has consistently shown that multitasking will make your studying dramatically less effective. Your study area should also be comfortable and well-lit so you don't have the distraction of straining your eyes or sitting on an uncomfortable chair.

The time of day you study is also important. You want to be rested and alert. Don't wait until just before bedtime. Study when you'll be most likely to comprehend and remember. Even better, if you know what time of day your test will be, set that time aside for study. That way your brain will be used to working on that subject at that specific time and you'll have a better chance of recalling information.

Finally, it can be helpful to team up with others who are studying for the same test. Your actual studying should be done in as isolated an environment as possible, but the work of organizing the information and setting up the study plan can be divided up. In between study sessions, you can discuss with your teammates the concepts that you're all studying and quiz each other on the details. Just be sure that your teammates are as serious about the test as you are. If you find that your study time is being replaced with social time, you might need to find a new team.

2

Secret Key #2 – Make Your Studying Count

You're devoting a lot of time and effort to preparing for this test, so you want to be absolutely certain it will pay off. This means doing more than just reading the content and hoping you can remember it on test day. It's important to make every minute of study count. There are two main areas you can focus on to make your studying count:

Retention

It doesn't matter how much time you study if you can't remember the material. You need to make sure you are retaining the concepts. To check your retention of the information you're learning, try recalling it at later times with minimal prompting. Try carrying around flashcards and glance at one or two from time to time or ask a friend who's also studying for the test to quiz you.

To enhance your retention, look for ways to put the information into practice so that you can apply it rather than simply recalling it. If you're using the information in practical ways, it will be much easier to remember. Similarly, it helps to solidify a concept in your mind if you're not only reading it to yourself but also explaining it to someone else. Ask a friend to let you teach them about a concept you're a little shaky on (or speak aloud to an imaginary audience if necessary). As you try to summarize, define, give examples, and answer your friend's questions, you'll understand the concepts better and they will stay with you longer. Finally, step back for a big picture view and ask yourself how each piece of information fits with the whole subject. When you link the different concepts together and see them working together as a whole, it's easier to remember the individual components.

Finally, practice showing your work on any multi-step problems, even if you're just studying. Writing out each step you take to solve a problem will help solidify the process in your mind, and you'll be more likely to remember it during the test.

Modality

Modality simply refers to the means or method by which you study. Choosing a study modality that fits your own individual learning style is crucial. No two people learn best in exactly the same way, so it's important to know your strengths and use them to your advantage.

For example, if you learn best by visualization, focus on visualizing a concept in your mind and draw an image or a diagram. Try color-coding your notes, illustrating them, or creating symbols that will trigger your mind to recall a learned concept. If you learn best by hearing or discussing information, find a study partner who learns the same way or read aloud to yourself. Think about how to put the information in your own words. Imagine that you are giving a lecture on the topic and record yourself so you can listen to it later.

For any learning style, flashcards can be helpful. Organize the information so you can take advantage of spare moments to review. Underline key words or phrases. Use different colors for different categories. Mnemonic devices (such as creating a short list in which every item starts with the same letter) can also help with retention. Find what works best for you and use it to store the information in your mind most effectively and easily.

Secret Key #3 – Practice the Right Way

Your success on test day depends not only on how many hours you put into preparing, but also on whether you prepared the right way. It's good to check along the way to see if your studying is paying off. One of the most effective ways to do this is by taking practice tests to evaluate your progress. Practice tests are useful because they show exactly where you need to improve. Every time you take a practice test, pay special attention to these three groups of questions:

- The questions you got wrong
- The questions you had to guess on, even if you guessed right
- The questions you found difficult or slow to work through

This will show you exactly what your weak areas are, and where you need to devote more study time. Ask yourself why each of these questions gave you trouble. Was it because you didn't understand the material? Was it because you didn't remember the vocabulary? Do you need more repetitions on this type of question to build speed and confidence? Dig into those questions and figure out how you can strengthen your weak areas as you go back to review the material.

Additionally, many practice tests have a section explaining the answer choices. It can be tempting to read the explanation and think that you now have a good understanding of the concept. However, an explanation likely only covers part of the question's broader context. Even if the explanation makes sense, **go back and investigate** every concept related to the question until you're positive you have a thorough understanding.

As you go along, keep in mind that the practice test is just that: practice. Memorizing these questions and answers will not be very helpful on the actual test because it is unlikely to have any of the same exact questions. If you only know the right answers to the sample questions, you won't be prepared for the real thing. **Study the concepts** until you understand them fully, and then you'll be able to answer any question that shows up on the test.

It's important to wait on the practice tests until you're ready. If you take a test on your first day of study, you may be overwhelmed by the amount of material covered and how much you need to learn. Work up to it gradually.

On test day, you'll need to be prepared for answering questions, managing your time, and using the test-taking strategies you've learned. It's a lot to balance, like a mental marathon that will have a big impact on your future. Like training for a marathon, you'll need to start slowly and work your way up. When test day arrives, you'll be ready.

Start with the strategies you've read in the first two Secret Keys—plan your course and study in the way that works best for you. If you have time, consider using multiple study resources to get different approaches to the same concepts. It can be helpful to see difficult concepts from more than one angle. Then find a good source for practice tests. Many times, the test website will suggest potential study resources or provide sample tests.

Practice Test Strategy

If you're able to find at least three practice tests, we recommend this strategy:

UNTIMED AND OPEN-BOOK PRACTICE

Take the first test with no time constraints and with your notes and study guide handy. Take your time and focus on applying the strategies you've learned.

TIMED AND OPEN-BOOK PRACTICE

Take the second practice test open-book as well, but set a timer and practice pacing yourself to finish in time.

TIMED AND CLOSED-BOOK PRACTICE

Take any other practice tests as if it were test day. Set a timer and put away your study materials. Sit at a table or desk in a quiet room, imagine yourself at the testing center, and answer questions as quickly and accurately as possible.

Keep repeating timed and closed-book tests on a regular basis until you run out of practice tests or it's time for the actual test. Your mind will be ready for the schedule and stress of test day, and you'll be able to focus on recalling the material you've learned.

Secret Key #4 – Pace Yourself

Once you're fully prepared for the material on the test, your biggest challenge on test day will be managing your time. Just knowing that the clock is ticking can make you panic even if you have plenty of time left. Work on pacing yourself so you can build confidence against the time constraints of the exam. Pacing is a difficult skill to master, especially in a high-pressure environment, so **practice is vital**.

Set time expectations for your pace based on how much time is available. For example, if a section has 60 questions and the time limit is 30 minutes, you know you have to average 30 seconds or less per question in order to answer them all. Although 30 seconds is the hard limit, set 25 seconds per question as your goal, so you reserve extra time to spend on harder questions. When you budget extra time for the harder questions, you no longer have any reason to stress when those questions take longer to answer.

Don't let this time expectation distract you from working through the test at a calm, steady pace, but keep it in mind so you don't spend too much time on any one question. Recognize that taking extra time on one question you don't understand may keep you from answering two that you do understand later in the test. If your time limit for a question is up and you're still not sure of the answer, mark it and move on, and come back to it later if the time and the test format allow. If the testing format doesn't allow you to return to earlier questions, just make an educated guess; then put it out of your mind and move on.

On the easier questions, be careful not to rush. It may seem wise to hurry through them so you have more time for the challenging ones, but it's not worth missing one if you know the concept and just didn't take the time to read the question fully. Work efficiently but make sure you understand the question and have looked at all of the answer choices, since more than one may seem right at first.

Even if you're paying attention to the time, you may find yourself a little behind at some point. You should speed up to get back on track, but do so wisely. Don't panic; just take a few seconds less on each question until you're caught up. Don't guess without thinking, but do look through the answer choices and eliminate any you know are wrong. If you can get down to two choices, it is often worthwhile to guess from those. Once you've chosen an answer, move on and don't dwell on any that you skipped or had to hurry through. If a question was taking too long, chances are it was one of the harder ones, so you weren't as likely to get it right anyway.

On the other hand, if you find yourself getting ahead of schedule, it may be beneficial to slow down a little. The more quickly you work, the more likely you are to make a careless mistake that will affect your score. You've budgeted time for each question, so don't be afraid to spend that time. Practice an efficient but careful pace to get the most out of the time you have.

Secret Key #5 – Have a Plan for Guessing

When you're taking the test, you may find yourself stuck on a question. Some of the answer choices seem better than others, but you don't see the one answer choice that is obviously correct. What do you do?

The scenario described above is very common, yet most test takers have not effectively prepared for it. Developing and practicing a plan for guessing may be one of the single most effective uses of your time as you get ready for the exam.

In developing your plan for guessing, there are three questions to address:

- When should you start the guessing process?
- How should you narrow down the choices?
- Which answer should you choose?

When to Start the Guessing Process

Unless your plan for guessing is to select C every time (which, despite its merits, is not what we recommend), you need to leave yourself enough time to apply your answer elimination strategies. Since you have a limited amount of time for each question, that means that if you're going to give yourself the best shot at guessing correctly, you have to decide quickly whether or not you will guess.

Of course, the best-case scenario is that you don't have to guess at all, so first, see if you can answer the question based on your knowledge of the subject and basic reasoning skills. Focus on the key words in the question and try to jog your memory of related topics. Give yourself a chance to bring the knowledge to mind, but once you realize that you don't have (or you can't access) the knowledge you need to answer the question, it's time to start the guessing process.

It's almost always better to start the guessing process too early than too late. It only takes a few seconds to remember something and answer the question from knowledge. Carefully eliminating wrong answer choices takes longer. Plus, going through the process of eliminating answer choices can actually help jog your memory.

Summary: Start the guessing process as soon as you decide that you can't answer the question based on your knowledge.

How to Narrow Down the Choices

The next chapter in this book (**Test-Taking Strategies**) includes a wide range of strategies for how to approach questions and how to look for answer choices to eliminate. You will definitely want to read those carefully, practice them, and figure out which ones work best for you. Here though, we're going to address a mindset rather than a particular strategy.

Your chances of guessing an answer correctly depend on how many options you are choosing from.

How many choices you have	How likely you are to guess correctly
5	20%
4	25%
3	33%
2	50%
1	100%

You can see from this chart just how valuable it is to be able to eliminate incorrect answers and make an educated guess, but there are two things that many test takers do that cause them to miss out on the benefits of guessing:

- Accidentally eliminating the correct answer
- Selecting an answer based on an impression

We'll look at the first one here, and the second one in the next section.

To avoid accidentally eliminating the correct answer, we recommend a thought exercise called **the $5 challenge**. In this challenge, you only eliminate an answer choice from contention if you are willing to bet $5 on it being wrong. Why $5? Five dollars is a small but not insignificant amount of money. It's an amount you could afford to lose but wouldn't want to throw away. And while losing $5 once might not hurt too much, doing it twenty times will set you back $100. In the same way, each small decision you make—eliminating a choice here, guessing on a question there—won't by itself impact your score very much, but when you put them all together, they can make a big difference. By holding each answer choice elimination decision to a higher standard, you can reduce the risk of accidentally eliminating the correct answer.

The $5 challenge can also be applied in a positive sense: If you are willing to bet $5 that an answer choice *is* correct, go ahead and mark it as correct.

Summary: Only eliminate an answer choice if you are willing to bet $5 that it is wrong.

8

Which Answer to Choose

You're taking the test. You've run into a hard question and decided you'll have to guess. You've eliminated all the answer choices you're willing to bet $5 on. Now you have to pick an answer. Why do we even need to talk about this? Why can't you just pick whichever one you feel like when the time comes?

The answer to these questions is that if you don't come into the test with a plan, you'll rely on your impression to select an answer choice, and if you do that, you risk falling into a trap. The test writers know that everyone who takes their test will be guessing on some of the questions, so they intentionally write wrong answer choices to seem plausible. You still have to pick an answer though, and if the wrong answer choices are designed to look right, how can you ever be sure that you're not falling for their trap? The best solution we've found to this dilemma is to take the decision out of your hands entirely. Here is the process we recommend:

Once you've eliminated any choices that you are confident (willing to bet $5) are wrong, select the first remaining choice as your answer.

Whether you choose to select the first remaining choice, the second, or the last, the important thing is that you use some preselected standard. Using this approach guarantees that you will not be enticed into selecting an answer choice that looks right, because you are not basing your decision on how the answer choices look.

This is not meant to make you question your knowledge. Instead, it is to help you recognize the difference between your knowledge and your impressions. There's a huge difference between thinking an answer is right because of what you know, and thinking an answer is right because it looks or sounds like it should be right.

Summary: To ensure that your selection is appropriately random, make a predetermined selection from among all answer choices you have not eliminated.

Test-Taking Strategies

This section contains a list of test-taking strategies that you may find helpful as you work through the test. By taking what you know and applying logical thought, you can maximize your chances of answering any question correctly!

It is very important to realize that every question is different and every person is different: no single strategy will work on every question, and no single strategy will work for every person. That's why we've included all of them here, so you can try them out and determine which ones work best for different types of questions and which ones work best for you.

Question Strategies

READ CAREFULLY

Read the question and answer choices carefully. Don't miss the question because you misread the terms. You have plenty of time to read each question thoroughly and make sure you understand what is being asked. Yet a happy medium must be attained, so don't waste too much time. You must read carefully, but efficiently.

CONTEXTUAL CLUES

Look for contextual clues. If the question includes a word you are not familiar with, look at the immediate context for some indication of what the word might mean. Contextual clues can often give you all the information you need to decipher the meaning of an unfamiliar word. Even if you can't determine the meaning, you may be able to narrow down the possibilities enough to make a solid guess at the answer to the question.

PREFIXES

If you're having trouble with a word in the question or answer choices, try dissecting it. Take advantage of every clue that the word might include. Prefixes and suffixes can be a huge help. Usually they allow you to determine a basic meaning. Pre- means before, post- means after, pro - is positive, de- is negative. From prefixes and suffixes, you can get an idea of the general meaning of the word and try to put it into context.

HEDGE WORDS

Watch out for critical hedge words, such as *likely, may, can, sometimes, often, almost, mostly, usually, generally, rarely,* and *sometimes.* Question writers insert these hedge phrases to cover every possibility. Often an answer choice will be wrong simply because it leaves no room for exception. Be on guard for answer choices that have definitive words such as *exactly* and *always.*

SWITCHBACK WORDS

Stay alert for *switchbacks.* These are the words and phrases frequently used to alert you to shifts in thought. The most common switchback words are *but, although,* and *however.* Others include *nevertheless, on the other hand, even though, while, in spite of, despite, regardless of.* Switchback words are important to catch because they can change the direction of the question or an answer choice.

FACE VALUE

When in doubt, use common sense. Accept the situation in the problem at face value. Don't read too much into it. These problems will not require you to make wild assumptions. If you have to go beyond creativity and warp time or space in order to have an answer choice fit the question, then you should move on and consider the other answer choices. These are normal problems rooted in reality. The applicable relationship or explanation may not be readily apparent, but it is there for you to figure out. Use your common sense to interpret anything that isn't clear.

Answer Choice Strategies

ANSWER SELECTION

The most thorough way to pick an answer choice is to identify and eliminate wrong answers until only one is left, then confirm it is the correct answer. Sometimes an answer choice may immediately seem right, but be careful. The test writers will usually put more than one reasonable answer choice on each question, so take a second to read all of them and make sure that the other choices are not equally obvious. As long as you have time left, it is better to read every answer choice than to pick the first one that looks right without checking the others.

ANSWER CHOICE FAMILIES

An answer choice family consists of two (in rare cases, three) answer choices that are very similar in construction and cannot all be true at the same time. If you see two answer choices that are direct opposites or parallels, one of them is usually the correct answer. For instance, if one answer choice says that quantity x increases and another either says that quantity x decreases (opposite) or says that quantity y increases (parallel), then those answer choices would fall into the same family. An answer choice that doesn't match the construction of the answer choice family is more likely to be incorrect. Most questions will not have answer choice families, but when they do appear, you should be prepared to recognize them.

ELIMINATE ANSWERS

Eliminate answer choices as soon as you realize they are wrong, but make sure you consider all possibilities. If you are eliminating answer choices and realize that the last one you are left with is also wrong, don't panic. Start over and consider each choice again. There may be something you missed the first time that you will realize on the second pass.

AVOID FACT TRAPS

Don't be distracted by an answer choice that is factually true but doesn't answer the question. You are looking for the choice that answers the question. Stay focused on what the question is asking for so you don't accidentally pick an answer that is true but incorrect. Always go back to the question and make sure the answer choice you've selected actually answers the question and is not merely a true statement.

EXTREME STATEMENTS

In general, you should avoid answers that put forth extreme actions as standard practice or proclaim controversial ideas as established fact. An answer choice that states the "process should be used in certain situations, if..." is much more likely to be correct than one that states the "process should be discontinued completely." The first is a calm rational statement and doesn't even make a definitive, uncompromising stance, using a hedge word *if* to provide wiggle room, whereas the second choice is a radical idea and far more extreme.

11

BENCHMARK

As you read through the answer choices and you come across one that seems to answer the question well, mentally select that answer choice. This is not your final answer, but it's the one that will help you evaluate the other answer choices. The one that you selected is your benchmark or standard for judging each of the other answer choices. Every other answer choice must be compared to your benchmark. That choice is correct until proven otherwise by another answer choice beating it. If you find a better answer, then that one becomes your new benchmark. Once you've decided that no other choice answers the question as well as your benchmark, you have your final answer.

PREDICT THE ANSWER

Before you even start looking at the answer choices, it is often best to try to predict the answer. When you come up with the answer on your own, it is easier to avoid distractions and traps because you will know exactly what to look for. The right answer choice is unlikely to be word-for-word what you came up with, but it should be a close match. Even if you are confident that you have the right answer, you should still take the time to read each option before moving on.

General Strategies

TOUGH QUESTIONS

If you are stumped on a problem or it appears too hard or too difficult, don't waste time. Move on! Remember though, if you can quickly check for obviously incorrect answer choices, your chances of guessing correctly are greatly improved. Before you completely give up, at least try to knock out a couple of possible answers. Eliminate what you can and then guess at the remaining answer choices before moving on.

CHECK YOUR WORK

Since you will probably not know every term listed and the answer to every question, it is important that you get credit for the ones that you do know. Don't miss any questions through careless mistakes. If at all possible, try to take a second to look back over your answer selection and make sure you've selected the correct answer choice and haven't made a costly careless mistake (such as marking an answer choice that you didn't mean to mark). This quick double check should more than pay for itself in caught mistakes for the time it costs.

PACE YOURSELF

It's easy to be overwhelmed when you're looking at a page full of questions; your mind is confused and full of random thoughts, and the clock is ticking down faster than you would like. Calm down and maintain the pace that you have set for yourself. Especially as you get down to the last few minutes of the test, don't let the small numbers on the clock make you panic. As long as you are on track by monitoring your pace, you are guaranteed to have time for each question.

DON'T RUSH

It is very easy to make errors when you are in a hurry. Maintaining a fast pace in answering questions is pointless if it makes you miss questions that you would have gotten right otherwise. Test writers like to include distracting information and wrong answers that seem right. Taking a little extra time to avoid careless mistakes can make all the difference in your test score. Find a pace that allows you to be confident in the answers that you select.

KEEP MOVING

Panicking will not help you pass the test, so do your best to stay calm and keep moving. Taking deep breaths and going through the answer elimination steps you practiced can help to break through a stress barrier and keep your pace.

Final Notes

The combination of a solid foundation of content knowledge and the confidence that comes from practicing your plan for applying that knowledge is the key to maximizing your performance on test day. As your foundation of content knowledge is built up and strengthened, you'll find that the strategies included in this chapter become more and more effective in helping you quickly sift through the distractions and traps of the test to isolate the correct answer.

Now it's time to move on to the test content chapters of this book, but be sure to keep your goal in mind. As you read, think about how you will be able to apply this information on the test. If you've already seen sample questions for the test and you have an idea of the question format and style, try to come up with questions of your own that you can answer based on what you're reading. This will give you valuable practice applying your knowledge in the same ways you can expect to on test day.

Good luck and good studying!

Reading Test

The reading portion of the SAT consists of one 65-minute section. It will contain 4 single passages and one pair of passages. There will be a total of 52 questions relating to these passages. The breakdown of passages and questions is in the table below.

U.S and World Literature	1 passage; 10 questions	20%
History/Social Studies	2 passages, or 1 passage and 1 pair;10-11 questions each	40%
Science	2 passages, or 1 passage and 1 pair;10-11 questions each	40%

The SAT Reading Test will contain a range of text complexities from grades 9-10 and post-secondary entry. The passages will cover U.S. and World Literature, History/Social Studies, and Science. The test will also contain 1-2 graphical representations. These may include tables, graphs, and charts. They will vary in level of difficulty as well as data density, and number of variables.

Information and Ideas

The questions tested in this section will focus on the informational content contained in the text.

READING CLOSELY

These questions will focus on the student's ability to read a passage and extrapolate beyond the information presented. They will look at both the explicit and implicit meanings of the text.

EXPLICITLY STATED INFORMATION

Identifying information stated explicitly in text means locating facts or opinions stated outright in the text and not requiring reader inference or interpretation. For example, when including factual information, an author might give specific names of people, places, or events; specific numbers; specific days of the week, names of months, or dates including the month, date, and year. In informational text, the author might state numerical measurements, (e.g., the size of a room or object; the distance between places; how many people live in a certain locality; how many people die annually from a certain cause; or the date, time, and/or place a certain event occurred). Abraham Lincoln began his Gettysburg Address, "Four score and seven years ago," which today is archaic language but does not require inference or interpretation; even a reader unfamiliar with the meaning of *score* can easily look up and find it. In a fictional novel, the author might state how many people are invited to, or were in attendance at, a party or other event.

DRAWING INFERENCES FROM TEXT

Some meanings in text are implicit rather than explicit; in other words, they are not directly stated (explicit), but implied (implicit). This means the reader needs to assume or draw an inference based on what is stated. Inferring meaning is often described by the saying *reading between the lines*, (i.e., determining what is unsaid through carefully observing what is said). For example, if an author writes, "Considering recent economic changes, what were once necessities are now luxuries for many businesses," the reader can infer that the "recent economic changes" the author refers to are economic decline, not economic prosperity. Describing things formerly viewed as necessary but now as unnecessary implies worse, not better changes. Or a novelist might write, "Trembling and flushing, she asked breathlessly, 'You saw him? How is he? Did he ask how I was? Did he mention

me at all?'" From the author's description of the character, the reader can infer she feels love/attraction for the person being referenced.

DETERMINING EXPLICIT MEANINGS

These questions will require the student to identify information explicitly stated in the text.

EXPLICIT DESCRIPTORS

Writers explicitly state not only factual information in their texts; they also explicitly state other kinds of information. For example, authors use description to give readers a better idea of the characteristics of whatever they are describing. If an author writes, "This sarcophagus is decorated with a vivid color illustration," the word *vivid* is more descriptive than factual. It communicates to the reader that the color illustration described is especially bright, vibrant, or intense visually. This is very helpful when there are no visual images of the object being described to accompany the text. Explicit descriptive words also apply to abstract concepts. For example, the author might write that the vivid color illustration depicts a famous figure's "brave actions." The word *brave* describes the actions of the person using an abstract concept. It communicates to the reader that the person's actions are considered brave or courageous by the author, and usually by other people as well.

EXPLICITLY STATED OPINIONS

An essayist might state an opinion; for example, "These people were not treated fairly." Since readers are expected to be able to distinguish opinion from fact, the essayist need not write, "*In my opinion*, these people were not treated fairly." It is a common practice of authors, especially those writing argumentative or persuasive types of text, to state opinions in the same way as facts. Even though not proven factual, opinions are stated just as explicitly as facts in these instances. Writers state ideas explicitly in text as well. For example, an author might write about how people historically believed that the Earth was flat, or that the Sun revolved around the Earth. These are not factual, but not simply opinions either; they were the prevailing beliefs at the time, (i.e., commonly held ideas). When an author explicitly states a *main idea*, he or she typically makes it the topic sentence of the paragraph, chapter, or piece. Topic sentences are also examples of explicitly stating ideas, (i.e., expressing them directly in text rather than implying them).

DETERMINING IMPLICIT MEANINGS

The questions in this section will require the student to read the text and then draw inferences from the text and form logical conclusions.

INFERENCES

Inferences are educated guesses that can be drawn from the facts and information available to a reader. Inferences are usually based upon a reader's own assumptions and beliefs. The ability to make inferences is often called reading between the lines. There are three basic types of inference: deductive reasoning, abductive reasoning, and inductive reasoning. Deductive reasoning is the ability to find an effect when given a cause and a rule. Abductive reasoning is the ability to find a cause when given a rule and an effect. Inductive reasoning is the ability to find a rule when given the cause and effect. Each type of reasoning can be used to make logical inferences from a piece of writing.

> **Review Video: Inference**
> Visit mometrix.com/academy and enter code: 379203

DRAWING CONCLUSIONS

Drawing logical conclusions is a way, along with making reasonable inferences, of determining implicit meanings, (i.e., meanings not directly or explicitly stated in the text but indirectly implied). For example, if an author of a fictional work has described a character who is emotionally distraught and hysterical running headlong toward a cliff without looking, without reading any further the reader can logically conclude that unless something happens in the interim—like another character appearing out of nowhere and stopping the first one—the character who is running will probably fall over the cliff. If a character in a novel talks about fighting and how they should all support their soldiers, the reader can logically conclude that the novel takes place during a war, even though the author does not explicitly state that a war is going on during the time period in which the author has set the novel's events.

WAYS THAT DRAWING INFERENCES ARE TESTED

One way a test might ask you to draw inferences or conclusions is asking what a character in text would likely react to a given event/circumstance based on a text passage. You would need to read closely for clues on which to base your inference. You might see a description of an earlier incident wherein this character reacted a certain way. For example, the author wrote, "The last time somebody hit her, she ran away." Based on this, you could infer she would do the same thing. Or one character says, "If he finds out what you did, he'll kill you," and the passage includes explicit description of the referenced character having killed people. You could then conclude if the third character finds out what the second character did, he will kill him or her. Some works, rather than providing a neat conclusion, seem to end in mid-action; yet readers can predict much from it.

USING ANALOGICAL REASONING

The student will be required to extrapolate information and idea from the text to answer these questions. They will also need to be able to this information and ideas to new, analogous situations.

Using analogical reasoning as described above involves thinking about situations that are comparable to one in the text and applying information from the text to those other parallel situations. For example, suppose a student reads that colonial Americans, dissatisfied with British laws and influenced by Enlightenment philosophy, wanted freedom to govern themselves instead of being ruled by the British monarchy, so they started the American Revolution to fight for their freedom and won, forming a democratic government. Suppose the student then further reads that the French, strongly influenced both by the same Enlightenment philosophy and by the Americans' success, started the French Revolution, also fighting for their freedom from an unfair monarchy, winning, and forming a democratic government. Then suppose the same student reads about people in other countries being ruled unfairly by a tyrannical monarchy. The student could reasonably apply the information about America and France to these other countries and expect revolutionary wars to break out in some of these other countries.

EXTRAPOLATE FROM TEXT

Even fictional text can be applied to analogous situations, particularly when the author's knowledge of human nature is sound and some of the text elements can be applied across settings. For example, reading William Shakespeare's tragedy *Romeo and Juliet,* one might first observe differences from today's real world: It is set centuries ago, in another country, and involves a family feud, which is rare today. However, one could then observe similarities: The main characters are teenagers; they fall madly in love; their families prohibit their seeing each other; and their families dislike each other, which is commoner today than actual feuds. Teen suicide and teen suicide pacts occur today. Thus, the student could extrapolate from this play, albeit fictional, that two teens today as fervently in love as Romeo and Juliet whose parents kept them apart, feeling there were no

17

better options, might take the same actions. Despite today's technology, the chance/accidental element (lack of timely information) causing the double tragedy could equally occur today.

<u>EXAMPLE</u>

Consider that a student reads in a biology text that mitosis is an asexual type of reproduction in which cells divide to produce more identical cells. The student reads further that mitosis takes place in all living organisms. From this information, the student can extrapolate that since mitosis occurs in all living organisms, mitosis must therefore occur in human beings. Since mitosis is an asexual type of reproduction, the student can further infer that mitosis is not the way in which humans reproduce sexually. By process of elimination, the student can then deduce that mitosis in humans must involve only the reproduction of cells within each individual human body. The student can further deduce that sexual reproduction in human beings must not be mitosis. The student cannot know that human sexual reproduction involves meiosis, or how this differs from mitosis, without reading about meiosis; however, he or she can determine all the aforementioned things just from reading about mitosis alone.

CITING TEXTUAL EVIDENCE

These questions will ask the student to support their answer with evidence from the text. The student should be able to specifically identify the information in the text and properly cite it.

CITING SUPPORTING EVIDENCE

Citing evidence from text that supports a point or claim in that text involves identifying which information is most directly related to that point or claim. As an example, if a writer makes the claim that the world population is increasing, that author might provide evidence to support this claim, such as census statistics from the past several consecutive years, decades, or centuries that give world population numbers larger than they were previously. In the same text, the author may also provide figures measuring poverty, hunger, and other ills related to overpopulation in certain parts of the world to make a case for the argument that population growth is bad and should be controlled. However, the student would be mistaken to cite those figures as evidence supporting the claim that the population is increasing; they are, rather, evidence supporting the claim that population growth is bad and should be controlled.

> **Review Video: <u>Text Evidence</u>**
> Visit mometrix.com/academy and enter code: 486236

CITING INFORMATION

Whereas informational and argumentative text may often use facts and/or figures as evidence to support various points or claims, fictional narration or description may use more descriptive details as supporting evidence. Moreover, the points or claims in such works may not be stated explicitly in words, but instead may be demonstrated through the actions or responses of characters. For example, an author of a play or novel may establish that a character is highly emotional by portraying or describing behaviors demonstrating this—flying into a rage, crying easily, becoming overjoyed readily, etc. The playwright or novelist need not write in another character's dialogue that this character is passionate or has mood swings; it is demonstrated through actions/behaviors. Subsequently in the play or novel, the character may do something which is not surprising but expected based on this established character trait. The character's previous actions are evidence supporting the credibility of the later action, (i.e., it was *in character*).

STEPS TO CITE TEXTUAL EVIDENCE

To cite evidence explicitly stated in text to support what they think about the text, students can take several steps. First, students should state their idea regarding the text. When answering a test question, students should also ensure his or her idea is or includes a restatement of the question. Then, to cite textual evidence supporting that idea, students can either paraphrase the evidence (i.e., restate or describe it in their own words) or quote part of the text directly, enclosing it in quotation marks and introducing it by referencing the paragraph or portion where it appears. Then students need to explain how the evidence they cited supports their idea about the text. For example, students might write that the evidence illustrates a similarity or difference between things, gives a reason for something, demonstrates a cause-and-effect relationship, explains what something means or how something works, etc. Students should also identify how the evidence cited contributed to their formulation of the idea answering the question. Students should cite at least two pieces of textual evidence per idea/question.

DETERMINING CENTRAL IDEAS AND THEMES

For these questions the student should be able to identify central ideas and themes that are explicitly stated in the text. They will also need to be able to determine implicit central ideas and themes from the text.

CENTRAL IDEAS

Central ideas are what a passage is mainly about. They are why the passage is written. The main idea is often found in a topic sentence or even a concluding sentence, and there are supporting details found in the passage that expand upon the main idea. There can, however, be more than one central idea, and these main ideas can be related and intertwined. For instance, the main or central idea of a passage may be that rainforests are drying out. A related main idea might be that the result of rainforest destruction is a loss of wildlife. These two central ideas are obviously related, and the passage may present both by focusing on one in one part of the passage and the other in another part of the passage. Another way they could be related is in a cause and effect relationship, with the loss of rainforests being the reason for losses of wildlife. It is important to always check to see if there is more than one central idea in a passage.

READ THE EXCERPT BELOW. IDENTIFY AND DISCUSS THE MAIN IDEA.

Students who have jobs while attending high school tend not to have as much time to complete their homework as other students. They also do not have time for other activities. We should try to persuade our young people to concentrate on doing well in school, not to concentrate on making money. Having a job while you are a student is harmful.

The main idea of the excerpt is actually the last sentence: "Having a job while you are a student is harmful." This is what the excerpt is mostly about. The other sentences contain supporting information: students who have jobs don't have as much time for homework; students with jobs don't have time for as many activities. These are both supporting details that tell more about the main idea. The third sentence deals with a persuasive argument; it is another kind of detail. Only the last sentence tells what the excerpt is mostly about. Main ideas are sometimes found in a topic sentence at the start of a text or in the concluding sentence, which is the case in this excerpt.

THEME

As opposed to a main idea, themes are seldom expressed directly in a text, so they can be difficult to identify. A theme is an issue, an idea, or a question raised by the text. For instance, a theme of William Shakespeare's *Hamlet* is indecision, as the title character explores his own psyche and the results of his failure to make bold choices. A great work of literature may have many themes, and

the reader is justified in identifying any for which he or she can find support. One common characteristic of themes is that they raise more questions than they answer. In a good piece of fiction, the author is not always trying to convince the reader, but is instead trying to elevate the reader's perspective and encourage him to consider the themes more deeply.

Review Video: Theme
Visit mometrix.com/academy and enter code: 732074

5 STEPS TO TAKE

As with all learning and development, reading should begin with concrete and gradually progress to abstract. Students must identify and understand literal information before they can make inferences. The first step is to identify the most important nouns and verbs in a sentence and define what the sentence is about. The second step is to identify the most important nouns, verbs, and adjectives in a whole paragraph, and define what that paragraph is about. The third step is to read brief passages, all of which use topic sentences with literal meanings. Students should be able to identify topic sentences not only at the beginning, but also anywhere else in a paragraph. In the fourth step, students can begin to make inferences by reading a single paragraph and then determining and articulating what the main idea is that the paragraph implies. The fifth step involves reading passages with more than one paragraph, gradually and slowly increasing the length of passages and identifying the implicit main idea each time. Students should be able to infer the main idea in shorter texts before proceeding to longer ones.

SUMMARIZING

These questions will test the student's ability to identify a summary of a text after reading the text. The student should be able to identify a reasonable summary of the text or of key information presented in the text.

It is also helpful to summarize the information you have read in a paragraph or passage format. This process is like creating an effective outline. To begin with, a summary should accurately define the main idea of the passage, though it does not need to explain this main idea in exhaustive detail. It should continue by laying out the most important supporting details or arguments from the passage. All the significant supporting details should be included, and none of the details included should be irrelevant or insignificant. Also, the summary should accurately report all of these details. Too often, the desire for brevity in a summary leads to the sacrifice of clarity or veracity. Summaries are often difficult to read, because they omit all graceful language, digressions, and asides that distinguish great writing. However, if the summary is effective, it should contain much the same message as the original text.

Review Video: Summarizing Text
Visit mometrix.com/academy and enter code: 172903

IMPROVING SUMMARIZATION SKILLS

For students to be able to identify good summaries of text or its key information, it will help if they learn how to summarize these themselves. Although they will find recognizing good summaries easier than making their own summaries, both processes require identifying subject matter through locating representative words and recalling significant information. One activity in which students can practice summarizing skills and teachers can provide scaffolding and guidance is using an ABC Chart. This is a simple square grid containing smaller squares, each labeled A, B, C, etc. through Z. Students read a passage; the teacher guides them to recall important phrases and words in the text, write each one on a Post-it Note, and attach it to the square labeled with the first letter

20

of the phrase/word. Students should try to recall as many details, facts, etc. as possible. Then they remove the Post-it Notes from the chart and stick them randomly on the board. The teacher helps them arrange the notes in some pattern, (e.g., into a web by ideas, chronologically along a timeline). This helps students organize their thoughts.

UNDERSTANDING RELATIONSHIPS

Texts will contain many different relationships between individuals, events, and ideas. These questions will test the student's ability to identify explicitly stated relationships as well as determine implicit ones.

> **Review Video: Relationships in a Story**
> Visit mometrix.com/academy and enter code: 929925

TEXTUAL FEATURES

Authors use various relationships as ways of organizing, presenting, and explaining information. For example, describing cause-and-effect relationships is a common technique in expository/informational text. The author describes some event(s), and then either explicitly states or implicitly establishes factors causing them. When authors use comparison-contrast, they typically compare similarities between/among ideas/things using similes (stated comparisons), metaphors (implied comparisons), and analogies (comparisons of similarities in two unrelated things). Authors identify contrasts by describing opposing qualities/characteristics in things/ideas. One example of using sequence or order is arranging events chronologically, beginning to end. Students can recognize sequential organization by observing specific dates, times, and signal words including *first, before, next, then, following, after, subsequently, finally*, etc. Sequence can also be spatial or by order of importance. Authors introduce some problem, describe its characteristics, and then offer solutions in problem-solution relationships. Descriptive writing provides sensory details to make information realer and easier for readers to imagine. How-to/instructional texts use serial directions to provide information.

COMPARE AND CONTRAST

Authors will use different stylistic and writing devices to make their meaning more clearly understood. One of those devices is comparison and contrast. When an author describes the ways in which two things are alike, he or she is comparing them. When the author describes the ways in which two things are different, he or she is contrasting them. The *compare and contrast* essay is one of the most common forms in nonfiction. It is often signaled with certain words: a comparison may be indicated with such words as *both, same, like, too*, and *as well*; while a contrast may be indicated by words like *but, however, on the other hand, instead*, and *yet*. Of course, comparisons and contrasts may be implicit without using any such signaling language. A single sentence may both compare and contrast. Consider the sentence *Brian and Sheila love ice cream, but Brian prefers vanilla and Sheila prefers strawberry*. In one sentence, the author has described both a similarity (love of ice cream) and a difference (favorite flavor).

> **Review Video: Compare and Contrast**
> Visit mometrix.com/academy and enter code: 798319

CAUSE AND EFFECT

One of the most common text structures is cause and effect. A cause is an act or event that makes something happen, and an effect is the thing that happens because of that cause. A cause-and-effect relationship is not always explicit, but there are some words in English that signal causality, such as

since, *because*, and *as a result*. As an example, consider the sentence *Because the sky was clear, Ron did not bring an umbrella*. The cause is the clear sky, and the effect is that Ron did not bring an umbrella. However, sometimes the cause-and-effect relationship will not be clearly noted. For instance, the sentence *He was late and missed the meeting* does not contain any signaling words, but it still contains a cause (he was late) and an effect (he missed the meeting). It is possible for a single cause to have multiple effects, or for a single effect to have multiple causes. Also, an effect can in turn be the cause of another effect, in what is known as a cause-and-effect chain.

> **Review Video: Cause and Effect**
> Visit mometrix.com/academy and enter code: 428037

TEXT SEQUENCE

A reader must be able to identify a text's sequence, or the order in which things happen. Often, and especially when the sequence is very important to the author, it is indicated with signal words like first, then, next, and last. However, sometimes a sequence is merely implied and must be noted by the reader. Consider the sentence He walked in the front door and switched on the hall lamp. Clearly, the man did not turn the lamp on before he walked in the door, so the implied sequence is that he first walked in the door and then turned on the lamp. Texts do not always proceed in an orderly sequence from first to last: sometimes, they begin at the end and then start over at the beginning. As a reader, it can be useful to make brief notes to clarify the sequence.

> **Review Video: Sequence**
> Visit mometrix.com/academy and enter code: 489027

INTERPRETING WORDS AND PHRASES IN CONTEXT

These questions will ask the student to determine the meaning of words and phrases from the text. The student must use context clues to help determine the meaning of these words and phrases.

CONTEXTUAL CLUES

Look for contextual clues. An answer can be right but not correct. The contextual clues will help you find the answer that is most right and is correct. Understand the context in which a phrase is stated.

When asked for the implied meaning of a statement made in the passage, immediately go find the statement and read the context. Also, look for an answer choice that has a similar phrase to the statement in question.

EXAMPLE:

> In the passage, what is implied by the phrase "Churches have become more or less part of the furniture"?

Find an answer choice that is similar or describes the phrase *part of the furniture* as that is the key phrase in the question. *Part of the furniture* is a saying that means something is fixed, immovable, or set in their ways. Those are all similar ways of saying *part of the furniture*. As such, the correct answer choice will probably include a similar rewording of the expression.

<u>EXAMPLE:</u>

Why was John described as "morally desperate"?

The answer will probably have some sort of definition of *morals* in it. *Morals* refers to a code of right and wrong behavior, so the correct answer choice will likely have words that mean something like that.

Review Video: Context
Visit mometrix.com/academy and enter code: 613660

WORD MEANING

Paying attention to the phrase, sentence, paragraph, or larger context surrounding a word gives students two distinct advantages: One, it can help figure out the meaning of a new or unfamiliar vocabulary word by the information its context provides; and two, it can help distinguish between/among different meanings of the same word according to which meaning makes sense within context. For example, when reading words like *nickelback* and *bootleg*, if the surrounding context is football, these refer to an additional, fifth defensive back position played by a safety or cornerback and a play run by the quarterback, respectively; but if the surrounding context is rock music, *Nickelback* refers to a Canadian band, and *bootleg* to unofficial or unauthorized recordings of musical performances. Students can look for contextual synonyms for unknown words; for example, a reader unfamiliar with the meaning of *prudent* may observe the words *careful*, *cautious*, *judicious*, etc. Antonyms also help; for example, if a text says, "Smug? On the contrary, he's the most self-critical person I know." This informs defining *smug* as self-congratulatory or overly self-satisfied.

Rhetoric

The questions in this section will focus on the rhetorical analysis of a text.

ANALYZING WORD CHOICE

Authors use specific words, phrases, and patterns of words in their writing. The student will be asked to determine how these help shape the meaning and tone in the text.

RHETORICAL ANALYSIS

When analyzing a text's rhetoric, students should aim to reveal the purpose of the text or the author's purpose in writing it; who the author's intended audience was; the decisions that the author made, and how these decisions may have influenced the final result of the text. Identifying the intended purpose and audience of a text is identifying two main components of its rhetorical situation, (i.e., the circumstances wherein communication occurs), which serves as a major basis for rhetorical analysis. The third main component is the context. Context can include many factors, such as the occasion of the work; the exigency (i.e., what motivated the author to write the text); the media and/or venue of its original appearance; the historical background and even the state of the world relative to the text's topic. As an example, texts written respectively before and after 9/11/2001 on the topic of air travel would have some marked differences.

WORD CHOICE OR DICTION IN RHETORIC

Word choice or diction affects the tone of a text and how readers perceive its meaning. Writers inform their diction in part by considering their intended audience and selecting words that will be understood by and appeal to this audience. For instance, language with more denotative meanings (i.e., straightforward dictionary definitions) is more suitable for informational texts, whereas language with more connotative meanings (i.e., words that carry implied associated meanings) is more suitable for descriptive and narrative texts to evoke images and emotions. As examples, describing a sound or noise as *extremely loud* or *at a volume of 100 dB* is more factual and denotative; describing it as *thunderous*, *deafening*, or in specific reference to a speaker's voice, *stentorian*, is more descriptive, connotative, and evocative. Audience also influences the relative formality of diction. For example, more formal text appropriate for an adult professional academic audience might describe size as *massive*, whereas more informal language appropriate for high school and younger students might use the blending neologism *ginormous*.

INFLUENCE ON MEANING AND UNDERSTANDING

When writers use good judgment in word choice, they communicate their messages more effectively for readers to understand. Poor word choice, as well as not considering the intended audience in one's diction, can distract readers to the point that they miss the message. Readers can consider the denotations (dictionary definition meanings) and connotations (implied associated meanings) of words used in text, as well as the rhythm and force of words and whether the author uses words concisely, includes verbiage, or appears to have logorrhea. When analyzing word choice in a text, students can consider whether the author has selected words that are comprehensible to the identified reading audience; whether words are chosen with precision and specificity; whether the author selected strong words to express meaning; whether the author placed more emphasis on positive than negative words in text; whether/how often the author included words that are overused, making the language cliché or trite; and whether the text incorporates words that are obsolete today, which readers may not recognize or understand.

ANALYZING TEXT STRUCTURE

For these questions, students will be asked to answer questions about why the author structured the text a certain way. They will also be asked about the relationship between a part of the text and the whole text.

ELEMENTS TO CONSIDER

Text structure is how a text is organized. In analyzing the overall structure of a text, the reader can consider its order, (e.g., what is written first, what follows, and how it ends) and how its sections and chapters are divided. The genre or type of text is another consideration. For example, consider whether the text is fictional or nonfictional; prose, poetry, drama, or oratory; in fictional prose, whether a novel is a romantic, adventure, action, graphic, historical, fantasy, science fiction novel, etc.; in nonfiction, whether it is an essay; research article, journalistic article, opinion-editorial article; how-to manual; travelogue, etc. The relationship or pattern organizing the text may be a timeline sequence, logical sequence, a priority sequence, or spatial sequence; an analysis of the balance of forces; an analysis of similarities and differences/comparison-contrast; a process of problem, solution, and resolution; simply a list of items; or a piece that seems to jump around without order. Consider also what tone the language establishes; vocabulary and imagery used; and the accuracy of text mechanics (grammar, punctuation, spelling, etc.).

ORGANIZATIONAL METHODS

Authors organize their writing based on the purpose of their text. Common organizational methods that authors use include: cause and effect, compare and contrast, inductive presentation of ideas, deductive presentation of ideas, and chronological order. Cause and effect is used to present the reasons that something happened. Compare and contrast is used to discuss the similarities and differences between two things. Inductive presentation of ideas starts with specific examples and moves to a general conclusion. Deductive presentation of ideas starts with a conclusion and then explains the examples used to arrive at the conclusion. Chronological order presents information in the order that it occurred.

Review Video: Organizational Methods to Structure Text
Visit mometrix.com/academy and enter code: 606263

Authors should organize information logically so the reader can follow what is being said and locate information in the text. Two common organizational structures are cause and effect and chronological order. In cause and effect, an author presents one thing that makes something else happen. For example, if you go to bed very late, you will be tired. The cause is going to bed late. The effect is being tired the next day. When using chronological order, the author presents information in the order that it happened. Biographies are written in chronological order. The subject's birth and childhood are presented first, followed by adult life, and then by events leading up to the person's death.

EXAMPLE 1

Read the following thesis statement and discuss the organizational pattern that the author will most likely use:

> Among people who are current on the latest technologies, there is a debate over whether DVD or Blu-ray Disc is a better choice for watching and recording video.

From the thesis statement the reader can assume that the author is most likely going to use a compare and contrast organizational structure. The compare and contrast structure is best used to

discuss the similarities and differences of two things. The author mentions two options for watching and recording video: DVD and Blu-ray Disc. During the rest of the essay, the author will most likely describe the two technologies, giving specific examples of how they are similar and different. The author may discuss the pros and cons of each technology.

EXAMPLE 2

Read the following thesis statement and discuss the organizational pattern that the author will most likely use:

> Throughout his life, Thomas Edison used his questioning and creative mind to become one of America's greatest inventors.

Based on the thesis statement, the reader can assume that the author is most likely going to use chronological order to organize the information in the rest of the essay. Chronological order presents information in the order that it occurred. It is often used as the organizational structure in biographies to logically present the important events in a person's life. The words "throughout his life" clue in the reader to the chronological organizational structure. The author will probably discuss Edison's childhood and initial inventions first and then move on to his later queries and inventions.

EXAMPLE 3

Read the following thesis statement and discuss the organizational pattern that the author will most likely use:

> Todd is writing an editorial on the need for more bus stops in his town. Discuss the type of organization he should use for his editorial and what each might look like.

Todd could organize the information in his editorial in a few different ways. An editorial is a persuasive text so Todd will want to keep that in mind. First, he could organize the information by making his most important points first, following with his lesser points towards the end. Alternatively, Todd could use a cause and effect structure. He could discuss the reasons that his town needs more bus stops and the effects they would have for the people living there. Finally, Todd could discuss the pros and cons of adding the bus stops, using a compare and contrast structure. The organizational structure Todd chooses will depend on the information he wants to write and the method he thinks will be most persuasive.

PART-WHOLE RELATIONSHIPS

Students should be able to recognize and explain how a portion of a text is related to the overall text to demonstrate they understand part-to-whole relationships when analyzing text. Every part of a text must serve essential purposes, including setting up/establishing the text at the beginning; fitting together logically with all other parts of the text; remaining focused on the point; supporting the overall text through introducing its topic, establishing evidence, supporting or countering a claim, outlining subtopics, aspects, or components, describing a characteristic or feature, etc.; and informing the reader—about the setting of the text, a character in it, a relationship between/among characters, a research study, an opinion, or something else relevant to the text. Test questions may ask about how words function within sentences, as these examples address; or sentence-to-paragraph relationships, which also include setup or setting the tone, logic, focus or point, including shifts in focus, and evidence supporting claims as functions; or paragraph-to-whole-text relationships, wherein paragraphs should establish a claim/situation; support or refute a claim; maintain focus; and/or inform readers.

ANALYZING POINT OF VIEW

These questions will ask the student to determine the author's point of view. They will also need to determine the influence that that this point of view has on the content and style of the text.

In expository text, authors apply various strategies for communicating their points of view about specific topics. As readers, students can identify author point of view readily in some texts; however, they will have to analyze other texts closely to determine point of view. To discern author viewpoint, students can ask themselves four questions: (1) The author is writing to persuade readers to agree with what main idea? (2) How does the author's word choice influence the reader perceptions about the topic? (3) How does the author's selection of examples and/or facts as supporting evidence influence reader thinking about the topic? And (4) What purpose does the author wish to achieve through the text? Students may find the main idea stated directly, as in a topic sentence found in the text, often somewhere in the first paragraph; or they may need to infer it by carefully reading to identify sentences or paragraphs implying it. Students can assess influences of word choice by identifying words/phrases with positive or negative connotations rather than only objective denotations, emphasis through repetition, etc. Examples/facts should illustrate the main idea/point. Author purpose coincides with point of view.

ANALYZING PURPOSE

These questions will ask the student to determine the purpose of a text or a piece of a text. The pieces of text are typically one paragraph of the text.

An author writes with four main purposes: to inform, to entertain, to describe, or to persuade. These purposes play into an author's motivation to create a text. If the author wants to entertain, he or she may write a novel or short story that has humorous elements and/or dramatic elements. Remember, entertainment does not have to mean comedy or humor; it can just as easily be drama. To determine an author's motives, think about the author's purpose. If the text is fiction, the author's purpose is most likely to entertain or describe. If the text is nonfiction, the author's purpose is most likely to inform. If the text is an editorial or advertisement, the author's purpose is most likely to persuade. Once you identify the author's purpose, you can determine the author's motives.

Review Video: Author's Main Point or Purpose
Visit mometrix.com/academy and enter code: 734339

USING CONTEXT CLUES

To determine the author's purpose in writing text, students can look for certain words as clues to various purposes. For example, if the author's purpose was to compare similarities between/among ideas, look for *clue words* including *like, similar(ly), same, in the same way*, and *just as*. If the author's purpose was to contrast differences between/among ideas, clue words include *but, however, on the other hand, dissimilar(ly)*, and *in contrast/contrastingly*. If the author's purpose was to criticize an idea, clue words connoting judgment/negative opinion include *poor, bad, inadequate, insufficient, lacking, excessive, wasteful, harmful, deleterious, disservice, unfair*, etc. If the purpose was to paint a picture illustrating an idea, descriptive clue words include *morose, crestfallen, lusty, glittering, exuberant*, etc. Explanatory purposes involve using simpler words to describe or explain more complex/abstract ideas. Identification purposes entail listing series of ideas without much accompanying opinion or description. To intensify an idea, authors add superlative (*-est*) adjectives, more specific details; and enlarge concepts. To suggest or propose an idea, authors typically express positive opinions and provide supporting evidence for points to convince readers to agree.

27

ANALYZING ARGUMENTS

Students will need to be able to analyze arguments in a text for their structure and content.

The best way to introduce an argument in a persuasive passage and to structure it is to begin by organizing your thoughts and researching the evidence carefully. You should write everything down in outline format to start. Make sure you put the claim at the beginning of the passage. Then, list the reasons and the evidence that you have to support the claim. It is important that you provide enough evidence. Reasons and evidence should follow each other in a logical order. Write the passage so that you hold the reader's attention; use a strong tone and choose words carefully for maximum effect. If you can get the reader to understand your claim, he or she will be more likely to agree with your argument. Restate your claim in the concluding paragraph to maximize the impact on the reader.

ANALYZING CLAIMS AND COUNTERCLAIMS

These questions will ask the student to identify explicitly stated claims and counter claims made in a text. They will also need to be able determine implicit claims and counterclaims made in a text.

DEFINING AND SUPPORTING CLAIMS

A claim/argument/proposition/thesis is anything a writer asserts in that is not a known/proven/accepted fact. As such, it is the author's opinion or at least includes an element of opinion. The writer usually will, or should, provide evidence to back up this claim. Some writers make claims without supporting them, but these are not as effective in convincing readers to believe or agree with them. Some may attempt to provide evidence but choose it poorly; if they cite evidence that is not related directly enough to the claim, or the *evidence* is information from untrustworthy sources or not verified as accurate, this is also less effective. Writers sometimes state their claims directly and clearly; in other instances, they may discuss a number of related topics from which the reader must infer the claims implied in the discussion. For example, suppose two writers take opposing positions, one that immigration to the USA is bad and the other that it is good. Rather than explicitly stating these claims, both may present information supporting negative/positive aspects/views of immigration. Critical readers can infer these claims from the information's negativity/positivity.

MAKING CLAIMS

A persuasive essay will likely focus on one central argument, but it may make many smaller claims along the way. These are subordinate arguments with which the reader must agree if he or she is going to agree with the central argument. The central argument will only be as strong as the subordinate claims. These claims should be rooted in fact and observation, rather than subjective judgment. The best persuasive essays provide enough supporting detail to justify claims without overwhelming the reader. Remember that a fact must be susceptible to independent verification: that is, it must be something the reader could confirm. Also, statistics are only effective when they take into account possible objections. For instance, a statistic on the number of foreclosed houses would only be useful if it was taken over a defined interval and in a defined area. Most readers are wary of statistics, because they are so often misleading. If possible, a persuasive essay should always include references so that the reader can obtain more information. Of course, this means that the writer's accuracy and fairness may be judged by the inquiring reader.

COUNTERCLAIMS

Whereas a claim represents a text's main argument, a counterclaim represents an argument that opposes that claim. Writers actually use counterclaims to support their claims. They do this by presenting their claim; introducing a counterclaim to it; and then definitively refuting the

28

counterclaim. Rather than only promoting and supporting the claim, which leaves the text open to being refuted or attacked by other writers who present their own counterclaims, authors who present both claim and counterclaim have anticipated opposing arguments before others can raise them; have given a voice to the opposition to their claim, and then discredited that voice; and, when they do this effectively, show that their ability to do so indicates how familiar and competent they are with respect to the topic they are discussing in their text. Words such as *but, yet, however, nevertheless, nonetheless, notwithstanding, despite, in spite of, on the contrary, contrastingly,* etc. indicating contrast/difference/disagreement signal counterclaims. If readers/students cannot locate a claim in text, they may identify a counterclaim by signal words and work backwards to discover what claim the counterclaim opposes.

DISCREDITING A COUNTERCLAIM

When writers present a claim, (i.e., a central argument in text), they may also introduce a counterclaim opposing that claim. When journalists do this, by presenting the other side to their argument they can demonstrate their objectivity. In a different use, writers of argumentative/persuasive text may find that furnishing evidence to support a claim, appealing to various reader responses, and other rhetorical devices may still not lend their claim as much strength as they would like. In such cases, another rhetorical technique they may use is presenting a counterclaim. This enables writers not only to anticipate opposing arguments to their claim, but also to rebut these opposing arguments, which in turn lends additional strength to their original claim. As an example, one might claim that using a dentist-approved mouthwash regularly can prevent gingivitis. A counterclaim might be that in a recent survey, dentists questioned the effectiveness of mouthwash. When the next sentence states that this survey included only three dentists, all of whose dental studies were incomplete, the writer has effectively discredited the counterclaim and opposition, reinforcing the original claim.

ASSESSING REASONING

ASSESSING SOUNDNESS

In addition to identifying claims and counterclaims that authors present in their texts, students must be able to evaluate whether those claims and counterclaims are sound. The PSAT, SAT, and other standardized tests ask questions that require students to assess the soundness of an author's reasoning in text. A valid argument is logical, (i.e., each premise or statement follows upon the previous one). However, test questions are not limited to requiring students to assess text logic/validity; they moreover require students to assess soundness, meaning whether the argument is true. Students will likely not have thorough knowledge of all text content on tests. They should assume the content of unfamiliar text is true, since the test will not try to trick students by providing false material. To assess a text argument, the student must first identify its central claim. The remainder of the argument should both answer why the central claim is true, and also prove or support that claim.

APPROACH FOR TEST QUESTIONS

Some text-based test questions may ask students not only what central claim or argument an author makes in a passage, but also what the author's reasoning behind that claim is. To help select the correct answer from among multiple choices on such questions, the student will need to follow the reasoning that the author uses in the text and relate it to the answer choices. The student can do this by reading each answer choice and then asking himself/herself whether this choice answers the question of why the author's central claim is true. For the student to be able to assess the author's reasoning for soundness, he or she must have the ability to cite evidence with accuracy to support that assessment of reasoning and its soundness or lack thereof. The best and easiest way of

justifying one's assessment of reasoning and its relative soundness by citing evidence is to ask oneself whether why the author makes the claim; how the author justifies the claim; and whether evidence supports the claim and answers the question of why.

LEVELS OF CRITICAL READING

Experts (cf. Elder and Paul, 2004) identify four levels of critical reading. The first level is paraphrasing the text one sentence at a time, which develops and demonstrates understanding. The second level is identifying and explicating a text paragraph's main idea. The third level is analyzing the author's logic and reasoning, including the main purpose, question, information, inferences, concepts, assumptions, implications, and viewpoints. The fourth level is assessing logic or reasoning. Since text quality varies among authors and texts, readers must assess author reasoning. Paraphrasing author meaning accurately on the first level is a prerequisite. To assess reasoning, consider whether the author states his or her meaning clearly; whether the author's claims are accurate; whether he or she offers specifics and/or details with enough precision when these are relevant; whether the author strays from his or her purpose by introducing irrelevant information; whether the text is written superficially or addresses the topic's inherent complexities; whether the author's perspective is narrow or considers other pertinent perspectives; whether the text has internal contradictions or is consistent; whether the text addresses the topic in a trivial or significant way; and whether the author's attitude is narrow/unilateral or fair.

ANALYZING EVIDENCE

For these questions the student will be asked to determine how the author uses evidence to support his claims and counterclaims.

PRESENTING EVIDENCE

When in a focused discussion, be prepared to present your claims, findings, and supporting evidence in a clear and distinct manner. This means being prepared. When compiling your data, make sure to create an outline that has the main ideas and then the supporting evidence, including graphics that you want to present. Attention to details will result in a successful presentation, one in which the diverse individuals in the group will come away with a feeling of having been part of something meaningful. Facts and examples should be stressed. Repetition creates retention. It is important for the speaker to choose the right words, and to build momentum by gradually building up to the strongest argument(s). Graphics are important, because participants will be more convinced if they can see evidence as well as hear it. By breaking up the flow of the discussion and introducing pauses before and after pertinent arguments, the speaker will make the presentation of facts more interesting.

IDENTIFYING EVIDENCE

To assess claims an author makes in text, the reader must be able to analyze the evidence the author supplies to support those claims and evaluate whether the evidence is convincing or not. Students should ask themselves why the author makes a given claim; how the author justifies that claim; and whether the evidence the author uses to justify the claim convincingly and thoroughly answers the *why* question, which means the evidence is effective. If the student can easily come up with counterclaims to the author's claims, the author's reasoning and/or evidence used to support it may not be as convincing as they could be. When answering text-based multiple-choice questions asking them to identify evidence supporting a central claim, students can determine the correct choice by identifying and eliminating choices citing text that extends the argument rather than supporting it because it does not answer why; and text that is related but not the main source of support, in addition to completely incorrect choices.

SUPPORTING EVIDENCE

Test questions will not only ask students to identify what evidence an author uses in text to support his or her claims; they will also ask students to evaluate an author's strategy for using evidence to support his or her argument. For example, a passage of text might be an author's review of a book, film, or other work. A review most commonly makes the main point that the work is either good or bad, or sometimes a combination of both. A review might also make, argue, and support the point that a movie or book demonstrates a particular central trait (e.g., that a movie identified in the romantic comedy genre is actually *anti-romantic*). In order to support his or her main point, the reviewer could use various tactics, such as comparing the work to others as evidence supporting the claim; stating and then effectively addressing a counterclaim to support the claim; or giving a number of examples from the work which can all be used to serve as support for the claim. Some reviewers combine all of these strategies, which when done well can be most effective.

ESSENTIAL CONSIDERATIONS

When analyzing the evidence that an author presents in a text to organize and back up his or her argument, as he or she reads, the student should remember to focus not only on what the author's central claim or point is, but also on what the actual content of that evidence is; how the author uses the evidence to prove the point or claim that he or she is making; and whether or not the evidence that the author provides is effective in supporting that central claim or point. A good way to evaluate whether a piece of evidence that an author uses is supportive of that author's central claim is whether that evidence answers the question of why the author is making that claim. The reader should also consider the questions of how the author justifies this claim and whether the evidence the author has presented to justify the claim is convincing or not.

Synthesis

The questions in this section will focus on synthesizing across multiple sources of information.

ANALYZING MULTIPLE TEXTS

The student will be required to synthesize information and ideas across multiple texts. This means that they will need to apply all the other skills above to analyze paired passages.

Synthesizing, (i.e., understanding and integrating), information from multiple texts can at times be among the most challenging skills for some students to succeed with on tests and in school, and yet it is also among the most important. Students who read at the highest cognitive levels can select related material from different text sources and construct coherent arguments that account for these varied information sources. Synthesizing ideas and information from multiple texts actually combines other reading skills that students should have mastered previously in reading one text at a time, and applies them in the context of reading more than one text. For example, students are required to read texts closely, including identifying explicit and implicit meanings; use critical thinking and reading; draw inferences; assess author reasoning; analyze supporting evidence; and formulate opinions they can justify, based on more passages than one. When two paired texts represent opposing sides of the same argument, students can find analyzing them easier; but this is not always the case.

> **Review Video: Synthesizing Text**
> Visit mometrix.com/academy and enter code: 187664

SIMILARITIES

When students are called upon to compare things two texts share, the most obvious commonality might be the same subject matter or specific topic. However, two texts need not be about the same thing to compare them. Some other features texts can share include structural characteristics. For example, they may both be written using a sequential format, such as narrating events or giving instructions in chronological order; listing and/or discussing subtopics by order of importance; or describing a place spatially in sequence from each point to the next. They may both use a comparison-contrast structure, identifying similarities and differences between, among, or within topics. They might both organize information by identifying cause-and-effect relationships. Texts can be similar in type, (e.g., description, narration, persuasion, or exposition). They can be similar in using technical vocabulary or using formal or informal language. They may share similar tones and/or styles, (e.g., humorous, satirical, serious). They can share similar purposes, (e.g., to alarm audiences, incite them to action, reassure them, inspire them, provoke strong emotional responses).

CONTRASTS

When analyzing paired or multiple texts, students might observe differences in tone; for example, one text might take a serious approach while another uses a humorous one. Even within approaches or treatments, style can differ: one text may be humorous in a witty, sophisticated, clever way while another may exercise broad, low-brow humor; another may employ mordant sarcasm; another may use satire, couching outrageous suggestions in a deadpan logical voice to lampoon social attitudes and behaviors as Jonathan Swift did in *A Modest Proposal*. Serious writing can range from darkly pessimistic to alarmist to objective and unemotional. Texts might have similar information, yet organize it using different structures. One text may support points or ideas using logical arguments, while another may seek to persuade its audience by appealing to their emotions. A very obvious difference in text is genre: for example, the same mythological or traditional stories have been told as oral folk tales, written dramas, written novels, etc.; and/or set

32

in different times and places (e.g., Shakespeare's *Romeo and Juliet* vs. Laurents, Bernstein, and Sondheim's *West Side Story*).

ANALYZING QUANTITATIVE INFORMATION

These questions will test the student's ability to analyze quantitative information. This information may be presented in graphs, tables, and charts and may relate to other information presented in the text.

When students read text, particularly informational text, authors may include graphs, charts, and/or tables to illustrate the written information under discussion. Students need to be able to understand these representations and how they are related to the text they supplement. For example, a line graph can show how some numerical value—like number or percentage of items, people, groups, dollars, births, deaths, cases of specific illnesses, etc. or amount of rainfall, products, waste matter, etc.—has increased, decreased, or stayed the same over designated periods of time. A bar graph may be used like a line graph to show the same chronological change; or to compare different numbers or proportions of things side by side without reference to time. A pie chart visualizes distribution and proportion by depicting percentages or fractions of a whole occupied by different categories, (e.g., how much money is allocated or spent for each division among services or products, what percentages or proportions of a population has certain characteristics). Tables and charts often list numbers by category; students must be able to identify largest and smallest quantities, order by quantity, etc.

INTERPRETING GRAPHICS

An author may organize information in a chart, a graph, in paragraph format, or as a list. Information may also be presented in a picture or a diagram. The information may be arranged according to the order in which it occurred over time, placed in categories, or it may be arranged in a cause-and-effect relationship. Information can also be presented according to where it occurs in a given space (spatial order), or organized through description. The way an author chooses to organize information is often based on the purpose of information that is being presented, the best way to present given information, and the audience that the information is meant to reach.

It is important to be able to interpret information presented in graphics and be able to translate it to text. These graphics can include maps, charts, illustrations, graphs, timelines, and tables. Each of these different graphics is used to present a different type of quantitative or technical information. Maps show a visual representation of a certain area. A map may contain a legend which helps to identify certain geographic features on the map. A graph or chart will usually contain two axes that show the relationship between two variables. A table can also be like this but may show the relationship between any number of variables. So, no matter how the information is presented it is important to be able to interpret it and explain what it means.

Review Video: Drawing Conclusions from Graphic Organizers
Visit mometrix.com/academy and enter code: 363785

Reading Passages

Some questions will be concerning sentence insertions. In those cases, do not look for the ones that simply restate what was in the previous sentence. New sentences should contain new information and new insights into the subject of the text. If asked for the paragraph to which a sentence would most naturally be added, find a key noun or word in that new sentence. Then find the paragraph containing exactly or another word closely related to that key noun or word. That is the paragraph that should include the new sentence.

Some questions will ask what purpose a phrase fulfilled in a text. It depends upon the subject of the text. If the text is dramatic, then the phrase was probably used to show drama. If the text is comedic, then the phrase was probably to show comedy.

In related cases, you may be asked to provide a sentence that summarizes the text, or to reorganize a paragraph. Simple sentences, without wordy phrases, are usually best. If asked for a succinct answer, then the shorter the answer, the more likely it is correct.

SKIMMING

Your first task when you begin reading is to answer the question "What is the topic of the selection?" This can best be answered by quickly skimming the passage for the general idea, stopping to read only the first sentence of each paragraph. A paragraph's first is usually the main topic sentence, and it gives you a summary of the content of the paragraph.

Once you've skimmed the passage, stopping to read only the first sentences, you will have a general idea about what it is about, as well as what is the expected topic in each paragraph.

Each question will contain clues as to where to find the answer in the passage. Do not just randomly search through the passage for the correct answer to each question. Search scientifically. Find key word(s) or ideas in the question that are going to either contain or be near the correct answer. These are typically nouns, verbs, numbers, or phrases in the question that will probably be duplicated in the passage. Once you have identified those key word(s) or idea, skim the passage quickly to find where those key word(s) or idea appears. The correct answer choice will be nearby.

EXAMPLE:

What caused Martin to suddenly return to Paris?

The key word is Paris. Skim the passage quickly to find where this word appears. The answer will be close by that word.

However, sometimes key words in the question are not repeated in the passage. In those cases, search for the general idea of the question.

Example:

Which of the following was the psychological impact of the author's childhood upon the remainder of his life?

Key words are *childhood* or *psychology*. While searching for those words, be alert for other words or phrases that have similar meaning, such as *emotional effect* or *mentally* which could be used in the passage, rather than the exact word *psychology*.

Numbers or years can be particularly good key words to skim for, as they stand out from the rest of the text.

Example:

Which of the following best describes the influence of Monet's work in the 20th century?

20th contains numbers and will easily stand out from the rest of the text. Use *20th* as the key word to skim for in the passage.

Other good key word(s) may be in quotation marks. These identify a word or phrase that is copied directly from the passage. In those cases, the word(s) in quotation marks are exactly duplicated in the passage.

EXAMPLE:

In her college years, what was meant by Margaret's "drive for excellence"?

Drive for excellence is a direct quote from the passage and should be easy to find.

DIRECTLY QUOTED ANSWERS

Once you've quickly found the correct section of the passage to find the answer, focus upon the answer choices. Sometimes a choice will repeat word for word a portion of the passage near the answer. However, beware of such duplication – it may be a trap! More than likely, the correct choice will paraphrase or summarize the related portion of the passage, rather than being exactly the same wording.

TRUE DOES NOT EQUAL CORRECT

For the answers that you think are correct, read them carefully and make sure that they answer the question. An answer can be factually correct, but it MUST answer the question asked. Additionally, two answers can both be seemingly correct, so be sure to read all of the answer choices, and make sure that you get the one that BEST answers the question.

NO KEY WORD?

Some questions will not have a key word.

EXAMPLE:

Which of the following would the author of this passage likely agree with?

In these cases, look for key words in the answer choices. Then skim the passage to find where the answer choice occurs. By skimming to find where to look, you can minimize the time required.

Sometimes it may be difficult to identify a good key word in the question to skim for in the passage. In those cases, look for a key word in one of the answer choices to skim for. Often the answer choices can all be found in the same paragraph, which can quickly narrow your search.

> **Review Video: When There's No Keyword**
> Visit mometrix.com/academy and enter code: 312791

PARAGRAPH FOCUS

Focus upon the first sentence of each paragraph, which is the most important. The main topic of the paragraph is usually there.

35

Once you've read the first sentence in the paragraph, you have a general idea about what each paragraph will be about. As you read the questions, try to determine which paragraph will have the answer. Paragraphs have a concise topic. The answer should either obviously be there or obviously not. It will save time if you can jump straight to the paragraph, so try to remember what you learned from the first sentences.

Example: The first paragraph is about poets; the second is about poetry. If a question asks about poetry, where will the answer be? The second paragraph.

The main idea of a passage is typically spread across all or most of its paragraphs. Whereas the main idea of a paragraph may be completely different than the main idea of the very next paragraph, a main idea for a passage affects all of the paragraphs in one form or another.

EXAMPLE:

What is the main idea of the passage?

For each answer choice, try to see how many paragraphs are related. It can help to count how many sentences are affected by each choice, but it is best to see how many paragraphs are affected by the choice. Typically, the answer choices will include incorrect choices that are main ideas of individual paragraphs, but not the entire passage. That is why it is crucial to choose ideas that are supported by the most paragraphs possible.

ELIMINATE CHOICES

Some choices can quickly be eliminated. "Andy Warhol lived there." Is Andy Warhol even mentioned in the article? If not, quickly eliminate it.

When trying to answer a question such as "the passage indicates all of the following EXCEPT" quickly skim the paragraph searching for references to each choice. If the reference exists, scratch it off as a choice. Similar choices may be crossed off simultaneously if they are close enough.

Watch for answers that are similarly worded. Since only one answer can be correct, if there are two answers that appear to mean the same thing, they must BOTH be incorrect, and can be eliminated.

EXAMPLE ANSWER CHOICES:

a. changing values and attitudes
b. a large population of mobile or uprooted people

These answer choices are similar; they both describe a fluid culture. Because of their similarity, they can be linked together. Since the answer can have only one choice, they can also be eliminated together.

FACT OR OPINION?

Remember that answer choices that are facts will typically have no ambiguous words. For example, how long is a long time? What defines an ordinary person? These ambiguous words of *long* and *ordinary* should not be in a factual statement. However, if all of the choices have ambiguous words, go to the context of the passage. Often a factual statement may be set out as a research finding.

> **Review Video: Fact or Opinion**
> Visit mometrix.com/academy and enter code: 870899

<u>EXAMPLE:</u>

"The scientist found that the eye reacts quickly to change in light."

Opinions may be set out in the context of words like thought, believed, understood, or wished.

<u>EXAMPLE:</u>

"He thought the Yankees should win the World Series."

TIME MANAGEMENT

Depending on your personal preference, try reading the questions before reading the passage. Doing so will help you be aware of what to look for while reading a passage and may even help with comprehension.

In technical passages, do not get lost on the technical terms. Skip them and move on. You want a general understanding of what is going on, not a mastery of the passage.

When you encounter material in the selection that seems difficult to understand, bracket it. It often may not be necessary and can be skipped. Only spend time trying to understand it if it is going to be relevant for a question. Understand difficult phrases only as a last resort.

Answer general questions before detail questions. A reader with a good understanding of the whole passage can often answer general questions without rereading a word. Get the easier questions out of the way before tackling the more time-consuming ones.

Identify each question by type. Usually the wording of a question will tell you whether you can find the answer by referring directly to the passage or by using your reasoning powers. You alone know which question types you customarily handle with ease and which give you trouble and will require more time. Save the difficult questions for last.

Final Warnings

HEDGE PHRASES

Once again, watch out for critical hedge phrases, such as likely, may, can, will often, mostly, usually, generally, rarely, sometimes, etc. Question writers insert these hedge phrases, to cover every possibility. Often an answer will be wrong simply because it leaves no room for exception.

EXAMPLE:

Animals live longer in cold places than animals in warm places.

This answer choice is wrong, because there are exceptions in which certain warm climate animals live longer. This answer choice leaves no possibility of exception. It states that every animal species in cold places live longer than animal species in warm places. Correct answer choices will typically have a key hedge word to leave room for exceptions.

EXAMPLE:

In severe cold, a polar bear cub is likely to survive longer than an adult polar bear.

This answer choice is correct, because not only does the passage imply that younger animals survive better in the cold, it also allows for exceptions to exist. The use of the word *likely* leaves room for cases in which a polar bear cub might not survive longer than the adult polar bear.

WORD USAGE

When asked how a word is used in the passage, don't use your existing knowledge of the word. The question is being asked precisely because there is some strange or unusual usage of the word in the passage. Go to the passage and use contextual clues to determine the answer. Don't simply use the popular definition you already know.

> **Review Video: Word Usage**
> Visit mometrix.com/academy and enter code: 197863

SWITCHBACK WORDS

Stay alert for *switchbacks*. These are the words and phrases frequently used to alert you to shifts in thought. The most common switchback word is *but*. Others include although, however, nevertheless, on the other hand, even though, while, in spite of, despite, regardless of.

FACT TRAPS

Once you know which paragraph the answer will be in, focus on that paragraph. However, don't get distracted by a choice that is factually true about the paragraph. Your search is for the answer that answers the question, which may be about a tiny aspect in the paragraph. Stay focused and don't fall for an answer that describes the larger picture of the paragraph. Always go back to the question and make sure you're choosing an answer that actually answers the question and is not just a true statement.

Writing and Language Test

The writing and language portion of the SAT consists of one 35-minute section. It will contain 4 passages and there will be a total of 44 questions relating to these passages. The breakdown of passages and questions is shown in the table below.

Careers	1 passage; 11 questions	25%
History/Social Studies	1 passage; 11 questions	25%
Humanities	1 passage; 11 questions	25%
Science	1 passage; 11 questions	25%

The SAT Writing and Language Test will contain a range of text complexities from grades 9-10 to post-secondary entry. The passages will cover the subjects from the table above. The test will also contain one or more graphics in one or more sets of questions. These may include tables, graphs, and charts. They will vary in level of difficulty as well as data density, and number of variables.

The questions on the Writing and Language portion of the test are divided into two categories. The first category, called **Expression of Ideas**, is essentially testing whether students understand how to effectively communicate ideas in writing. The second category, called **Standard English Conventions**, is essentially testing whether students are able to practically apply their knowledge of the conventions of standard written English. Both types of questions are set in the context of revising a sample written passage. Students are asked to modify specific portions of the passage by selecting the best words, phrases, concepts, order, and structure to ensure that the final version of the passage adheres to the conventions of writing, is consistent with the author's style and purpose, and effectively conveys the message the author intends.

Expression of Ideas

The questions in this section will focus on the revision of text. They will ask the student to revise for topic development, accuracy, logic, cohesion, and rhetorically effective use of language. Many of the skills needed for these questions are the same skills as are needed for the Reading Test, or are built upon those skills.

DEVELOPMENT

PROPOSITION AND SUPPORT

Proposition questions will require the student to add, retain, or revise central ideas, main claims, counterclaims, and topic sentences. These revisions should be made to convey arguments, information, and ideas more clearly and effectively. *Support* questions will ask the student to add, revise, or retain information and ideas with the intention of supporting claims in the text.

TOPICS AND MAIN IDEAS

The topic is the **subject** of a text (i.e., what the text is all about). The main idea, on the other hand, is the **most important point** being made by the author. The topic is usually expressed in a few words at the most while the main idea often needs a full sentence to be completely defined. As an example, a short passage might have the topic of penguins and the main idea could be written as: *Penguins are different from other birds in many ways*. In most nonfiction writing, the topic and the main idea will be stated directly and often appear in a sentence at the very **beginning** or **end** of the text. When being tested on an understanding of the author's topic, you may be able to **skim** the passage

39

for the general idea, by reading only the first sentence of each paragraph. A body paragraph's first sentence is often—but not always—the main topic sentence which gives you a summary of the content in the paragraph. However, there are cases in which the reader must figure out an **unstated** topic or main idea. In these instances, you must read every sentence of the text and try to come up with an overarching idea that is supported by each of those sentences.

Be aware though that identifying the main idea is only the first step. Once you've determined what it is, you have to decide how to express it in the most effective way.

> **Review Video: Topics and Main Ideas**
> Visit mometrix.com/academy and enter code: 407801

SUPPORTING DETAILS

Effective supporting details provide **evidence** and backing for the main point. In order to show that a main idea is correct, or valid, authors add details that prove their point. All texts contain details, but they are only classified as **supporting details** when they serve to reinforce some larger point. Supporting details are most commonly found in **informative** and **persuasive** texts. In some cases, they will be clearly indicated with terms like *for example* or *for instance*, or they will be enumerated with terms like *first*, *second*, and *last*. However, you need to be prepared for texts that do not contain those indicators. In considering which supporting details to include, you should consider whether the details *effectively* support the main point. **Ineffective supporting details** can be factual and correct, yet they may not be relevant to the author's point. Conversely, ineffective supporting details can seem pertinent, but may be ineffective because they are based on opinion or unprovable assertions.

> **Review Video: Supporting Details**
> Visit mometrix.com/academy and enter code: 396297

TOPIC AND SUMMARY SENTENCES

Topic and summary sentences are a convenient way to encapsulate the **main idea** of a text. In some textbooks and academic articles, the author will place a **topic** or **summary sentence** at the beginning of each section as a means of preparing the reader for what is to come. A good topic sentence will be **clear** and not contain any **jargon**. When topic or summary sentences are not provided, good readers can jot down their own so that they can find their place in a text and refresh their memory.

FOCUS

For these questions, students will be asked to add, revise, retain, or delete information for the sake of relevance. These revisions should make the text more relevant and focused.

These questions are generally straightforward and do not require any special skills to answer. The correct answer will be the one that best stays on topic and coherently contributes to the author's main point in the paragraph or passage.

QUANTITATIVE INFORMATION

These questions will ask the student to relate information presented quantitatively to information presented in the text. The quantitative information may be in the form of graphs, charts, and tables.

The only particular skill needed for these questions is the ability to read and understand the information contained within a graphic. Questions will typically require you to select the choice that

accurately reflects the quantitative information conveyed by the graphic. Answer choices for this type of question are often long, so reading through them can be time-consuming. However, you should be able to scan the answer choices for numbers, and quickly determine which ones match the quantities with their correct values. In general, there should be only one choice that uses the correct values (i.e., a single question won't ask you to both determine the correct quantitative information and decide how to state it in the most concise way).

ORGANIZATION

LOGICAL SEQUENCE

For these questions the student should revise the text with the intention of improving the logical order that the information is presented in.

These questions generally come at the end of a paragraph (or the whole passage) and ask you to decide whether a sentence (or a paragraph) should be moved to a different location. Since these questions come at the end of the paragraph, you will already have read the paragraph when you get to them, so start by mentally relocating the sentence into each of the suggested positions to see what makes the most sense. In some cases, the sentence may fit into a logical progression within the paragraph that will give you a clue about where it ought to go. Does the sentence refer back to anything that has already been said? At other times, there may be grammatical clues within the sentence that offer hints. Do the verb tenses transition from past to present or present to future over the course of the paragraph? Even if you can't determine exactly which choice would be considered the best, you can usually use these techniques to rule out some of them.

INTRODUCTIONS, CONCLUSIONS, AND TRANSITIONS

These questions require the student to revise the beginning or ending of passages, paragraphs, and sentences. Students will ensure that transition words, phrases, or sentences are used effectively to connect the information and ideas being presented in the passage.

This is often the largest single category of questions on the Writing and Language test. There will usually be 5-7 of these questions on each test.

INTRODUCTIONS AND CONCLUSIONS

An ideal introduction to a paragraph or passage sets up the reader to understand what is coming. In some cases, you may have to read the entire paragraph to see where the author is going before you can knowledgeably select the best way to introduce it.

The conclusion of a text is typically found in the last one or two paragraphs of the text. A conclusion wraps-up the text and reminds the reader of the main point of the text. The conclusion is the author's way of leaving the reader with a final note to remember about the paper and comes after all the supporting points of the text have been presented. For example, a paper about the importance of avoiding too much sunlight may have a conclusion that reads: By limiting sun exposure to 15 minutes a day and wearing sunscreen of at least SPF 15, a person can reduce their risk of getting skin cancer later in life.

TRANSITIONS

Appropriate transition words help clarify the relationships between sentences and paragraphs, and they create a much more cohesive passage. Below are listed several categories of transitions that you will need to be familiar with along with the associated transition words:

- **Logical Continuation**: therefore, as such, for this reason, thus, consequently, as a result
- **Extended Argument**: moreover, furthermore, also
- **Example or Illustration**: for instance, for example
- **Comparison**: similarly, likewise, in like manner
- **Contrast**: however, nevertheless, by contrast
- **Restatement or Clarification**: in other words, to put it another way
- **Generalization or General Application**: in broad terms, broadly speaking, in general

EFFECTIVE LANGUAGE USE

PRECISION

For these questions, students will revise the text to improve the exactness or context-appropriateness of word choice.

This is as close as the Writing and Language test gets to testing your vocabulary directly. As with everything on the test, these questions are asked within the context of the passage, but you will have to select the word from among the answer choices that most closely means what the author intends. Connotation and tone will play some role here, but rarely will you be presented with more than one choice whose dictionary definition fits the situation.

CONCISION

For these questions, students will revise the text to improve the economy of word choice. This means they should cut out wordiness and redundancy.

In general, these questions can be solved by feel. The incorrect choices on these questions tend to be rambling or awkward. If you pick the answer that uses a simple construction, does not repeat itself, and carries a reasonable meaning, you'll get it right just about every time.

EXAMPLE

Edit the following sentence so that it expresses ideas precisely and concisely, and wordiness and redundancy are eliminated.

> If you go to the library on Sunday, you will find that the library doors are locked and that the facility is closed on Sunday.

Here is one possible revision:

> If you go to the library on Sunday, you will find the doors locked and the facility closed.

STYLE AND TONE

These questions require the student to revise the style and tone of the text. These revisions are made primarily to ensure consistency of style and tone throughout the passage but also to improve the appropriateness of the style and tone to the author's purpose.

If the author has been using formal words and tone throughout, maintain that pattern. If the author has been writing relatively informally, don't suddenly transition to formal language. Most passages on the test will be on the formal side, but you should be able to distinguish between slightly formal and overly formal. Don't choose fancy words just because they're fancy. If there are simpler more precise words available, go with those.

SYNTAX

These questions will require the student to use varied sentence structure to achieve the desired rhetorical purpose.

Syntax is the order of the words in a sentence. When writing, it is important to make sure not only that the syntax is correct, but also that it is not repetitive. There is nothing worse than reading a passage that has sentences that are all alike: noun, verb, object. These need to be interspersed with sentences that use a variety of clause constructions. This will lend a musicality to the writing, and will allow for greater flow of language and ideas.

EXAMPLE:
Rewrite the following sentences by varying their syntax.

> Marilyn and Rosemary worked together. They were having a party. They had to get all the food done first. They cleaned the house and decorated. They invited about 20 people. The people were all work associates. They were having the party in Marilyn's backyard. This is where she had many similar parties. They were always fun.

This is one way to rewrite the sentences so that the syntax is varied:

> Marilyn and Rosemary were coworkers who decided to throw a party. To prepare, they had to get all the food ready, as well as clean and decorate the house. They invited about 20 people, all work associates, and held the party in Marilyn's backyard, where they had hosted many fun parties before.

The rewritten sentences provide a greater variety of syntax, and consequently, greater rhythm. The language is more engaging as a result.

Standard English Conventions

The questions in this section focus on editing the text to make sure that it conforms to the conventions of standard written English. This includes the editing of sentences, usage, and punctuation. While this part of the test does not specifically require a detailed knowledge of technical grammar, it would be next to impossible to excel on these questions without it. We will therefore be reviewing the basics of grammar and using that vocabulary as we discuss what to do on the test.

THE EIGHT PARTS OF SPEECH

NOUNS

When you talk about a person, place, thing, or idea, you are talking about **nouns**. The two main types of nouns are **common** and **proper** nouns. Also, nouns can be abstract (i.e., general) or concrete (i.e., specific).

Common nouns are the class or group of people, places, and things (Note: Do not capitalize common nouns). Examples of common nouns:

> *People*: boy, girl, worker, manager

> *Places*: school, bank, library, home

> *Things*: dog, cat, truck, car

Proper nouns are the names of a specific person, place, or thing (Note: Capitalize all proper nouns). Examples of proper nouns:

> *People*: Abraham Lincoln, George Washington, Martin Luther King, Jr.

> *Places*: Los Angeles, California / New York / Asia

> *Things*: Statue of Liberty, Earth*, Lincoln Memorial

> *Note: When you talk about the planet that we live on, you capitalize *Earth*. When you mean the dirt, rocks, or land, you lowercase *earth*.

General nouns are the names of conditions or ideas. **Specific nouns** name people, places, and things that are understood by using your senses.

General nouns:

> *Condition*: beauty, strength

> *Idea*: truth, peace

Specific nouns:

> *People*: baby, friend, father

> *Places*: town, park, city hall

> *Things*: rainbow, cough, apple, silk, gasoline

44

Collective nouns are the names for a person, place, or thing that may act as a whole. The following are examples of collective nouns: *class, company, dozen, group, herd, team,* and *public.*

PRONOUNS

Pronouns are words that are used to stand in for a noun. A pronoun may be grouped as personal, intensive, relative, interrogative, demonstrative, indefinite, and reciprocal.

Personal: *Nominative* is the case for nouns and pronouns that are the subject of a sentence. *Objective* is the case for nouns and pronouns that are an object in a sentence. *Possessive* is the case for nouns and pronouns that show possession or ownership.

Singular

	Nominative	Objective	Possessive
First Person	I	me	my, mine
Second Person	you	you	your, yours
Third Person	he, she, it	him, her, it	his, her, hers, its

Plural

	Nominative	Objective	Possessive
First Person	we	us	our, ours
Second Person	you	you	your, yours
Third Person	they	them	their, theirs

Intensive: I myself, you yourself, he himself, she herself, the (thing) itself, we ourselves, you yourselves, they themselves

Relative: which, who, whom, whose

Interrogative: what, which, who, whom, whose

Demonstrative: this, that, these, those

Indefinite: all, any, each, everyone, either/neither, one, some, several

Reciprocal: each other, one another

Review Video: Nouns and Pronouns
Visit mometrix.com/academy and enter code: 312073

VERBS

If you want to write a sentence, then you need a verb in your sentence. Without a verb, you have no sentence. The verb of a sentence explains action or being. In other words, the verb shows the subject's movement or the movement that has been done to the subject.

TRANSITIVE AND INTRANSITIVE VERBS

A transitive verb is a verb whose action (e.g., drive, run, jump) points to a receiver (e.g., car, dog, kangaroo). Intransitive verbs do not point to a receiver of an action. In other words, the action of the verb does not point to a subject or object.

> **Transitive**: He plays the piano. | The piano was played by him.

> **Intransitive**: He plays. | John writes well.

A dictionary will let you know whether a verb is transitive or intransitive. Some verbs can be transitive and intransitive.

ACTION VERBS AND LINKING VERBS

An action verb is a verb that shows what the subject is doing in a sentence. In other words, an action verb shows action. A sentence can be complete with one word: an action verb. Linking verbs are intransitive verbs that show a condition (i.e., the subject is described but does no action).

Linking verbs link the subject of a sentence to a noun or pronoun, or they link a subject with an adjective. You always need a verb if you want a complete sentence. However, linking verbs are not able to complete a sentence.

Common linking verbs include *appear, be, become, feel, grow, look, seem, smell, sound,* and *taste.* However, any verb that shows a condition and has a noun, pronoun, or adjective that describes the subject of a sentence is a linking verb.

Action: He sings. | Run! | Go! | I talk with him every day. | She reads.

Linking:

> Incorrect: I am.

> Correct: I am John. | I smell roses. | I feel tired.

Note: Some verbs are followed by words that look like prepositions, but they are a part of the verb and a part of the verb's meaning. These are known as phrasal verbs and examples include *call off, look up,* and *drop off.*

VOICE

Transitive verbs come in active or passive voice. If the subject does an action or receives the action of the verb, then you will know whether a verb is active or passive. When the subject of the sentence is doing the action, the verb is **active voice**. When the subject receives the action, the verb is **passive voice**.

Active: Jon drew the picture. (The subject *Jon* is doing the action of *drawing a picture.*)

Passive: The picture is drawn by Jon. (The subject *picture* is receiving the action from Jon.)

VERB TENSES

A verb tense shows the different form of a verb to point to the time of an action. The present and past tense are shown by changing the verb's form. An action in the present *I talk* can change form for the past: *I talked.* However, for the other tenses, an auxiliary (i.e., helping) verb is needed to show the change in form. These helping verbs include *am, are, is | have, has, had | was, were, will* (or *shall*).

Present: I talk	Present perfect: I have talked
Past: I talked	Past perfect: I had talked
Future: I will talk	Future perfect: I will have talked

Present: The action happens at the current time.

Example: He *walks* to the store every morning.

To show that something is happening right now, use the progressive present tense: I *am walking*.

Past: The action happened in the past.

Example: He *walked* to the store an hour ago.

Future: The action is going to happen later.

Example: I *will walk* to the store tomorrow.

Present perfect: The action started in the past and continues into the present.

Example: I *have walked* to the store three times today.

Past perfect: The second action happened in the past. The first action came before the second.

Example: Before I walked to the store (Action 2), I *had walked* to the library (Action 1).

Future perfect: An action that uses the past and the future. In other words, the action is complete before a future moment.

Example: When she comes for the supplies (future moment), I *will have walked* to the store (action completed in the past).

CONJUGATING VERBS

When you need to change the form of a verb, you are **conjugating** a verb. The key parts of a verb are first person singular, present tense (dream); first person singular, past tense (dreamed); and the past participle (dreamed). Note: the past participle needs a helping verb to make a verb tense. For example, I *have dreamed* of this day. | I *am dreaming* of this day.

Present Tense: Active Voice

	Singular	Plural
First Person	I dream	We dream
Second Person	You dream	You dream
Third Person	He, she, it dreams	They dream

MOOD

There are three moods in English: the indicative, the imperative, and the subjunctive.

The **indicative mood** is used for facts, opinions, and questions.

> Fact: You can do this.

> Opinion: I think that you can do this.

> Question: Do you know that you can do this?

The **imperative** is used for orders or requests.

> Order: You are going to do this!

> Request: Will you do this for me?

The **subjunctive mood** is for wishes and statements that go against fact.

> Wish: I wish that I were going to do this.

> Statement against fact: If I were you, I would do this. (This goes against fact because I am not you. You have the chance to do this, and I do not have the chance.)

The mood that causes trouble for most people is the subjunctive mood. If you have trouble with any of the moods, then be sure to practice.

ADJECTIVES

An adjective is a word that is used to modify a noun or pronoun. An adjective answers a question: *Which one?, What kind of?*, or *How many?*. Usually, adjectives come before the words that they modify.

> Which one?: The *third* suit is my favorite.

> What kind?: The *navy blue* suit is my favorite.

> How many?: Can I look over the *four* neckties for the suit?

ARTICLES

Articles are adjectives that are used to mark nouns. There are only three: the **definite** (i.e., limited or fixed amount) article *the*, and the **indefinite** (i.e., no limit or fixed amount) articles *a* and *an*. Note: *An* comes before words that start with a vowel sound (i.e., vowels include *a, e, i, o, u,* and *y*). For example, "Are you going to get an **u**mbrella?"

> **Definite**: I lost *the* bottle that belongs to me.

> **Indefinite**: Does anyone have *a* bottle to share?

COMPARISON WITH ADJECTIVES

Some adjectives are relative and other adjectives are absolute. Adjectives that are **relative** can show the comparison between things. Adjectives that are **absolute** can show comparison. However, they show comparison in a different way. Let's say that you are reading two books. You think that one book is perfect, and the other book is not exactly perfect. It is <u>not</u> possible for the book to be more perfect than the other. Either you think that the book is perfect, or you think that the book is not perfect.

The adjectives that are relative will show the different degrees of something or someone to something else or someone else. The three degrees of adjectives include positive, comparative, and superlative.

The **positive** degree is the normal form of an adjective.

Example: This work is *difficult*. | She is *smart*.

The **comparative** degree compares one person or thing to another person or thing.

Example: This work is *more difficult* than your work. | She is *smarter* than me.

The **superlative** degree compares more than two people or things.

Example: This is the *most difficult* work of my life. | She is the *smartest* lady in school.

> **Review Video: What is an Adjective?**
> Visit mometrix.com/academy and enter code: 470154

ADVERBS

An adverb is a word that is used to modify a verb, adjective, or another adverb. Usually, adverbs answer one of these questions: *When?*, *Where?*, *How?*, and *Why?*. The negatives *not* and *never* are known as adverbs. Adverbs that modify adjectives or other adverbs **strengthen** or **weaken** the words that they modify.

Examples:

He walks quickly through the crowd.

The water flows smoothly on the rocks.

Note: While many adverbs end in -*ly*, you need to remember that not all adverbs end in -*ly*. Also, some words that end in -*ly* are adjectives, not adverbs. Some examples include: *early, friendly, holy, lonely, silly*, and *ugly*. To know if a word that ends in -*ly* is an adjective or adverb, you need to check your dictionary.

Examples:

He is *never* angry.

You talk *too* loudly.

COMPARISON WITH ADVERBS

The rules for comparing adverbs are the same as the rules for adjectives.

The **positive** degree is the standard form of an adverb.

Example: He arrives soon. | She speaks softly to her friends.

The **comparative** degree compares one person or thing to another person or thing.

Example: He arrives sooner than Sarah. | She speaks more softly than him.

The **superlative** degree compares more than two people or things.

Example: He arrives soonest of the group. | She speaks most softly of any of her friends.

Review Video: Adverbs
Visit mometrix.com/academy and enter code: 713951

PREPOSITIONS

A preposition is a word placed before a noun or pronoun that shows the relationship between an object and another word in the sentence.

Common prepositions:

about	before	during	on
under	after	beneath	for
over	until	against	between
from	past	up	among
beyond	in	through	with
around	by	of	to
within	at	down	off
toward	without		

Examples:

The napkin is *in* the drawer.

The Earth rotates *around* the Sun.

The needle is *beneath* the haystack.

Can you find me *among* the words?

Review Video: What is a Preposition?
Visit mometrix.com/academy and enter code: 946763

CONJUNCTIONS

Conjunctions join words, phrases, or clauses, and they show the connection between the joined pieces. There are coordinating conjunctions that connect equal parts of sentences. Correlative conjunctions show the connection between pairs. Subordinating conjunctions join subordinate (i.e., dependent) clauses with independent clauses.

COORDINATING CONJUNCTIONS

The coordinating conjunctions include: *and, but, yet, or, nor, for,* and *so*

Examples:

The rock was small, but it was heavy.

She drove in the night, and he drove in the day.

CORRELATIVE CONJUNCTIONS

The correlative conjunctions are: *either...or* | *neither...nor* | *not only... but also*

Examples:

Either you are coming, *or* you are staying. | He ran *not only* three miles, *but also* swam 200 yards.

> **Review Video: Coordinating and Correlative Conjunctions**
> Visit mometrix.com/academy and enter code: 390329

SUBORDINATING CONJUNCTIONS

Common subordinating conjunctions include:

after	since	whenever
although	so that	where
because	unless	wherever
before	until	whether
in order that	when	while

Examples:

I am hungry *because* I did not eat breakfast.

He went home *when* everyone left.

> **Review Video: Subordinating Conjunctions**
> Visit mometrix.com/academy and enter code: 958913

INTERJECTIONS

An interjection is a word for exclamation (i.e., great amount of feeling) that is used alone or as a piece to a sentence. Often, they are used at the beginning of a sentence for an introduction. Sometimes, they can be used in the middle of a sentence to show a change in thought or attitude.

Common Interjections: Hey! | Oh,... | Ouch! | Please! | Wow!

Conventions of Punctuation

END PUNCTUATION

PERIODS

Use a period to end all sentences except direct questions, exclamations, and questions.

DECLARATIVE SENTENCE

A declarative sentence gives information or makes a statement.

> Examples: I can fly a kite. | The plane left two hours ago.

IMPERATIVE SENTENCE

An imperative sentence gives an order or command.

> Examples: You are coming with me. | Bring me that note.

PERIODS FOR ABBREVIATIONS

> Examples: 3 P.M. | 2 A.M. | Mr. Jones | Mrs. Stevens | Dr. Smith | Bill Jr. | Pennsylvania Ave.

> Note: an abbreviation is a shortened form of a word or phrase.

QUESTION MARKS

Question marks should be used following a direct question. A polite request can be followed by a period instead of a question mark.

> **Direct Question**: What is for lunch today? | How are you? | Why is that the answer?

> **Polite Requests**: Can you please send me the item tomorrow. | Will you please walk with me on the track.

EXCLAMATION MARKS

Exclamation marks are used after a word group or sentence that shows much feeling or has special importance. Exclamation marks should not be overused. They are saved for proper **exclamatory interjections**.

> Examples: We're going to the finals! | You have a beautiful car! | That's crazy!

COMMAS

The comma is a punctuation mark that can help you understand connections in a sentence. Not every sentence needs a comma. However, if a sentence needs a comma, you need to put it in the right place. A comma in the wrong place (or an absent comma) will make a sentence's meaning unclear. These are some of the rules for commas:

1. Use a comma before a coordinating conjunction joining independent clauses
   Example: Bob caught three fish, and I caught two fish.
2. Use a comma after an introductory phrase or an adverbial clause
   Examples:
   > *After the final out,* we went to a restaurant to celebrate.
   > *Studying the stars,* I was surprised at the beauty of the sky.

3. Use a comma between items in a series.

    Example: I will bring the turkey, the pie, and the coffee.

4. Use a comma between coordinate adjectives not joined with *and*

    Incorrect: The kind, brown dog followed me home.
    Correct: The *kind, loyal* dog followed me home.
    Not all adjectives are **coordinate** (i.e., equal or parallel). There are two simple ways to know if your adjectives are coordinate. One, you can join the adjectives with *and*: *The kind and loyal dog*. Two, you can change the order of the adjectives: *The loyal, kind dog.*

5. Use commas for interjections and after *yes* and *no* responses

    Examples:

    Interjection: Oh, I had no idea. | Wow, you know how to play this game.
    Yes and No: *Yes,* I heard you. | *No,* I cannot come tomorrow.

6. Use commas to separate nonessential modifiers and nonessential appositives

    Examples:

    Nonessential Modifier: John Frank, who is coaching the team, was promoted today.

    Nonessential Appositive: Thomas Edison, an American inventor, was born in Ohio.

7. Use commas to set off nouns of direct address, interrogative tags, and contrast

    Examples:

    Direct Address: You, *John,* are my only hope in this moment.
    Interrogative Tag: This is the last time, *correct?*
    Contrast: You are my friend, *not my enemy.*

8. Use commas with dates, addresses, geographical names, and titles

    Examples:

    Date: *July 4, 1776,* is an important date to remember.
    Address: He is meeting me at *456 Delaware Avenue, Washington, D.C.,* tomorrow morning.
    Geographical Name: *Paris, France,* is my favorite city.
    Title: John Smith, *Ph. D.,* will be visiting your class today.

9. Use commas to separate expressions like *he said* and *she said* if they come between a sentence of a quote

    Examples:

    "I want you to know," he began, "that I always wanted the best for you."
    "You can start," Jane said, "with an apology."

    > **Review Video: Commas**
    > Visit mometrix.com/academy and enter code: 786797

SEMICOLONS

The semicolon is used to connect major sentence pieces of equal value. Some rules for semicolons include:

1. Use a semicolon between closely connected independent clauses that are not connected with a coordinating conjunction.

    Examples:

    > She is outside; we are inside.
    > You are right; we should go with your plan.

2. Use a semicolon between independent clauses linked with a transitional word.

    Examples:

    > I think that we can agree on this; *however,* I am not sure about my friends.
    > You are looking in the wrong places; *therefore,* you will not find what you need.

3. Use a semicolon between items in a series that has internal punctuation.

    Example: I have visited New York, New York; Augusta, Maine; and Baltimore, Maryland.

> **Review Video: Semicolon Usage**
> Visit mometrix.com/academy and enter code: 370605

COLONS

The colon is used to call attention to the words that follow it. A colon must come after an independent clause. The rules for colons are as follows:

1. Use a colon after an independent clause to make a list

    Example: I want to learn many languages: Spanish, German, and Italian.

2. Use a colon for explanations or to give a quote

    Examples:

    > **Quote**: He started with an idea: "We are able to do more than we imagine."
    > **Explanation**: There is one thing that stands out on your resume: responsibility.

3. Use a colon after the greeting in a formal letter, to show hours and minutes, and to separate a title and subtitle

    Examples:

    > **Greeting in a formal letter**: Dear Sir: | To Whom It May Concern:
    > **Time**: It is 3:14 P.M.
    > **Title**: The essay is titled "America: A Short Introduction to a Modern Country"

PARENTHESES

Parentheses are used for additional information. Also, they can be used to put labels for letters or numbers in a series. Parentheses should be not be used very often. If they are overused, parentheses can be a distraction instead of a help.

Examples:

Extra Information: The rattlesnake (see Image 2) is a dangerous snake of North and South America.

Series: Include in the email (1) your name, (2) your address, and (3) your question for the author.

QUOTATION MARKS

Use quotation marks to close off direct quotations of a person's spoken or written words. Do not use quotation marks around indirect quotations. An indirect quotation gives someone's message without using the person's exact words. Use **single quotation marks** to close off a quotation inside a quotation.

Direct Quote: Nancy said, "I am waiting for Henry to arrive."

Indirect Quote: Henry said that he is going to be late to the meeting.

Quote inside a Quote: The teacher asked, "Has everyone read 'The Gift of the Magi'?"

Quotation marks should be used around the titles of **short works**: newspaper and magazine articles, poems, short stories, songs, television episodes, radio programs, and subdivisions of books or web sites.

Examples:

"Rip van Winkle" (short story by Washington Irving)

"O Captain! My Captain!" (poem by Walt Whitman)

Quotation marks may be used to set off words that are being used in a different way from a dictionary definition. Also, they can be used to highlight **irony**.

Examples:

The boss warned Frank that he was walking on "thin ice."

(Frank is not walking on real ice. Instead, Frank is being warned to avoid mistakes.)

The teacher thanked the young man for his "honesty."

(Honesty and truth are not always the same thing. In this example, the quotation marks around *honesty* show that the teacher does not believe the young man's explanation.)

Review Video: Quotation Marks
Visit mometrix.com/academy and enter code: 884918

Note: Periods and commas are put **inside** quotation marks. Colons and semicolons are put **outside** the quotation marks. Question marks and exclamation points are placed inside quotation marks when they are part of a quote. When the question or exclamation mark goes with the whole sentence, the mark is left outside of the quotation marks.

Examples:

> *Period and comma*: We read "The Gift of the Magi," "The Skylight Room," and "The Cactus."

> *Semicolon*: They watched "The Nutcracker"; then, they went home.

> *Exclamation mark that is a part of a quote*: The crowd cheered, "Victory!"

> *Question mark that goes with the whole sentence*: Is your favorite short story "The Tell-Tale Heart"?

APOSTROPHES

An apostrophe is used to show **possession** or the **deletion** of letters in contractions. An apostrophe is not needed with the possessive pronouns *his, hers, its, ours, theirs, whose*, and *yours*.

> Singular Nouns: David's car | a book's theme | my brother's board game

> Plural Nouns with -*s*: the scissors' handle | boys' basketball

> Plural Nouns without -*s*: Men's department | the people's adventure

Review Video: <u>Apostrophes</u>
Visit mometrix.com/academy and enter code: 213068

HYPHENS

The hyphen is used to separate **compound words**. The following are the rules for hyphens:

1. Compound numbers come with a hyphen

    > Example: This team needs *twenty-five* points to win the game.

2. Fractions need a hyphen if they are used as an adjective

    > Correct: The recipe says that we need a *three-fourths* cup of butter.
    > Incorrect: *One-fourth* of the road is under construction.

3. Compound words used as adjectives that come before a noun need a hyphen

    > Correct: The *well-fed* dog took a nap.
    > Incorrect: The dog was *well-fed* for his nap.

4. To avoid confusion with some words, use a hyphen

    > Examples: semi-irresponsible | Re-collect | Re-claim

Note: This is not a complete set of the rules for hyphens. A dictionary is the best tool for knowing if a compound word needs a hyphen.

DASHES

Dashes are used to show a **break** or a **change** in thought in a sentence or to act as parentheses in a sentence. When typing, use two hyphens to make a dash. Do not put a space before or after the dash. The following are the rules for dashes:

1. To set off parenthetical statements or an appositive that has internal punctuation.

   Example: The three trees--oak, pine, and magnolia--are coming on a truck tomorrow.

2. To show a break or change in tone or thought.

   Example: The first question--how silly of me--does not have a correct answer.

ELLIPSIS MARKS

The ellipsis mark has three periods (...) to show when words have been removed from a quotation. If a full sentence or more is removed from a quoted passage, you need to use four periods to show the removed text and the end punctuation mark. The ellipsis mark should not be used at the beginning of a quotation. Also, the ellipsis should not be used at the end of a quotation. The exception is when some words have been deleted from the end of the final sentence.

The following sentence provides an example:

   "...Then he picked up the groceries...paid for them...later he went home...."

BRACKETS

There are two main ways to use brackets:

1. When you need to place parentheses inside of parentheses, you use brackets instead of parentheses.

   Example: The hero of this story, Paul Revere (a silversmith and industrialist [see Ch. 4]), rode through towns of Massachusetts to warn of advancing British troops.

2. You can use brackets when you need to add material that is being quoted.

   Example: The father explained, "My children are planning to attend my alma mater [State University]."

Conventions of Usage

SUBJECTS AND PREDICATES

SUBJECTS

Every sentence has two things: a subject and a verb. The **subject** of a sentence names who or what the sentence is all about. The subject may be directly stated in a sentence, or the subject may be the implied *you*.

The **complete subject** has the simple subject and all of the modifiers. To find the complete subject, ask *Who* or *What* and insert the verb to complete the question. The answer is the complete subject. To find the **simple subject**, remove all of the modifiers in the complete subject. When you can find the subject of a sentence, you can correct many problems. These problems include sentence fragments and subject-verb agreement.

Examples:

> The small red car is the one that he wants for Christmas.

> (The complete subject is *the small red car.*)

> The young artist is coming over for dinner.

> (The complete subject is *the young artist.*)

> **Review Video: Subjects**
> Visit mometrix.com/academy and enter code: 444771

In **imperative** sentences, the verb's subject is understood (e.g., |You| Run to the store). So, the subject may not be in the sentence. Normally, the subject comes before the verb. However, the subject comes after the verb in sentences that begin with *There are* or *There was*.

Direct:

> John knows the way to the park.

> (Who knows the way to the park? Answer: John)

> The cookies need ten more minutes.

> (What needs ten minutes? Answer: The cookies)

> By five o' clock, Bill will need to leave.

> (Who needs to leave? Answer: Bill)

Remember: The subject can come after the verb.

> There are five letters on the table for him.

> (What is on the table? Answer: Five letters)

There were coffee and doughnuts in the house.

(What was in the house? Answer: Coffee and doughnuts)

Implied:

Go to the post office for me.

(Who is going to the post office? Answer: You are.)

Come and sit with me, please?

(Who needs to come and sit? Answer: You do.)

PREDICATES

In a sentence, you always have a predicate and a subject. A **predicate** is what remains when you have found the subject. The subject tells what the sentence is about, and the predicate explains or describes the subject.

Think about the sentence: *He sings*. In this sentence, we have a subject (He) and a predicate (sings). This is all that is needed for a sentence to be complete. Would we like more information? Of course, we would like to know more. However, if this all the information that you are given, you have a complete sentence.

Now, let's look at another sentence:

John and Jane sing on Tuesday nights at the dance hall.

What is the subject of this sentence?

Answer: John and Jane.

What is the predicate of this sentence?

Answer: Everything else in the sentence besides John and Jane.

SUBJECT-VERB AGREEMENT

Verbs **agree** with their subjects in number. In other words, *singular* subjects need *singular* verbs. *Plural* subjects need *plural* verbs. Singular is for one person, place, or thing. Plural is for more than one person, place, or thing. Subjects and verbs must also agree in person: first, second, or third. The present tense ending *-s* is used on a verb if its subject is third person singular; otherwise, the verb takes no ending.

> **Review Video: Subject Verb Agreement**
> Visit mometrix.com/academy and enter code: 479190

NUMBER AGREEMENT EXAMPLES:

Single Subject and Verb: *Dan calls home.*

(Dan is one person. So, the singular verb *calls* is needed.)

Plural Subject and Verb: *Dan and Bob call home.*

(More than one person needs the plural verb *call*.)

PERSON AGREEMENT EXAMPLES:

First Person: I *am* walking.

Second Person: You *are* walking.

Third Person: He *is* walking.

PROBLEMS WITH SUBJECT-VERB AGREEMENT

WORDS BETWEEN SUBJECT AND VERB

The joy of my life returns home tonight.

(**Singular Subject**: joy. **Singular Verb**: returns)

The phrase *of my life* does not influence the verb *returns*.

The question that still remains unanswered is "Who are you?"

(**Singular Subject**: question. **Singular Verb**: is)

Don't let the phrase "*that still remains…*" trouble you. The subject *question* goes with *is*.

COMPOUND SUBJECTS

You and Jon are invited to come to my house.

(**Plural Subject**: You and Jon. **Plural Verb**: are)

The pencil and paper belong to me.

(**Plural Subject**: pencil and paper. **Plural Verb**: belong)

SUBJECTS JOINED BY OR AND NOR

Today or tomorrow is the day.

(**Subject**: Today / tomorrow. **Verb**: is)

Stan or Phil wants to read the book.

(**Subject**: Stan / Phil. **Verb**: wants)

Neither the books nor the *pen is* on the desk.

(**Subject**: Books / Pen. **Verb**: is)

Either the blanket or *pillows arrive* this afternoon.

(**Subject**: Blanket / Pillows. **Verb**: arrive)

Note: Singular subjects that are joined with the conjunction *or* need a singular verb. However, when one subject is singular and another is plural, you make the verb agree with the **closer subject**. The example about books and the pen has a singular verb because the pen (singular subject) is closer to the verb.

INDEFINITE PRONOUNS: EITHER, NEITHER, AND EACH

Is either of you ready for the game?

(**Singular Subject**: Either. **Singular Verb**: is)

Each man, woman, and child is unique.

(**Singular Subject**: Each. **Singular Verb**: is)

THE ADJECTIVE EVERY AND COMPOUNDS: EVERYBODY, EVERYONE, ANYBODY, ANYONE

Every day passes faster than the last.

(**Singular Subject**: Every day. **Singular Verb**: passes)

Anybody is welcome to bring a tent.

(**Singular Subject**: Anybody. **Singular Verb**: is)

COLLECTIVE NOUNS

The family eats at the restaurant every Friday night.

(The members of the family are one at the restaurant.)

The team are leaving for their homes after the game.

(The members of the team are leaving as individuals to go to their own homes.)

WHO, WHICH, AND THAT AS SUBJECTS

This is the man who is helping me today.

He is a good man who serves others before himself.

This painting that is hung over the couch is very beautiful.

PLURAL FORM AND SINGULAR MEANING

Some nouns are singular in meaning but plural in form: news, mathematics, physics, and economics.

The news is coming on now.

Mathematics is my favorite class.

Some nouns are always plural in meaning: athletics, gymnastics, scissors, and pants.

> Do these pants come with a shirt?

> The scissors are for my project.

Note: Look to your dictionary for help when you aren't sure whether a noun with a plural form has a singular or plural meaning.

Addition, Multiplication, Subtraction, and Division are normally singular.

> One plus one is two.

> Three times three is nine.

COMPLEMENTS

A complement is a noun, pronoun, or adjective that is used to give more information about the verb in the sentence.

DIRECT OBJECTS

A direct object is a noun that takes or receives the **action** of a verb. Remember: a complete sentence does not need a direct object. A sentence needs only a subject and a verb. When you are looking for a direct object, find the verb and ask *who* or *what*.

> I took the blanket. (Who or what did I take? *The blanket*)

> Jane read books. (Who or what does Jane read? *Books*)

INDIRECT OBJECTS

An indirect object is a word or group of words that show how an action had an **influence** on someone or something. If there is an indirect object in a sentence, then you always have a direct object in the sentence. When you are looking for the indirect object, find the verb and ask *to/for whom or what*.

> We taught the old dog a new trick.

> (To/For Whom or What was taught? *The old dog*)

> I gave them a math lesson.

> (To/For Whom or What was given? *Them*)

Predicate Nouns are nouns that modify the subject and finish linking verbs.

> My father is a lawyer.

> Father is the subject. Lawyer is the predicate noun.

Predicate Adjectives are adjectives that modify the subject and finish linking verbs.

> Your mother is patient.

> Mother is the subject. Patient is the predicate adjective.

PRONOUN USAGE

Pronoun - Antecedent Agreement - The **antecedent** is the noun that has been replaced by a pronoun. A pronoun and the antecedent agree when they are singular or plural.

Singular agreement: *John* came into town, and *he* played for us.

(The word *He* replaces *John.*)

Plural agreement: *John and Rick* came into town, and *they* played for us.

(The word *They* replaces *John* and *Rick.*)

To know the correct pronoun for a compound subject, try each pronoun **separately** with the verb. Your knowledge of pronouns will tell you which one is correct.

Example:

Bob and (I, me) will be going.

Answer: Bob and I will be going.

Test: (1) *I will be going* or (2) *Me will be going.* The second choice cannot be correct because *me* is not used as a subject of a sentence. Instead, *me* is used as an object.

When a pronoun is used with a noun immediately following (as in "we boys"), try the sentence without the added noun.

Example:

(We/Us) boys played football last year.

Answer: We boys played football last year.

Test: (1) *We* played football last year or (2) *Us* played football last year. Again, the second choice cannot be correct because *us* is not used as a subject of a sentence. Instead, *us* is used as an object.

> **Review Video: Pronoun Usage**
> Visit mometrix.com/academy and enter code: 666500

Pronoun Reference - A pronoun should point clearly to the **antecedent**. Here is how a pronoun reference can be unhelpful if it is not directly stated or puzzling.

Unhelpful: Ron and Jim went to the store, and he bought soda.

(Who bought soda? Ron or Jim?)

Helpful: Jim went to the store, and he bought soda.

(The sentence is clear. Jim bought the soda.)

Personal Pronouns - Some pronouns change their form by their placement in a sentence. A pronoun that is a subject in a sentence comes in the **subjective case**. Pronouns that serve as objects appear in the **objective case**. Finally, the pronouns that are used as possessives appear in the **possessive case**.

> **Subjective case**: *He* is coming to the show.
>
> (The pronoun *He* is the subject of the sentence.)
>
> **Objective case**: Josh drove *him* to the airport.
>
> (The pronoun *him* is the object of the sentence.)
>
> **Possessive case**: The flowers are *mine*.
>
> (The pronoun *mine* shows ownership of the flowers.)

Who or whom - *Who*, a subjective-case pronoun, can be used as a **subject**. *Whom*, an objective case pronoun, can be used as an **object**. The words *who* and *whom* are common in subordinate clauses or in questions.

> **Subject**: He knows who wants to come.
>
> (*Who* is the subject of the verb *wants*.)
>
> **Object**: He knows whom we want at the party.
>
> (*Whom* is the object of *we want*.)

CLAUSES

There are two groups of clauses: independent and dependent. Unlike phrases, a clause has a subject and a verb. So, what is the difference between a clause that is independent and one that is dependent? An **independent clause** gives a complete thought. A **dependent clause** does not share a complete thought. Instead, a dependent clause has a subject and a verb, but it needs an independent clause. **Subordinate** (i.e., dependent) clauses look like sentences. They may have a subject, a verb, and objects or complements. They are used within sentences as adverbs, adjectives, or nouns.

Examples:

> **Independent Clause**: I am running outside.
>
> (The sentence has a subject *I* and a verb *am running*.)
>
> **Dependent Clause**: I am running because I want to stay in shape.
>
> The clause *I am running* is an independent clause. The underlined clause is dependent. Remember: a dependent clause does not give a complete thought. Think about the dependent clause: *because I want to stay in shape*.

Without any other information, you think: So, you want to stay in shape. What are you are doing to stay in shape? Answer: *I am running*.

Types of Dependent Clauses

An **adjective clause** is a dependent clause that modifies nouns and pronouns. Adjective clauses begin with a relative pronoun (*who, whose, whom, which,* and *that*) or a relative adverb (*where, when,* and *why*).

Also, adjective clauses come after the noun that the clause needs to explain or rename. This is done to have a clear connection to the independent clause.

Examples:

> I learned the reason *why I won the award.*

> This is the place *where I started my first job.*

An adjective clause can be an essential or nonessential clause. An essential clause is very important to the sentence. **Essential clauses** explain or define a person or thing. **Nonessential clauses** give more information about a person or thing. However, they are not necessary to the sentence.

Examples:

> **Essential**: A person *who works hard at first* can rest later in life.

> **Nonessential**: Neil Armstrong, *who walked on the moon*, is my hero.

An **adverb clause** is a dependent clause that modifies verbs, adjectives, and other adverbs. To show a clear connection to the independent clause, put the adverb clause immediately before or after the independent clause. An adverb clause can start with *after, although, as, as if, before, because, if, since, so, so that, unless, when, where,* or *while.*

Examples:

> *When you walked outside*, I called the manager.

> I want to go with you *unless you want to stay.*

A **noun clause** is a dependent clause that can be used as a subject, object, or complement. Noun clauses can begin with *how, that, what, whether, which, who,* or *why.* These words can also come with an adjective clause.

Remember that the entire clause makes a noun or an adjective clause, not the word that starts a clause. So, be sure to look for more than the word that begins the clause. To show a clear connection to the independent clause, be sure that a noun clause comes after the verb. The exception is when the noun clause is the subject of the sentence.

Examples:

> The fact *that you were alone* alarms me.

> *What you learn from each other* depends on your honesty with others.

Copyright © Mometrix Media. You have been licensed one copy of this document for personal use only. Any other reproduction or redistribution is strictly prohibited. All rights reserved.

PHRASES

A phrase is not a complete sentence. So, a phrase cannot be a statement and cannot give a complete thought. Instead, a phrase is a group of words that can be used as a noun, adjective, or adverb in a sentence. Phrases strengthen sentences by adding **explanation** or **renaming** something.

PREPOSITIONAL PHRASES

A phrase that can be found in many sentences is the prepositional phrase. A prepositional phrase begins with a preposition and ends with a noun or pronoun that is used as an object. Normally, the prepositional phrase works as an **adjective** or an **adverb**.

Examples:

The picnic is *on the blanket.*

I am sick *with a fever* today.

Among the many flowers, a four-leaf clover was found by John.

VERBALS AND VERBAL PHRASES

A verbal looks like a verb, but it is not used as a verb. Instead, a verbal is used as a noun, adjective, or adverb. Be careful with verbals. They do **not** replace a verb in a sentence.

Correct: Walk a mile daily.

(*Walk* is the verb of this sentence. As in, "*You* walk a mile daily.")

Incorrect: To walk a mile.

(*To walk* is a type of verbal. But, verbals cannot be a verb for a sentence.)

A **verbal phrase** is a verb form that does not function as the verb of a clause. There are three major types of verbal phrases: participial, gerund, and infinitive phrases.

PARTICIPLES

A participle is a verbal that is used as an adjective. The present participle always ends with *-ing*. Past participles end with *-d, -ed, -n,* or *-t.*

Examples: Verb: *dance* | Present Participle: *dancing* | Past Participle: *danced*

Participial phrases are made of a participle and any complements or modifiers. Often, they come right after the noun or pronoun that they modify.

Examples:

Shipwrecked on an island, the boys started to fish for food.

Having been seated for five hours, we got out of the car to stretch our legs.

Praised for their work, the group accepted the first-place trophy.

GERUNDS

A gerund is a verbal that is used as a noun. Gerunds can be found by looking for their *-ing* endings. However, you need to be careful that you have found a gerund, not a present participle. Since

66

gerunds are nouns, they can be used as a subject of a sentence and the object of a verb or preposition.

Gerund Phrases are built around present participles (i.e., *-ing* endings to verbs) and they are always used as nouns. The gerund phrase has a gerund and any complements or modifiers.

Examples:

We want to be known for *teaching the poor*. (Object of Preposition)

Coaching this team is the best job of my life. (Subject)

We like *practicing our songs* in the basement. (Object of the verb: *like*)

INFINITIVES

An infinitive is a verbal that can be used as a noun, an adjective, or an adverb. An infinitive is made of the basic form of a verb with the word *to* coming before the verb.

Infinitive Phrases are made of an infinitive and all complements and modifiers. They are used as nouns, adjectives, or adverbs.

Examples:

To join the team is my goal in life. (Noun)

The animals have enough food *to eat for the night*. (Adjective)

People lift weights *to exercise their muscles*. (Adverb)

APPOSITIVE PHRASES

An appositive is a word or phrase that is used to explain or rename nouns or pronouns. In a sentence they can be noun phrases, prepositional phrases, gerund phrases, or infinitive phrases.

Examples:

Terriers, *hunters at heart*, have been dressed up to look like lap dogs.

(The phrase *hunters at heart* renames the noun *terriers*.)

His plan, *to save and invest his money*, was proven as a safe approach.

(The italicized infinitive phrase renames the plan.)

Appositive phrases can be essential or nonessential. An appositive phrase is essential if the person, place, or thing being described or renamed is too general.

Essential: Two Founding Fathers George Washington and Thomas Jefferson served as presidents.

Nonessential: George Washington and Thomas Jefferson, two Founding Fathers, served as presidents.

ABSOLUTE PHRASES

An absolute phrase is a phrase with a participle that comes after a noun. The absolute phrase is never the subject of a sentence. Also, the phrase does not explain or add to the meaning of a word in a sentence. Absolute phrases are used *independently* from the rest of the sentence. However, they are still phrases, and phrases cannot give a complete thought.

Examples:

> *The alarm ringing*, he pushed the snooze button.

> *The music paused*, she continued to dance through the crowd.

Note: Appositive and absolute phrases can be confusing in sentences. So, don't be discouraged if you have a difficult time with them.

MODES OF SENTENCE PATTERNS

Sentence patterns fall into five common modes with some exceptions. They are:

- Subject + linking verb + subject complement
- Subject + transitive verb + direct object
- Subject + transitive verb + indirect object + direct object
- Subject + transitive verb + direct object + object complement
- Subject + intransitive verb

Common exceptions to these patterns are questions and commands, sentences with delayed subjects, and passive transformations.

TYPES OF SENTENCES

For a sentence to be complete, it must have a subject and a verb or predicate. A complete sentence will express a complete thought, otherwise it is known as a fragment. An example of a fragment is: *As the clock struck midnight.* A complete sentence would be: *As the clock struck midnight, she ran home.* The types of sentences are declarative, imperative, interrogative, and exclamatory.

A declarative sentence states a fact and ends with a period. The following is an example:

> *The football game starts at seven o'clock.*

An imperative sentence tells someone to do something and ends with a period. The following is an example:

> *Go to the store and buy milk.*

An interrogative sentence asks a question and ends with a question mark. The following is an example:

> *Are you going to the game on Friday?*

An exclamatory sentence shows strong emotion and ends with an exclamation point. The following is an example:

> *I can't believe we won the game!*

SENTENCE STRUCTURES

The four major types of sentence structure are:

1. **Simple Sentences** - Simple sentences have one independent clause with no subordinate clauses. A simple sentence can have compound elements (e.g., a compound subject or verb).

   Examples:

   > Judy watered the lawn. (Singular Subject & Singular Predicate)

   > Judy and Alan watered the lawn. (Compound Subject: Judy and Alan)

2. **Compound Sentences** - Compound sentences have two or more independent clauses with no dependent clauses. Usually, the independent clauses are joined with a comma and a coordinating conjunction, or they can be joined with a semicolon.
   Example:

   > The time has come, and we are ready.

   > I woke up at dawn; then I went outside to watch the sun rise.

3. **Complex Sentences** - A complex sentence has one independent clause and one or more dependent clauses.
   Examples:

   > Although he had the flu, Harry went to work.

   > Marcia got married after she finished college.

4. **Compound-Complex Sentences** - A compound-complex sentence has at least two independent clauses and at least one dependent clause.
   Examples:

   > John is my friend who went to India, and he brought souvenirs for us.

   > You may not know, but we heard the music that you played last night.

> **Review Video: Sentence Structure**
> Visit mometrix.com/academy and enter code: 700478

SENTENCE FRAGMENTS

A part of a sentence should not be treated like a complete sentence. A sentence must be made of at least one **independent clause**. An independent clause has a subject and a verb. Remember that the independent clause can stand alone as a sentence. Some **fragments** are independent clauses that begin with a subordinating word (e.g., as, because, so, etc.). Other fragments may not have a subject, a verb, or both.

A sentence fragment can be **repaired** in several ways. One way is to put the fragment with a neighbor sentence. Another way is to be sure that punctuation is not needed. You can also turn the fragment into a sentence by adding any missing pieces. Sentence fragments are allowed for writers who want to show off their art. However, for your exam, sentence fragments are not allowed.

Fragment: Because he wanted to sail for Rome.

Correct: He dreamed of Europe because he wanted to sail for Rome.

RUN-ON SENTENCES

Run-on sentences are independent clauses that have not been joined by a conjunction. When two or more independent clauses appear in one sentence, they must be **joined** in one of these ways:

1. Correction with a comma and a coordinating conjunction.
   Incorrect: I went on the trip and I had a good time.
   Correct: I went on the trip, and I had a good time.
2. Correction with a semicolon, a colon, or a dash. Used when independent clauses are closely related and their connection is clear without a coordinating conjunction.
   Incorrect: I went to the store and I bought some eggs.
   Correct: I went to the store; I bought some eggs.
3. Correction by separating sentences. This correction may be used when both independent clauses are long. Also, this can be used when one sentence is a question and one is not.
   Incorrect: The drive to New York takes ten hours it makes me very tired.
   Correct: The drive to New York takes ten hours. So, I become very tired.
4. Correction by changing parts of the sentence. One way is to turn one of the independent clauses into a phrase or subordinate clause.
   Incorrect: The drive to New York takes ten hours it makes me very tired.
   Correct: During the ten-hour drive to New York, I become very tired.

Note: Normally, one of these choices will be a clear correction to a run-on sentence. The fourth way can be the best correction but needs the most work.

> **Review Video: Fragments and Run-on Sentences**
> Visit mometrix.com/academy and enter code: 541989

DANGLING AND MISPLACED MODIFIERS

DANGLING MODIFIERS

A dangling modifier is a verbal phrase that does not have a **clear connection** to a word. A dangling modifier can also be a dependent clause (the subject and/or verb are not included) that does not have a clear connection to a word.

Examples:

Dangling: *Reading each magazine article*, the stories caught my attention.

Corrected: Reading each magazine article, *I* was entertained by the stories.

In this example, the word *stories* cannot be modified by *Reading each magazine article*. People can read, but stories cannot read. So, the pronoun *I* is needed for the modifying phrase *Reading each magazine article*.

Dangling: Since childhood, my grandparents have visited me for Christmas.

Corrected: Since childhood, I have been visited by my grandparents for Christmas.

In this example, the dependent adverb clause *Since childhood* cannot modify grandparents. So, the pronoun *I* is needed for the modifying adverb clause.

MISPLACED MODIFIERS

In some sentences, a **modifier** can be put in more than one place. However, you need to be sure that there is no confusion about which word is being explained or given more detail.

Incorrect: He read the book to a crowd that was filled with beautiful pictures.

Correct: He read the book that was filled with beautiful pictures to a crowd.

The crowd is not filled with pictures. The book is filled with pictures.

Incorrect: John only ate fruits and vegetables for two weeks.

Correct: John ate *only* fruits and vegetables for two weeks.

John may have done nothing else for two weeks but eat fruits and vegetables and sleep. However, it is reasonable to think that John had fruits and vegetables for his meals. Then, he continued to work on other things.

SPLIT INFINITIVES

A split infinitive occurs when a modifying word comes between the word *to* and the verb that pairs with *to*.

Example: To *clearly* explain vs. *To explain* clearly | To *softly* sing vs. *To sing* softly

Though still considered improper by some, split infinitives may provide better clarity and simplicity than the alternatives. As such, avoiding them should not be considered a universal rule.

DOUBLE NEGATIVES

Standard English allows **two negatives** when a **positive** meaning is intended. For example, "The team was not displeased with their performance." Double negatives that are used to emphasize negation are not part of Standard English.

Negative modifiers (e.g., never, no, and not) should not be paired with other negative modifiers or negative words (e.g., none, nobody, nothing, or neither). The modifiers *hardly, barely*, and *scarcely* are also considered negatives in Standard English. So, they should not be used with other negatives.

PARALLELISM AND SUBORDINATION

PARALLELISM

Parallel structures are used in sentences to highlight similar ideas and to connect sentences that give similar information. **Parallelism** pairs parts of speech, phrases, or clauses together with a matching piece. To write, *I enjoy reading and to study* would be incorrect. An infinitive does not match with a gerund. Instead, you should write *I enjoy reading and studying*.

Be sure that you continue to use certain words (e.g., articles, linking verbs, prepositions, infinitive sign (to), and the introductory word for a dependent clause) in sentences.

> Incorrect: Will you bring the paper and pen with you?
>
> Correct: Will you bring *the* paper and *a* pen with you?

> Incorrect: The animals can come to eat and play.
>
> Correct: The animals can come *to* eat and *to* play.

> Incorrect: You are the person who remembered my name and cared for me.
>
> Correct: You are the person *who* remembered my name and *who* cared for me.

SUBORDINATION

When two items are not equal to each other, you can join them by making the more important piece an **independent clause**. The less important piece can become **subordinate**. To make the less important piece subordinate, you make it a phrase or a dependent clause. The piece of more importance should be the one that readers want or will need to remember.

Example:

> (1) The team had a perfect regular season. (2) The team lost the championship.

> Despite having a perfect regular season, *the team lost the championship.*

WORD CONFUSION

Which is used for things only.

> Example: John's dog, *which was called Max,* is large and fierce.

That is used for people or things.

> Example: Is this the only book *that Louis L'Amour wrote?*

> Example: Is Louis L'Amour the author *that wrote Western novels?*

Who is used for people only.

> Example: Mozart was the composer *who wrote those operas.*

HOMOPHONES

Homophones are words that sound alike, but they have different **spellings** and **definitions**.

TO, TOO, AND TWO

To can be an adverb or a preposition for showing direction, purpose, and relationship. See your dictionary for the many other ways use *to* in a sentence.

> Examples: I went to the store. | I want to go with you.

Too is an adverb that means *also, as well, very, or more than enough*.

> Examples: I can walk a mile too. | You have eaten too much.

Two is the second number in the series of numbers (e.g., one (1), two, (2), three (3)…)

> Example: You have two minutes left.

THERE, THEIR, AND THEY'RE

There can be an adjective, adverb, or pronoun. Often, *there* is used to show a place or to start a sentence.

> Examples: I went there yesterday. | There is something in his pocket.

Their is a pronoun that is used to show ownership.

> Examples: He is their father. | This is their fourth apology this week.

They're is a contraction of *they are*.

> Example: Did you know that they're in town?

KNEW AND NEW

Knew is the past tense of *know*.

> Example: I knew the answer.

New is an adjective that means something is current, has not been used, or modern.

> Example: This is my new phone.

ITS AND IT'S

Its is a pronoun that shows ownership.

> Example: The guitar is in its case.

It's is a contraction of *it is*.

> Example: It's an honor and a privilege to meet you.

Note: The *h* in honor is silent, so the sound of the vowel *o* must have the article *an*.

73

YOUR AND YOU'RE

Your is a pronoun that shows ownership.

Example: This is your moment to shine.

You're is a contraction of you are.

Example: Yes, you're correct.

AFFECT AND EFFECT

There are two main reasons that **affect** and **effect** are so often confused: 1) both words can be used as either a noun or a verb, and 2) unlike most homophones, their usage and meanings are closely related to each other. Here is a quick rundown of the four usage options:

Affect (n): feeling, emotion, or mood that is displayed

Example: The patient had a flat *affect*. (i.e., his face showed little or no emotion)

Affect (v): to alter, to change, to influence

Example: The sunshine *affects* the plant's growth.

Effect (n): a result, a consequence

Example: What *effect* will this weather have on our schedule?

Effect (v): to bring about, to cause to be

Example: These new rules will *effect* order in the office.

The noun form of *affect* is rarely used outside of technical medical descriptions, so if a noun form is needed on the test, you can safely select *effect*. The verb form of *effect* is not as rare as the noun form of *affect*, but it's still not all that likely to show up on your test. If you need a verb and you can't decide which to use based on the definitions, choosing *affect* is your best bet.

HOMOGRAPHS

Homographs are words that share the same spelling, and they have multiple meanings. To figure out which meaning is being used, you should be looking for context clues. The context clues give hints to the meaning of the word. For example, the word *spot* has many meanings. It can mean "a place" or "a stain or blot." In the sentence "After my lunch, I saw a spot on my shirt," the word *spot* means "a stain or blot." The context clues of "After my lunch…" and "on my shirt" guide you to this decision.

BANK

(noun): an establishment where money is held for savings or lending

(verb): to collect or pile up

CONTENT

(noun): the topics that will be addressed within a book

(adjective): pleased or satisfied

FINE

(noun): an amount of money that acts a penalty for an offense

(adjective): very small or thin

INCENSE

(noun): a material that is burned in religious settings and makes a pleasant aroma

(verb): to frustrate or anger

LEAD

(noun): the first or highest position

(verb): to direct a person or group of followers

OBJECT

(noun): a lifeless item that can be held and observed

(verb): to disagree

PRODUCE

(noun): fruits and vegetables

(verb): to make or create something

REFUSE

(noun): garbage or debris that has been thrown away

(verb): to not allow

SUBJECT

(noun): an area of study

(verb): to force or subdue

TEAR

(noun): a fluid secreted by the eyes

(verb): to separate or pull apart

Mathematics Test

The math portion of the SAT consists of a 55-minute section in which a calculator may be used and a 25-minute section in which no calculator may be used. The calculator portion contains 38 questions and the no-calculator portion contains 20 questions.

CONCEPTS COVERED

SAT questions fall into four categories:

- Heart of Algebra
- Problem Solving and Data Analysis
- Passport to Advanced Math
- Additional Topics in Math

The table below gives a complete breakdown of questions:

Calculator Portion	Number of Questions	% of Test
Total Questions	*38*	*100%*
Multiple Choice	30	79%
Student-Produced Response	8	21%
Content Categories		
Heart of Algebra	11	29%
Problem Solving and Data Analysis	17	45%
Passport to Advanced Math	7	18%
Additional Math Topics	3	8%
No-Calculator Portion	**Number of Questions**	**% of Test**
Total Questions	*20*	*100%*
Multiple Choice	15	75%
Student-Produced Response	5	25%
Content Categories		
Heart of Algebra	8	40%
Passport to Advanced Math	9	45%
Additional Math Topics	3	15%

USE THE PRACTICE TESTS

The best thing you can do to prepare for the SAT is to take several practice tests and review all your wrong answers very carefully. Work back through those problems until you understand how the answer was derived and you're confident you could answer a similar problem on your own.

This guide includes a practice test with answer key and explanations. Examples are also available on the College Board website. If you feel uncertain on a particular concept or problem type, use these tests to practice.

How to Approach the Math Questions

TAKE AN APPROVED CALCULATOR YOU'RE FAMILIAR WITH. CHECK ITS BATTERIES

If you normally use a scientific or graphic calculator, check the SAT website to make sure it's one you'll be allowed to use. Use that calculator as you work through the practice tests.

REMEMBER THAT THE TEST PROVIDES ALL THE INFORMATION YOU NEED

There's even a handy chart of "reference information" in the test booklet with geometry formulas you might need, including the Pythagorean Theorem and special right triangles. The chart even tells you that the sum of angles in a triangle equals 180. Don't worry about cramming to memorize the formula for calculating the area of a circle. All you need to know is that A = area, C = circumference, and r = radius.

READ CAREFULLY

Yes, it's a math test, but these questions require careful reading. Look for key words such as "is" (equals), "more than," "less than," "of" (percentage, ratio, or multiplication), and so forth. Ask yourself:

- "What do I know?"
- "What information does the problem provide?"
- "What is the question asking, exactly?"

REMEMBER THAT YOU DON'T ALWAYS HAVE TO SOLVE THE WHOLE PROBLEM TO ANSWER THE QUESTION

Especially with algebra problems, answering the question may not actually require solving the entire equation or finding all the variables. This is another example of "read carefully"—be sure you understand what the question is asking for.

LOOK AT THE ANSWERS BEFORE YOU BEGIN CALCULATING

What form do the possible answers take? If they're fractions, then work in fractions rather than decimals. Do they include negative numbers? (Negative numbers are an often-forgotten option for many problems involving exponents, roots, and absolute values.)

TAKE IT ONE STEP AT A TIME

If a problem seems overwhelming at first, just look for the first step. Write down what information you know. Break it down. And remember that by just using logic and basic techniques, you can work through even the most complex multi-step problems.

DRAW A PICTURE OR WRITE DOWN EXPRESSIONS AS YOU READ

Many of the problems require more logic than raw mathematical knowledge. As you read a problem, make a sketch in the margin, draw on the figure in the test book, or write out the mathematical expression described. (For example, if you read "The area of Circle A is twice the area of Circle B," write down "A = 2B.")

SUBSTITUTE NUMBERS FOR VARIABLES

Sometimes the easiest thing to do is pick a value for *x*, *n*, or another variable, and work through the problem using that number. It may be easier to work through that way, especially for geometry problems. (Just remember that the value isn't "true," merely convenient.)

USE ELIMINATION

As with all SAT questions, the first thing to do is eliminate obviously wrong answers. Are there choices that are clearly too big or too small? In an impossible form? Based on a common error, such as a sign or exponent error?

CHECK YOUR ANSWERS

When you solve a problem, plug the answer back in to confirm it makes sense. Make sure you haven't made careless mistakes such as skipping a step or making an arithmetic error.

FILL IN ALL THE CIRCLES, THEN DOUBLE-CHECK

For the "student-produced" responses, where you have to supply the actual number instead of selecting from multiple choices, make sure to fill in all the circles. You get no credit for the number written at the top — those boxes are only there to help you mark the circles accurately. Make sure you've filled in the right spots.

GIVE AN EDUCATED GUESS

The SAT no longer penalizes students for wrong answers. This means that you should always narrow down your answer choices by eliminating anything you know is wrong and then give an educated guess at the answer.

DON'T GET MIRED DOWN ON ANY ONE QUESTION

The first, easiest problem on the test is worth the same points as the last, hardest question. If one problem is taking a long time, move on. You can come back to it later if you have time.

Foundational Math Concepts

NUMBERS AND OPERATIONS

Numbers are the basic building blocks of mathematics. The following terms identify specific features of numbers:

- Integers – The set of whole positive and negative numbers, including zero. Integers do not include fractions ($\frac{1}{3}$), decimals (0.56), or mixed numbers ($7\frac{3}{4}$).
- Prime number – A whole number greater than 1 that has only two factors, itself and 1; that is, a number that can be divided evenly only by 1 and itself.
- Composite number – A whole number greater than 1 that has more than two different factors; in other words, any whole number that is not a prime number. For example: The composite number 8 has the factors of 1, 2, 4, and 8.
- Even number – Any integer that can be divided by 2 without leaving a remainder. For example: 2, 4, 6, 8, and so on.
- Odd number – Any integer that cannot be divided evenly by 2. For example: 3, 5, 7, 9, and so on.
- Decimal number – a number that uses a decimal point to show the part of the number that is less than one. Example: 1.234.
- Decimal point – a symbol used to separate the ones place from the tenths place in decimals or dollars from cents in currency.
- Decimal place – the position of a number to the right of the decimal point. In the decimal 0.123, the 1 is in the first place to the right of the decimal point, indicating tenths; the 2 is in the second place, indicating hundredths; and the 3 is in the third place, indicating thousandths.

The decimal, or base 10, system is a number system that uses ten different digits (0, 1, 2, 3, 4, 5, 6, 7, 8, 9). An example of a number system that uses something other than ten digits is the binary, or base 2, number system, used by computers, which uses only the numbers 0 and 1. It is thought that the decimal system originated because people had only their 10 fingers for counting.

Rational, irrational, and real numbers can be described as follows:

- Rational numbers include all integers, decimals, and fractions. Any terminating or repeating decimal number is a rational number.
- Irrational numbers cannot be written as fractions or decimals because the number of decimal places is infinite and there is no recurring pattern of digits within the number. For example, pi (π) begins with 3.141592 and continues without terminating or repeating, so pi is an irrational number.
- Real numbers are the set of all rational and irrational numbers.

OPERATIONS

There are four basic mathematical operations:

- Addition increases the value of one quantity by the value of another quantity. Example: $2 + 4 = 6; 8 + 9 = 17$. The result is called the sum. With addition, the order does not matter. $4 + 2 = 2 + 4$.
- Subtraction is the opposite operation to addition; it decreases the value of one quantity by the value of another quantity. Example: $6 - 4 = 2; 17 - 8 = 9$. The result is called the difference. Note that with subtraction, the order does matter. $6 - 4 \neq 4 - 6$.

- Multiplication can be thought of as repeated addition. One number tells how many times to add the other number to itself. Example: 3×2 (three times two) $= 2 + 2 + 2 = 6$. With multiplication, the order does not matter. $2 \times 3 = 3 \times 2$ or $3 + 3 = 2 + 2 + 2$.
- Division is the opposite operation to multiplication; one number tells us how many parts to divide the other number into. Example: $20 \div 4 = 5$; if 20 is split into 4 equal parts, each part is 5. With division, the order of the numbers does matter. $20 \div 4 \neq 4 \div 20$.

An exponent is a superscript number placed next to another number at the top right. It indicates how many times the base number is to be multiplied by itself. Exponents provide a shorthand way to write what would be a longer mathematical expression. Example: $a^2 = a \times a$; $2^4 = 2 \times 2 \times 2 \times 2$. A number with an exponent of 2 is said to be "squared," while a number with an exponent of 3 is said to be "cubed." The value of a number raised to an exponent is called its power. So, 8^4 is read as "8 to the 4th power," or "8 raised to the power of 4." A negative exponent is the same as the reciprocal of a positive exponent. Example: $a^{-2} = \frac{1}{a^2}$.

> **Review Video: Exponents**
> Visit mometrix.com/academy and enter code: 600998

Parentheses are used to designate which operations should be done first when there are multiple operations. Example: $4 - (2 + 1) = 1$; the parentheses tell us that we must add 2 and 1, and then subtract the sum from 4, rather than subtracting 2 from 4 and then adding 1 (this would give us an answer of 3).

Order of Operations is a set of rules that dictates the order in which we must perform each operation in an expression so that we will evaluate it accurately. If we have an expression that includes multiple different operations, Order of Operations tells us which operations to do first. The most common mnemonic for Order of Operations is PEMDAS, or "Please Excuse My Dear Aunt Sally." PEMDAS stands for Parentheses, Exponents, Multiplication, Division, Addition, Subtraction. It is important to understand that multiplication and division have equal precedence, as do addition and subtraction, so those pairs of operations are simply worked from left to right in order.

> **Review Video: Order of Operations**
> Visit mometrix.com/academy and enter code: 259675

Example: Evaluate the expression $5 + 20 \div 4 \times (2 + 3)^2 - 6$ using the correct order of operations.

P: Perform the operations inside the parentheses, $(2 + 3) = 5$.

E: Simplify the exponents, $(5)^2 = 25$.
The equation now looks like this: $5 + 20 \div 4 \times 25 - 6$.

MD: Perform multiplication and division from left to right, $20 \div 4 = 5$; then $5 \times 25 = 125$.
The equation now looks like this: $5 + 125 - 6$.

AS: Perform addition and subtraction from left to right, $5 + 125 = 130$; then $130 - 6 = 124$.

The laws of exponents are as follows:

1. Any number to the power of 1 is equal to itself: $a^1 = a$.
2. The number 1 raised to any power is equal to 1: $1^n = 1$.
3. Any number raised to the power of 0 is equal to 1: $a^0 = 1$.

4. Add exponents to multiply powers of the same base number: $a^n \times a^m = a^{n+m}$.
5. Subtract exponents to divide powers of the same number; that is $a^n \div a^m = a^{n-m}$.
6. Multiply exponents to raise a power to a power: $(a^n)^m = a^{n \times m}$.
7. If multiplied or divided numbers inside parentheses are collectively raised to a power, this is the same as each individual term being raised to that power: $(a \times b)^n = a^n \times b^n$; $(a \div b)^n = a^n \div b^n$.

Note: Exponents do not have to be integers. Fractional or decimal exponents follow all the rules above as well. Example: $5^{\frac{1}{4}} \times 5^{\frac{3}{4}} = 5^{\frac{1}{4}+\frac{3}{4}} = 5^1 = 5$.

A root, such as a square root, is another way of writing a fractional exponent. Instead of using a superscript, roots use the radical symbol ($\sqrt{}$) to indicate the operation. A radical will have a number underneath the bar, and may sometimes have a number in the upper left: $\sqrt[n]{a}$, read as "the nth root of a." The relationship between radical notation and exponent notation can be described by this equation: $\sqrt[n]{a} = a^{\frac{1}{n}}$. The two special cases of $n = 2$ and $n = 3$ are called square roots and cube roots. If there is no number to the upper left, it is understood to be a square root ($n = 2$). Nearly all the roots you encounter will be square roots. A square root is the same as a number raised to the one-half power. When we say that a is the square root of b ($a = \sqrt{b}$), we mean that a multiplied by itself equals b: ($a \times a = b$).

> **Review Video: Square Root and Perfect Square**
> Visit mometrix.com/academy and enter code: 648063

A perfect square is a number that has an integer for its square root. There are 10 perfect squares from 1 to 100: 1, 4, 9, 16, 25, 36, 49, 64, 81, 100 (the squares of integers 1 through 10).

Scientific notation is a way of writing large numbers in a shorter form. The form $a \times 10^n$ is used in scientific notation, where a is greater than or equal to 1, but less than 10, and n is the number of places the decimal must move to get from the original number to a.

Example: The number 230,400,000 is cumbersome to write. To write the value in scientific notation, place a decimal point between the first and second numbers, and include all digits through the last non-zero digit ($a = 2.304$). To find the appropriate power of 10, count the number of places the decimal point had to move ($n = 8$). The number is positive if the decimal moved to the left, and negative if it moved to the right. We can then write 230,400,000 as 2.304×10^8. If we look instead at the number 0.00002304, we have the same value for a, but this time the decimal moved 5 places to the right ($n = -5$). Thus, 0.00002304 can be written as 2.304×10^{-5}. Using this notation makes it simple to compare very large or very small numbers. By comparing exponents, it is easy to see that 3.28×10^4 is smaller than 1.51×10^5, because 4 is less than 5.

> **Review Video: Scientific Notation**
> Visit mometrix.com/academy and enter code: 976454

POSITIVE AND NEGATIVE NUMBERS

A precursor to working with negative numbers is understanding what absolute values are. A number's *Absolute Value* is simply the distance away from zero a number is on the number line. The absolute value of a number is always positive and is written $|x|$.

When adding signed numbers, if the signs are the same simply add the absolute values of the addends and apply the original sign to the sum. For example, $(+4) + (+8) = +12$ and $(-4) + (-8) = -12$. When the original signs are different, take the absolute values of the addends and subtract the smaller value from the larger value, then apply the original sign of the larger value to the difference. For instance, $(+4) + (-8) = -4$ and $(-4) + (+8) = +4$.

For subtracting signed numbers, change the sign of the number after the minus symbol and then follow the same rules used for addition. For example, $(+4) - (+8) = (+4) + (-8) = -4$.

If the signs are the same the product is positive when multiplying signed numbers. For example, $(+4) \times (+8) = +32$ and $(-4) \times (-8) = +32$. If the signs are opposite, the product is negative. For example, $(+4) \times (-8) = -32$ and $(-4) \times (+8) = -32$. When more than two factors are multiplied together, the sign of the product is determined by how many negative factors are present. If there are an odd number of negative factors then the product is negative, whereas an even number of negative factors indicates a positive product. For instance, $(+4) \times (-8) \times (-2) = +64$ and $(-4) \times (-8) \times (-2) = -64$.

The rules for dividing signed numbers are similar to multiplying signed numbers. If the dividend and divisor have the same sign, the quotient is positive. If the dividend and divisor have opposite signs, the quotient is negative. For example, $(-4) \div (+8) = -0.5$.

FACTORS AND MULTIPLES

Factors are numbers that are multiplied together to obtain a product. For example, in the equation $2 \times 3 = 6$, the numbers 2 and 3 are factors. A prime number has only two factors (1 and itself), but other numbers can have many factors.

A common factor is a number that divides exactly into two or more other numbers. For example, the factors of 12 are 1, 2, 3, 4, 6, and 12, while the factors of 15 are 1, 3, 5, and 15. The common factors of 12 and 15 are 1 and 3.

A prime factor is also a prime number. Therefore, the prime factors of 12 are 2 and 3. For 15, the prime factors are 3 and 5.

The greatest common factor (GCF) is the largest number that is a factor of two or more numbers. For example, the factors of 15 are 1, 3, 5, and 15; the factors of 35 are 1, 5, 7, and 35. Therefore, the greatest common factor of 15 and 35 is 5.

> **Review Video: Greatest Common Factor (GCF)**
> Visit mometrix.com/academy and enter code: 838699

The least common multiple (LCM) is the smallest number that is a multiple of two or more numbers. For example, the multiples of 3 include 3, 6, 9, 12, 15, etc.; the multiples of 5 include 5, 10, 15, 20, etc. Therefore, the least common multiple of 3 and 5 is 15.

FRACTIONS AND RELATED CONCEPTS

A fraction is a number that is expressed as one integer written above another integer, with a dividing line between them $\left(\frac{x}{y}\right)$. It represents the quotient of the two numbers "x divided by y." It can also be thought of as x out of y equal parts.

The top number of a fraction is called the numerator, and it represents the number of parts under consideration. The 1 in $\frac{1}{4}$ means that 1 part out of the whole is being considered in the calculation. The bottom number of a fraction is called the denominator, and it represents the total number of equal parts. The 4 in $\frac{1}{4}$ means that the whole consists of 4 equal parts. A fraction cannot have a denominator of zero; this is referred to as "undefined."

Review Video: Fractions
Visit mometrix.com/academy and enter code: 262335

Fractions can be manipulated, without changing the value of the fraction, by multiplying or dividing (but not adding or subtracting) both the numerator and denominator by the same number. If you divide both numbers by a common factor, you are reducing or simplifying the fraction. Two fractions that have the same value, but are expressed differently are known as equivalent fractions. For example, $\frac{2}{10}, \frac{3}{15}, \frac{4}{20}$, and $\frac{5}{25}$ are all equivalent fractions. They can also all be reduced or simplified to $\frac{1}{5}$.

When two fractions are manipulated so that they have the same denominator, this is known as finding a common denominator. The number chosen to be that common denominator should be the least common multiple of the two original denominators. Example: $\frac{3}{4}$ and $\frac{5}{6}$; the least common multiple of 4 and 6 is 12. Manipulating to achieve the common denominator: $\frac{3}{4} = \frac{9}{12}; \frac{5}{6} = \frac{10}{12}$.

If two fractions have a common denominator, they can be added or subtracted simply by adding or subtracting the two numerators and retaining the same denominator. Example: $\frac{1}{2} + \frac{1}{4} = \frac{2}{4} + \frac{1}{4} = \frac{3}{4}$. If the two fractions do not already have the same denominator, one or both must be manipulated to achieve a common denominator before they can be added or subtracted.

Two fractions can be multiplied by multiplying the two numerators to find the new numerator and the two denominators to find the new denominator.

Example: $\frac{1}{3} \times \frac{2}{3} = \frac{1 \times 2}{3 \times 3} = \frac{2}{9}$.

Review Video: Multiplying Fractions
Visit mometrix.com/academy and enter code: 638849

Two fractions can be divided flipping the numerator and denominator of the second fraction and then proceeding as though it were a multiplication. Example: $\frac{2}{3} \div \frac{3}{4} = \frac{2}{3} \times \frac{4}{3} = \frac{8}{9}$.

Review Video: Dividing Fractions
Visit mometrix.com/academy and enter code: 300874

A fraction whose denominator is greater than its numerator is known as a proper fraction, while a fraction whose numerator is greater than its denominator is known as an improper fraction. Proper fractions have values less than one and improper fractions have values greater than one.

A mixed number is a number that contains both an integer and a fraction. Any improper fraction can be rewritten as a mixed number. Example: $\frac{8}{3} = \frac{6}{3} + \frac{2}{3} = 2 + \frac{2}{3} = 2\frac{2}{3}$. Similarly, any mixed number can be rewritten as an improper fraction. Example: $1\frac{3}{5} = 1 + \frac{3}{5} = \frac{5}{5} + \frac{3}{5} = \frac{8}{5}$.

Review Video: Improper Fractions and Mixed Numbers
Visit mometrix.com/academy and enter code: 731507

ALGEBRA, FUNCTIONS, AND GRAPHS

POLYNOMIAL ALGEBRA

To multiply two binomials, follow the *FOIL* method. FOIL stands for:

- First: Multiply the first term of each binomial
- Outer: Multiply the outer terms of each binomial
- Inner: Multiply the inner terms of each binomial
- Last: Multiply the last term of each binomial

Using FOIL $(Ax + By)(Cx + Dy) = ACx^2 + ADxy + BCxy + BDy^2$.

Review Video: Multiplying Terms Using the FOIL Method
Visit mometrix.com/academy and enter code: 854792

EQUATIONS AND GRAPHING

When algebraic functions and equations are shown graphically, they are usually shown on a *Cartesian Coordinate Plane*. The Cartesian coordinate plane consists of two number lines placed perpendicular to each other, and intersecting at the zero point, also known as the origin. The horizontal number line is known as the *x*-axis, with positive values to the right of the origin, and negative values to the left of the origin. The vertical number line is known as the *y*-axis, with positive values above the origin, and negative values below the origin. Any point on the plane can be identified by an ordered pair in the form (x, y), called coordinates. The *x*-value of the coordinate is called the abscissa, and the *y*-value of the coordinate is called the ordinate. The two number lines divide the plane into four quadrants: I, II, III, and IV.

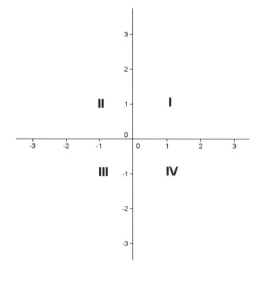

84

Before learning the different forms equations can be written in, it is important to understand some terminology. A ratio of the change in the vertical distance to the change in horizontal distance is called the *Slope*. On a graph with two points, (x_1, y_1) and (x_2, y_2), the slope is represented by the formula $= \frac{y_2-y_1}{x_2-x_1}$; $x_1 \neq x_2$. If the value of the slope is positive, the line slopes upward from left to right. If the value of the slope is negative, the line slopes downward from left to right. If the y-coordinates are the same for both points, the slope is 0 and the line is a *Horizontal Line*. If the x-coordinates are the same for both points, there is no slope and the line is a *Vertical Line*. Two or more lines that have equal slopes are *Parallel Lines*. *Perpendicular Lines* have slopes that are negative reciprocals of each other, such as $\frac{a}{b}$ and $\frac{-b}{a}$.

Equations are made up of monomials and polynomials. A *Monomial* is a single variable or product of constants and variables, such as x, $2x$, or $\frac{2}{x}$. There will never be addition or subtraction symbols in a monomial. Like monomials have like variables, but they may have different coefficients. *Polynomials* are algebraic expressions which use addition and subtraction to combine two or more monomials. Two terms make a binomial; three terms make a trinomial; etc. The *Degree of a Monomial* is the sum of the exponents of the variables. The *Degree of a Polynomial* is the highest degree of any individual term.

As mentioned previously, equations can be written many ways. Below is a list of the many forms equations can take.

- Standard Form: $Ax + By = C$; the slope is $\frac{-A}{B}$ and the y-intercept is $\frac{C}{B}$
- *Slope Intercept Form*: $y = mx + b$, where m is the slope and b is the y-intercept
- Point-Slope Form: $y - y_1 = m(x - x_1)$, where m is the slope and (x_1, y_1) is a point on the line
- Two-Point Form: $\frac{y-y_1}{x-x_1} = \frac{y_2-y_1}{x_2-x_1}$, where (x_1, y_1) and (x_2, y_2) are two points on the given line
- *Intercept Form*: $\frac{x}{x_1} + \frac{y}{y_1} = 1$, where $(x_1, 0)$ is the point at which a line intersects the x-axis, and $(0, y_1)$ is the point at which the same line intersects the y-axis

Review Video: Slope-Intercept and Point-Slope Forms
Visit mometrix.com/academy and enter code: 113216

Equations can also be written as $ax + b = 0$, where $a \neq 0$. These are referred to as *One Variable Linear Equations*. A solution to such an equation is called a *Root*. In the case where we have the equation $5x + 10 = 0$, if we solve for x we get a solution of $x = -2$. In other words, the root of the equation is -2. This is found by first subtracting 10 from both sides, which gives $5x = -10$. Next, simply divide both sides by the coefficient of the variable, in this case 5, to get $x = -2$. This can be checked by plugging -2 back into the original equation $(5)(-2) + 10 = -10 + 10 = 0$.

The *Solution Set* is the set of all solutions of an equation. In our example, the solution set would simply be -2. If there were more solutions (there usually are in multivariable equations) then they would also be included in the solution set. When an equation has no true solutions, this is referred to as an *Empty Set*. Equations with identical solution sets are *Equivalent Equations*. An *Identity* is a term whose value or determinant is equal to 1.

CALCULATIONS USING POINTS

Sometimes you need to perform calculations using only points on a graph as input data. Using points, you can determine what the midpoint and distance are. If you know the equation for a line you can calculate the distance between the line and the point.

To find the *Midpoint* of two points (x_1, y_1) and (x_2, y_2), average the x-coordinates to get the x-coordinate of the midpoint, and average the y-coordinates to get the y-coordinate of the midpoint. The formula is Midpoint $= \left(\frac{x_1+x_2}{2}, \frac{y_1+y_2}{2}\right)$.

The *Distance* between two points is the same as the length of the hypotenuse of a right triangle with the two given points as endpoints, and the two sides of the right triangle parallel to the x-axis and y-axis, respectively. The length of the segment parallel to the x-axis is the difference between the x-coordinates of the two points. The length of the segment parallel to the y-axis is the difference between the y-coordinates of the two points. Use the Pythagorean Theorem $a^2 + b^2 = c^2$ or $c = \sqrt{a^2 + b^2}$ to find the distance. The formula is Distance $= \sqrt{(x_2 - x_1)^2 + (y_2 - y_1)^2}$.

When a line is in the format $Ax + By + C = 0$, where A, B, and C are coefficients, you can use a point (x_1, y_1) not on the line and apply the formula $d = \frac{|Ax_1 + By_1 + C|}{\sqrt{A^2 + B^2}}$ to find the distance between the line and the point (x_1, y_1).

GEOMETRY

LINES AND PLANES

A point is a fixed location in space; has no size or dimensions; commonly represented by a dot.

A line is a set of points that extends infinitely in two opposite directions. It has length, but no width or depth. A line can be defined by any two distinct points that it contains. A line segment is a portion of a line that has definite endpoints. A ray is a portion of a line that extends from a single point on that line in one direction along the line. It has a definite beginning, but no ending.

A plane is a two-dimensional flat surface defined by three non-collinear points. A plane extends an infinite distance in all directions in those two dimensions. It contains an infinite number of points, parallel lines and segments, intersecting lines and segments, as well as parallel or intersecting rays. A plane will never contain a three-dimensional figure or skew lines. Two given planes will either be parallel or they will intersect to form a line. A plane may intersect a circular conic surface, such as a cone, to form conic sections, such as the parabola, hyperbola, circle or ellipse.

Perpendicular lines are lines that intersect at right angles. They are represented by the symbol ⊥. The shortest distance from a line to a point not on the line is a perpendicular segment from the point to the line.

Parallel lines are lines in the same plane that have no points in common and never meet. It is possible for lines to be in different planes, have no points in common, and never meet, but they are not parallel because they are in different planes.

A bisector is a line or line segment that divides another line segment into two equal lengths. A perpendicular bisector of a line segment is composed of points that are equidistant from the endpoints of the segment it is dividing.

Intersecting lines are lines that have exactly one point in common. Concurrent lines are multiple lines that intersect at a single point.

A transversal is a line that intersects at least two other lines, which may or may not be parallel to one another. A transversal that intersects parallel lines is a common occurrence in geometry.

General Rules

The Triangle Inequality Theorem states that the sum of the measures of any two sides of a triangle is always greater than the measure of the third side. If the sum of the measures of two sides were equal to the third side, a triangle would be impossible because the two sides would lie flat across the third side and there would be no vertex. If the sum of the measures of two of the sides was less than the third side, a closed figure would be impossible because the two shortest sides would never meet.

The sum of the measures of the interior angles of a triangle is always 180°. Therefore, a triangle can never have more than one angle greater than or equal to 90°.

In any triangle, the angles opposite congruent sides are congruent, and the sides opposite congruent angles are congruent. The largest angle is always opposite the longest side, and the smallest angle is always opposite the shortest side.

The line segment that joins the midpoints of any two sides of a triangle is always parallel to the third side and exactly half the length of the third side.

Area and Perimeter Formulas

The perimeter of any triangle is found by summing the three side lengths; $P = a + b + c$. For an equilateral triangle, this is the same as $P = 3s$, where s is any side length, since all three sides are the same length.

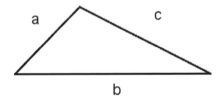

The area of any triangle can be found by taking half the product of one side length (base or b) and the perpendicular distance from that side to the opposite vertex (height or h). In equation form, $A = \frac{1}{2}bh$. For many triangles, it may be difficult to calculate h, so using one of the other formulas given here may be easier.

Another formula that works for any triangle is $A = \sqrt{s(s - a)(s - b)(s - c)}$, where A is the area, s is the semiperimeter $s = \frac{a+b+c}{2}$, and a, b, and c are the lengths of the three sides.

The area of an equilateral triangle can be found by the formula $A = \frac{\sqrt{3}}{4}s^2$, where A is the area and s is the length of a side. You could use the $30° - 60° - 90°$ ratios to find the height of the triangle and then use the standard triangle area formula, but this is faster.

The area of an isosceles triangle can be found by the formula, $A = \frac{1}{2}b\sqrt{a^2 - \frac{b^2}{4}}$, where A is the area, b is the base (the unique side), and a is the length of one of the two congruent sides. If you do not remember this formula, you can use the Pythagorean Theorem to find the height so you can use the standard formula for the area of a triangle.

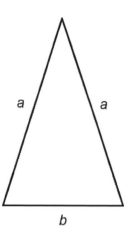

Congruent figures are geometric figures that have the same size and shape. All corresponding angles are equal, and all corresponding sides are equal. It is indicated by the symbol ≅.

Congruent polygons

Similar figures are geometric figures that have the same shape, but do not necessarily have the same size. All corresponding angles are equal, and all corresponding sides are proportional, but they do not have to be equal. It is indicated by the symbol ~.

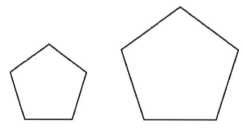

Similar polygons

Note that all congruent figures are also similar, but not all similar figures are congruent.

Line of Symmetry: The line that divides a figure or object into two symmetric parts. Each symmetric half is congruent to the other. An object may have no lines of symmetry, one line of symmetry, or more than one line of symmetry.

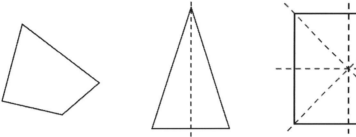

No lines of symmetry   One line of symmetry   Multiple lines of symmetry

Quadrilateral: A closed two-dimensional geometric figure composed of exactly four straight sides. The sum of the interior angles of any quadrilateral is 360°.

Parallelogram: A quadrilateral that has exactly two pairs of opposite parallel sides. The sides that are parallel are also congruent. The opposite interior angles are always congruent, and the consecutive interior angles are supplementary. The diagonals of a parallelogram bisect each other. Each diagonal divides the parallelogram into two congruent triangles.

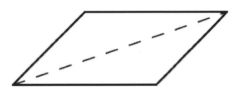

Trapezoid: Traditionally, a quadrilateral that has exactly one pair of parallel sides. Some math texts define trapezoid as a quadrilateral that has at least one pair of parallel sides. Because there are no rules governing the second pair of sides, there are no rules that apply to the properties of the diagonals of a trapezoid.

Rectangles, rhombuses, and squares are all special forms of parallelograms.

Rectangle: A parallelogram with four right angles. All rectangles are parallelograms, but not all parallelograms are rectangles. The diagonals of a rectangle are congruent.

Rhombus: A parallelogram with four congruent sides. All rhombuses are parallelograms, but not all parallelograms are rhombuses. The diagonals of a rhombus are perpendicular to each other.

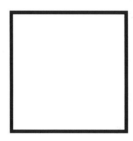

Square: A parallelogram with four right angles and four congruent sides. All squares are also parallelograms, rhombuses, and rectangles. The diagonals of a square are congruent and perpendicular to each other.

A quadrilateral whose diagonals bisect each other is a parallelogram. A quadrilateral whose opposite sides are parallel (2 pairs of parallel sides) is a parallelogram.

A quadrilateral whose diagonals are perpendicular bisectors of each other is a rhombus. A quadrilateral whose opposite sides (both pairs) are parallel and congruent is a rhombus.

A parallelogram that has a right angle is a rectangle. (Consecutive angles of a parallelogram are supplementary. Therefore, if there is one right angle in a parallelogram, there are four right angles in that parallelogram.)

A rhombus with one right angle is a square. Because the rhombus is a special form of a parallelogram, the rules about the angles of a parallelogram also apply to the rhombus.

AREA AND PERIMETER FORMULAS

The area of a square is found by using the formula $A = s^2$, where and s is the length of one side.

The perimeter of a square is found by using the formula $P = 4s$, where s is the length of one side. Because all four sides are equal in a square, it is faster to multiply the length of one side by 4 than to add the same number four times. You could use the formulas for rectangles and get the same answer.

The area of a rectangle is found by the formula $A = lw$, where A is the area of the rectangle, l is the length (usually considered to be the longer side) and w is the width (usually considered to be the shorter side). The numbers for l and w are interchangeable.

The perimeter of a rectangle is found by the formula $P = 2l + 2w$ or $P = 2(l + w)$, where l is the length, and w is the width. It may be easier to add the length and width first and then double the result, as in the second formula.

The area of a parallelogram is found by the formula $A = bh$, where b is the length of the base, and h is the height. Note that the base and height correspond to the length and width in a rectangle, so this formula would apply to rectangles as well. Do not confuse the height of a parallelogram with the length of the second side. The two are only the same measure in the case of a rectangle.

> **Review Video: Finding Areas in Geometry**
> Visit mometrix.com/academy and enter code: 663492

The perimeter of a parallelogram is found by the formula $P = 2a + 2b$ or $P = 2(a + b)$, where a and b are the lengths of the two sides.

The area of a trapezoid is found by the formula $A = \frac{1}{2}h(b_1 + b_2)$, where h is the height (segment joining and perpendicular to the parallel bases), and b_1 and b_2 are the two parallel sides (bases). Do not use one of the other two sides as the height unless that side is also perpendicular to the parallel bases.

The perimeter of a trapezoid is found by the formula $P = a + b_1 + c + b_2$, where a, b_1, c, and b_2 are the four sides of the trapezoid.

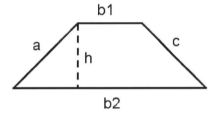

DATA ANALYSIS, STATISTICS, AND PROBABILITY

STATISTICS

Statistics is the branch of mathematics that deals with collecting, recording, interpreting, illustrating, and analyzing large amounts of data. The following terms are often used in the discussion of data and statistics:

- Data – the collective name for pieces of information (singular is datum).
- Quantitative data – measurements (such as length, mass, and speed) that provide information about quantities in numbers
- Qualitative data – information (such as colors, scents, tastes, and shapes) that cannot be measured using numbers
- Discrete data – information that can be expressed only by a specific value, such as whole or half numbers; For example, since people can be counted only in whole numbers, a population count would be discrete data.
- Continuous data – information (such as time and temperature) that can be expressed by any value within a given range
- Primary data – information that has been collected directly from a survey, investigation, or experiment, such as a questionnaire or the recording of daily temperatures; Primary data that has not yet been organized or analyzed is called raw data.
- Secondary data – information that has been collected, sorted, and processed by the researcher

- Ordinal data – information that can be placed in numerical order, such as age or weight
- Nominal data – information that cannot be placed in numerical order, such as names or places

DISPLAYING DATA

A bar graph is a graph that uses bars to compare data, as if each bar were a ruler being used to measure the data. The graph includes a scale that identifies the units being measured.

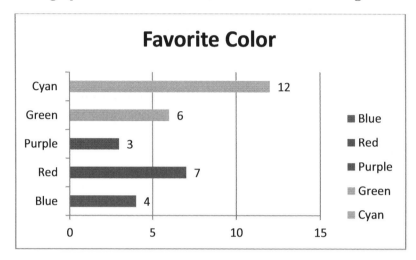

A line graph is a graph that connects points to show how data increases or decreases over time. The time line is the horizontal axis. The connecting lines between data points on the graph are a way to more clearly show how the data changes.

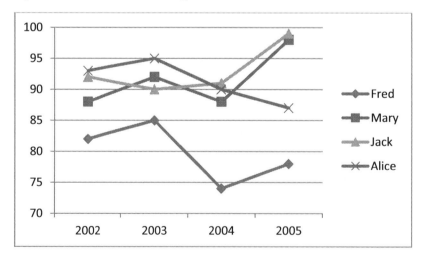

A pictograph is a graph that uses pictures or symbols to show data. The pictograph will have a key to identify what each symbol represents. Generally, each symbol stands for one or more objects.

A pie chart or circle graph is a diagram used to compare parts of a whole. The full pie represents the whole, and it is divided into sectors that each represent something that is a part of the whole. Each sector or slice of the pie is either labeled to indicate what it represents, or explained on a key associated with the chart. The size of each slice is determined by the percentage of the whole that

92

the associated quantity represents. Numerically, the angle measurement of each sector can be computed by solving the proportion: x/360 = part/whole.

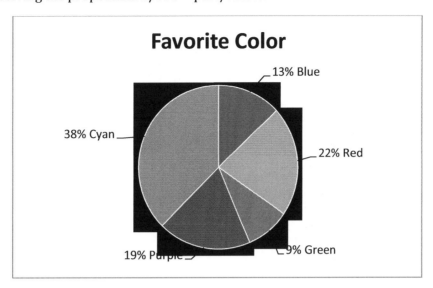

A histogram is a special type of bar graph where the data are grouped in intervals (for example 20-29, 30-39, 40-49, etc.). The frequency, or number of times a value occurs in each interval, is indicated by the height of the bar. The intervals do not have to be the same amount but usually are (all data in ranges of 10 or all in ranges of 5, for example). The smaller the intervals, the more detailed the information.

4.5		
4.1		
4.0		
4.9	5.0	
4.6	5.1	
4.3	5.6	
4.8	5.9	6.2
4.7	5.8	6.1

| 4 | 5 | 6 | 7 |

A stem-and-leaf plot is a way to organize data visually so that the information is easy to understand. A stem-and-leaf plot is simple to construct because a simple line separates the stem (the part of the plot listing the tens digit, if displaying two-digit data) from the leaf (the part that shows the ones digit). Thus, the number 45 would appear as 4 | 5. The stem-and-leaf plot for test scores of a group of 11 students might look like the following:

$$9 \mid 5$$
$$8 \mid 1, 3, 8$$
$$7 \mid 0, 2, 4, 6, 7$$
$$6 \mid 2, 8$$

A stem-and-leaf plot is like a histogram or other frequency plot, but with a stem-and-leaf plot, all the original data is preserved. In this example, it can be seen at a glance that nearly half the students scored in the 70's, yet all the data has been maintained. These plots can be used for larger

numbers as well, but they tend to work better for small sets of data as they can become unwieldy with larger sets.

Heart of Algebra

The questions in this section will cover a range of topics in algebra. Students will be tested on their ability to analyze and solve linear equations and systems of equations. They will also need to be able to create these equations to represent a relationship between two or more quantities and solve problems. Along with linear equations, students will need to be able to create and solve linear inequalities. Some questions will also require the student to interpret formulas and rearrange them to solve the problem.

LINEAR EQUATION IN ONE VARIABLE, INFINITELY MANY SOLUTIONS

When solving a linear equation in one variable, if the process results in a true equation of the form $a = a$ where a is a real number, the equation has infinitely many solutions. This is because the equation is always true, independent of the value of the variable. For example, consider the solution of the equation below:

$$2x - 3(x + 1) = 2 - (x + 5)$$
$$2x - 3x - 3 = 2 - x - 5$$
$$-x - 3 = -x - 3$$
$$-3 = -3$$

For any value of x, each side of the equation evaluates to 3. So the solution is x = any real number, and there are infinitely many solutions.

LINEAR EQUATION IN ONE VARIABLE, NO SOLUTIONS

When solving a linear equation in one variable, if the process results in a false equation of the form $a = b$ where a and b are different (not equal) numbers, the equation has no solution. This is because the equation is always false, independent of the value of the variable. For example, consider the solution of the equation below:

$$2x - 3(x + 1) = 2 - (x + 4)$$
$$2x - 3x - 3 = 2 - x - 4$$
$$-x - 3 = -x - 2$$
$$-3 = -2$$

For any value of x, each side of the equation evaluates to two different values. The equation therefore has no solution.

TYPES OF QUESTIONS – LINEAR EXPRESSIONS

You should expect to create, solve, or interpret a linear equation in one variable. These equations will have rational coefficients and may require multiple steps to simplify or solve. Linear equations in one variable have just one unknown variable. That variable has an exponent of one. For example, $2m + 3 = 3m + 7$ and $1.2(2.5x + 3.2) = 6.7x$ are linear equations in one variable. Typically, a question asks you to translate a verbal expression into an algebraic expression or a word problem into an equation. Then, you may need to solve the equation or answer another question related to that equation. The problems may include questions about any topic that lends itself to a linear expression or equation in one variable. For instance, you may see a question that says, "Jacob rents a car during his vacation. The rental agency's daily charge is $49.95, which is taxed at a rate of 7%.

Jacob is also charged a one-time nonrefundable rental fee of $50. Which of the following represents Jacob's total car rental expenses, in dollars, for use of the car for *x* days?" You would then need to create the expression that computes the total cost for *x* days.

MATHEMATICAL SYMBOLS

You must be able to translate verbal expressions or "math words" into math symbols. This chart contains several "math words" and their appropriate symbols:

equal, is, was, will be, has, costs, gets to, is the same as, becomes	=
time, of, multiplied by, product of, twice, doubles, halves, triples	×
divided by, per, ratio of/to, out of	÷
plus, added to, sum, combined, and, more than, totals of	+
subtracted from, less than, decreased by, minus, difference between	-
what, how much, original value, how many, a number, a variable	x, n, etc.

For example, the phrase *four more than twice a number* can be written algebraically as $2x + 4$. The phrase *half a number decreased by six* can be written algebraically as $\frac{1}{2}x - 6$. The phrase *the sum of a number and the product of five and that number* can be written algebraically as $x + 5x$. You may see a test question that says, "Olivia is constructing a bookcase from seven boards. Two of them are for vertical supports and five are for shelves. The height of the bookcase is twice the width of the bookcase. If the seven boards total 36 feet in length, what will be the height of Olivia's bookcase?" You would need to make a sketch and then create the equation to determine the width of the shelves. The height can be represented as double the width. (If *x* represents the width of the shelves in feet, then the height of the book shelf is $2x$. Since the seven boards total 36 feet, $2x + 2x + x + x + x + x + x = 36$; $9x = 36$; $x = 4$. The height is twice the width, or 8 feet.)

INEQUALITIES

Commonly in algebra and other upper-level fields of math you find yourself working with mathematical expressions that do not equal each other. The statement comparing such expressions with symbols such as < (less than) or > (greater than) is called an *Inequality*. An example of an inequality is $7x > 5$. To solve for *x*, simply divide both sides by 7 and the solution is shown to be $x > \frac{5}{7}$. Graphs of the solution set of inequalities are represented on a number line. Open circles are used to show that an expression approaches a number but is never quite equal to that number.

> **Review Video: Inequalities**
> Visit mometrix.com/academy and enter code: 347842

Conditional Inequalities are those with certain values for the variable that will make the condition true and other values for the variable where the condition will be false. *Absolute Inequalities* can have any real number as the value for the variable to make the condition true, while there is no real number value for the variable that will make the condition false. Solving inequalities is done by following the same rules as for solving equations with the exception that when multiplying or dividing by a negative number the direction of the inequality sign must be flipped or reversed. *Double Inequalities* are situations where two inequality statements apply to the same variable expression. An example of this is $-c < ax + b < c$.

A *Weighted Mean*, or weighted average, is a mean that uses "weighted" values. The formula is weighted mean $= \frac{w_1 x_1 + w_2 x_2 + w_3 x_3 \ldots + w_n x_n}{w_1 + w_2 + w_3 + \cdots + w_n}$. Weighted values, such as $w_1, w_2, w_3, \ldots w_n$ are assigned to each member of the set $x_1, x_2, x_3, \ldots x_n$. If calculating weighted mean, make sure a weight value for each member of the set is used.

SOLVING LINEAR INEQUALITIES

Solving linear inequalities is very similar to solving linear equations. You must isolate the variable on one side of the inequality by using the inverse, or opposite operations. To undo addition, you use subtraction and vice versa. To undo multiplication, you use division and vice versa. The only difference in solving linear inequalities occurs when you multiply or divide by a negative number. When this is the case, you must flip the inequality symbol. This means that less than becomes greater than, greater than becomes less than, etc. Another type of inequality is called a compound inequality. A compound inequality contains two inequalities separated by an "and" or an "or" statement. An "and" statement can also consist of a variable sandwiched in the middle of two inequality symbols. To solve this type of inequality, simply separate it into two inequalities applying the middle terms to each. Then, follow the steps to isolate the variable.

TYPES OF QUESTIONS – LINEAR INEQUALITIES

You should expect to create, solve, or interpret a linear inequality in one variable. Linear inequalities in one variable are inequalities with just one unknown variable. That variable has an exponent of one. For example, $4x + 2 > 10$ and $100 - 2x \geq 27$ are both linear equalities in one variable. Typically, the questions ask you to translate verbal expressions or word problems into algebraic inequalities. Then, you may be expected to solve the inequality or answer another question related to that inequality. Examples of key words and phrases indicating an inequality include *at least* ($\geq$), *no more than* ($\leq$), *more than* ($>$) and *less than* ($<$). You may see a test question that says, "Emily and Madison sold tickets to the school play. Emily sold 70 more tickets than Madison, but together they sold fewer than 200 tickets. Which of the following represents the number of tickets Madison sold?" You would then need to create an inequality from the given information and simplify that inequality using correct algebraic procedures; afterwards, when solving, remember to flip the inequality symbol if dividing or multiplying both sides by negative numbers.

TYPES OF QUESTIONS – LINEAR FUNCTIONS

You should expect to build or create a linear function or equation in two variables that models a context. Linear functions or equations in two variables are equations with two unknown variables. Both variables have an exponent of one. You might be required to express the relationship in functional notation. For example, $y = 3x + 12$ and $p = 0.5d + 14.7$ are both linear equations in two variables and can be expressed in functional notation as $f(x) = 3x + 12$ and $f(d) = 0.5d + 14.7$, respectively. You may be expected to simplify your equation or function. You may see a test question that says, "The pressure in a tank which contains an industrial chemical and which is open to the atmosphere increases linearly with the height of the chemical in the tank. The measured pressure is due to the combined hydrostatic pressure of the chemical and the atmospheric pressure. A pressure gauge at a depth of five feet beneath the surface reads 17.2 pounds per square inch (psi), and at a depth of ten feet reads 19.7 psi. Which of the following linear models best describes the pressure p in psi at a depth of d feet?" You must determine the relationship between pressure p and depth d. First, determine the rate at which the pressure changes with depth; then, consider the contribution of the atmospheric pressure to the total pressure.

MODELING LINEAR RELATIONSHIPS IN TWO VARIABLES

The key idea when modeling linear relationships in two variables is to determine which quantity is the independent variable and which quantity is the dependent variable. For example, you might be asked to build a function to model the pressure at the bottom of a lake in terms of the depth of the lake. Since pressure depends on depth, depth is the independent variable, and pressure is the dependent variable. Your function would have the form of $p(d) = (rate)d + constant$. It helps to recognize that these functions typically fall into the slope-intercept form of a linear equation $y = mx + b$, where y represents the dependent variable, m represents the rate, x represents the independent variable, and b represents the constant. You may need to determine if the independent variable and dependent variable are directly or inversely related. Ask yourself, "As the dependent variable increases, does the dependent variable increase or decrease?" This will determine if the sign associated with your rate is positive or negative.

TYPES OF QUESTIONS – LINEAR INEQUALITIES IN TWO VARIABLES

You should expect to create, solve, or interpret systems of linear inequalities in two variables. Linear inequalities in two variables resemble systems of equations except the equal signs are replaced with inequality symbols ($<, >, \leq, \geq$). You may be asked to solve a system of linear equalities. To solve a system of linear inequalities, each inequality must be graphed on the same coordinate plane. If both inequalities are written in slope intercept form, they can be graphed using the slope-intercept method. A dotted line is used when the inequality includes a $<$ or $>$ symbol. A solid line is used when the inequality includes a $\leq$ or $\geq$ symbol. Shade above the line if $y <$ or $\leq mx + b$ and above if $y >$ or $\geq mx + b$. The region where the two shaded areas overlap is the solution to the original system of inequalities; if there is no overlap, there is no solution. You may be asked to determine whether a given point is in the solution set of a system of linear inequalities. If a graph is provided, simply check to see if the given point is located in the region where the regions of the inequalities overlap. If you are not given a graph, see if the point satisfies each of the given inequalities. If the given point satisfies both inequalities, it is in the solution set for the system of inequalities.

SYSTEMS OF EQUATIONS

Systems of Equations are a set of simultaneous equations that all use the same variables. A solution to a system of equations must be true for each equation in the system. *Consistent Systems* are those with at least one solution. *Inconsistent Systems* are systems of equations that have no solution.

> **Review Video: Systems of Equations**
> Visit mometrix.com/academy and enter code: 658153

To solve a system of linear equations by *substitution*, start with the easier equation and solve for one of the variables. Express this variable in terms of the other variable. Substitute this expression in the other equation, and solve for the other variable. The solution should be expressed in the form (x, y). Substitute the values into both original equations to check your answer. Consider the following problem.

Solve the system using substitution:

$$x + 6y = 15$$
$$3x - 12y = 18$$

Solve the first equation for x:

$$x = 15 - 6y$$

Substitute this value in place of x in the second equation, and solve for y:

$$3(15 - 6y) - 12y = 18$$

$$45 - 18y - 12y = 18$$

$$30y = 27$$

$$y = \frac{27}{30} = \frac{9}{10} = 0.9$$

Plug this value for y back into the first equation to solve for x:

$$x = 15 - 6(0.9) = 15 - 5.4 = 9.6$$

Check both equations if you have time:

$$9.6 + 6(0.9) = 9.6 + 5.4 = 15$$

$$3(9.6) - 12(0.9) = 28.8 - 10.8 = 18$$

Therefore, the solution is $(9.6, 0.9)$.

To solve a system of equations using *elimination*, begin by rewriting both equations in standard form $Ax + By = C$. Check to see if the coefficients of one pair of like variables add to zero. If not, multiply one or both equations by a non-zero number to make one set of like variables add to zero. Add the two equations to solve for one of the variables. Substitute this value into one of the original equations to solve for the other variable. Check your work by substituting into the other equation. Next, we will solve the same problem as above, but using the addition method.

Solve the system using elimination:

$$x + 6y = 15$$
$$3x - 12y = 18$$

If we multiply the first equation by 2, we can eliminate the y terms:

$$2x + 12y = 30$$
$$3x - 12y = 18$$

Add the equations together and solve for x:

$$5x = 48$$

$$x = \frac{48}{5} = 9.6$$

Plug the value for x back into either of the original equations and solve for y:

$$9.6 + 6y = 15$$

$$y = \frac{15 - 9.6}{6} = 0.9$$

Check both equations if you have time:

$$9.6 + 6(0.9) = 9.6 + 5.4 = 15$$

$$3(9.6) - 12(0.9) = 28.8 - 10.8 = 18$$

Therefore, the solution is (9.6, 0.9).

SOLVING SYSTEMS OF EQUATIONS VS SOLVING SYSTEMS OF INEQUALITIES

Solving systems of inequalities is very similar to solving systems of equations in that you are looking for a solution or a range of solutions that satisfy all of the equations in the system. Since solutions to inequalities are within a certain interval, it is best to solve this type of system by graphing. Follow the same steps to graph an inequality as you would an equation, but in addition, shade the portion of the graph that represents the solution. Recall that when graphing an inequality on the coordinate plane, you replace the inequality symbol with an equal sign and draw a solid line if the points are included (greater than or equal to or less than or equal to) or a dashed line if the points are not included (greater than or less than). Then replace the inequality symbol and shade the portion of the graph that is included in the solution. Choose a point that is not on the line and test it in the inequality to see if it is makes sense. In a system, you repeat this process for all of the equations and the solution is the region in which the graphs overlap. This is unlike solving a system of equations, in which the solution is a single point where the lines intersect.

POSSIBILITIES OF A SYSTEM OF 2 LINEAR EQUATIONS IN 2 VARIABLES

There are 3 possibilities that can occur graphically for a given system of two linear equations in two variables:

1. The graphs intersect. The point at which they intersect is the solution of the system of equations.
2. The graphs are the same, or coincide with each other. This means that the two equations are actually the same equation. The solution of the system is all points on the line.
3. The graphs do not intersect, and the system has no solution. This occurs when the two equations have the same slope, or the two lines are distinct vertical lines. These lines are parallel.

TYPES OF QUESTIONS – SYSTEMS OF EQUATIONS

You should expect to be asked to write and solve a system of linear equations from a word problem. You may see a test question that says, "Alyssa's scout troop is selling tickets for the community fun fair. Adult tickets cost \$8.50 each, and child tickets cost \$5.50 each. The troop sells a total of 375 tickets and collects \$2,512.50 in revenue. Solving which of these systems of equations yields the number of adult tickets, x, and the number of child tickets, y, sold by Alyssa's scout troop? How many of each ticket type are sold?" First, write an equation for the number of tickets sold ($x + y = 375$) and a second equation for revenue generated ($8.50x + 5.50y = 2512.50$). Then, solve the system of equations and answer the question that is asked. The methods used in solving systems of linear equations include elimination (addition), substitution, and graphing. To solve by elimination, write the equations in a way that the like variables line up when one equation is placed above the other. The goal is to add the two equations together to eliminate one of the variables. If necessary, multiply one or both equations by a constant to enable such elimination. To solve by substitution, select one of the equations and solve it for one of the variables; then, substitute this into the other equation and solve. To solve by graphing, find the point of intersection of the two lines graphed on the same coordinate plane.

SOLVING LINEAR EQUATIONS IN ONE VARIABLE

You should expect to be asked to solve linear equations in one variable without the use of a calculator. Linear equations in one variable are equations with just one unknown variable that has an exponent of one. The equation may be complicated with rational coefficients. For example, $\frac{10x-8}{6} = \frac{3x+12}{3}$ and $\frac{x-2}{x+3} = \frac{6}{8}$ are both linear equations in one variable that require several steps to solve. If any of the terms in the given equation has/have a denominator, first clear the equation of fractions by multiplying the entire equation by the least common denominator of all of the fractional terms. Then, simplify each side by collecting like terms. Finally, solve for the unknown variable by isolating the variable on one side.

SOLVING LINEAR EQUATIONS IN TWO VARIABLES

You should expect to be given a system of linear equations in two variables to solve without a calculator. For example, $\begin{cases} \frac{1}{2}x + \frac{1}{4}y = \frac{-1}{2} \\ 5x + 3y = -3 \end{cases}$ is a system of linear equations which you might be asked to solve. One of the coefficients may be replaced with a variable as shown here: $\begin{cases} \frac{1}{2}x + \frac{1}{4}y = \frac{-1}{2} \\ ax + 3y = -3 \end{cases}$; you may be asked to solve for a. You can solve systems of equations algebraically by elimination or substitution. Systems of equations may have no solution, one solution, or an infinite number of solutions. If when graphed the two lines are parallel, there is no solution. If the lines intersect at one point, there is one solution. If the lines graph as the same line, there are an infinite number of solutions.

INTERPRETING VARIABLES AND CONSTANTS

You should expect to be given a real-world scenario and the linear function associated with that scenario. You may be asked to identify variable terms or constant terms from the given function as well as interpret their meanings in the given real-world situation. You may see a test question like "The school van begins a field trip with 14 gallons of gasoline. After travelling 120 miles, the van has 8 gallons of gasoline. If this relationship is modeled by the linear function $f(x) = -20x + 280$, what does the x represent?" Or you might be asked what -20 and 280 represent in the given function.

UNDERSTANDING THE BASIC FORMAT

Understanding the basic format of a linear function is very helpful. A linear function has an input and an output. The value of the output is determined by substituting the value of the independent variable into the equation. If the function notation is $f(x)$, the x is the input, and the $f(x)$ is the output. Linear functions are just linear equations written with functional notation. For example, the linear equation $y = 4x + 7$ can be written as the function $f(x) = 4x + 7$. You can compare this to the slope-intercept form of a line in which y represents the output, m represents the rate, x represents the input, and b represents a constant. You may see a test question with a word problem that says, "A school play has $200 in production costs. If tickets are sold at $5.75, how many tickets must be sold before the play makes a profit?" In addition, you may be given a function $p(x) = 5.75x - 200$ and asked a question such as, "What does the x represent?" or "Describe why the operator before the 200 is a minus sign."

ASSESSING UNDERSTANDING OF THE CONNECTION BETWEEN ALGEBRAIC AND GRAPHICAL REPRESENTATIONS

You should expect five types of questions about the connections between algebraic and graphical representations. First, you may be given a linear equation and asked to select from several choices the graph which corresponds to that equation. Key features such as slope and y-intercept provide clues. Second, you may be given the graph of a linear equation and asked to select from several choices the equation which corresponds with that graph. Note the slant of the line, which indicates the slope, and the line's intercepts. Third, you may be given a verbal description of a linear graph and be asked to write the equation that matches the given description. Fourth, you may be given a graph of a linear equation and asked to determine key features such as slope (rate) and intercepts. Fifth, you may be given the graph of a linear equation and asked how a change in the equation impacts the graph. For example, you might be asked how a change in the slope or y-intercept affects the slant or position of the line graphed.

HELPFUL KNOWLEDGE ABOUT CONNECTIONS BETWEEN ALGEBRAIC AND GRAPHICAL REPRESENTATIONS

Understanding the term *slope* and the various forms of linear equations, such as slope-intercept form, is very useful. Slope indicates the slant of the line. Lines with positive slopes slant up and to the right. Lines with negative slopes slant down and to the right. A horizontal line has a slope of zero, and the slope of a vertical line is undefined. If a linear equation is written in the slope-intercept form $y = mx + b$, the slope of the line is given by m. Slope may be determined from a graph as $m = \frac{\Delta y}{\Delta x}$. This often referred to as "rise over run." Also, the b in the slope-intercept form $y = mx + b$ is the y-intercept of the line. The intercepts are the places where the graphed line crosses the axes. The y-intercept has coordinates $(0, b)$, and the x-intercept has coordinates $(a, 0)$. The two-intercept form of a line is given by $\frac{x}{a} + \frac{y}{b} = 1$, where a is the x-intercept and b is the y-intercept. The point-slope form of a line is given by $y - y_1 = m(x - x_1)$, where m is the slope and (x_1, y_1) is a point on the line. A vertical line has the form $x = a$, and a horizontal line has the form $y = b$.

Problem Solving and Data Analysis

The questions in this section will require students to create and analyze relationships. They will solve single- and multistep problems using ratios, rates, proportions, and percentages. Some questions will also require students to describe relationships that are presented graphically. In addition, students should be able to analyze and summarize both qualitative and quantitative data.

RATIOS

A ratio is a comparison of two quantities in a particular order. Example: If there are 14 computers in a lab, and the class has 20 students, there is a student to computer ratio of 20 to 14, commonly written as 20:14. Ratios are normally reduced to their smallest whole number representation, so 20:14 would be reduced to 10:7 by dividing both sides by 2.

> **Review Video: Ratios**
> Visit mometrix.com/academy and enter code: 996914

PROPORTIONS

A proportion is a relationship between two quantities that dictates how one changes when the other changes. A direct proportion describes a relationship in which a quantity increases by a set amount for every increase in the other quantity, or decreases by that same amount for every decrease in the other quantity.

Example: Assuming a constant driving speed, the time required for a car trip increases as the distance of the trip increases. The distance to be traveled and the time required to travel are directly proportional.

> **Review Video: Proportions**
> Visit mometrix.com/academy and enter code: 505355

PERCENTAGES

Percentages can be thought of as fractions that are based on a whole of 100; that is, one whole is equal to 100%. The word percent means "per hundred." Fractions can be expressed as percentages by finding equivalent fractions with a denomination of 100. Example: $\frac{7}{10} = \frac{70}{100} = 70\%$; $\frac{1}{4} = \frac{25}{100} = 25\%$.

> **Review Video: Percentages**
> Visit mometrix.com/academy and enter code: 141911

A percentage problem can be presented three main ways: (1) Find what percentage of some number another number is. Example: What percentage of 40 is 8? (2) Find what number is some percentage of a given number. Example: What number is 20% of 40? (3) Find what number another number is a given percentage of.

Example: What number is 8 20% of? The three components in these cases are the same: a whole (W), a part (P), and a percentage (%). These are related by the equation: $P = W \times \%$. This is the form of the equation you would use to solve problems of type (2). To solve types (1) and (3), you would use these two forms: $\% = \frac{P}{W}$ and $W = \frac{P}{\%}$.

The thing that frequently makes percentage problems difficult is that they are most often also word problems, so a large part of solving them is figuring out which quantities are what. Example: In a school cafeteria, 7 students choose pizza, 9 choose hamburgers, and 4 choose tacos. Find the percentage that chooses tacos. To find the whole, you must first add all the parts: 7 + 9 + 4 = 20. The percentage can then be found by dividing the part by the whole $(\% = \frac{P}{W})$: $\frac{4}{20} = \frac{20}{100} = 20\%$.

UNIT RATE

Unit rate expresses a quantity of one thing in terms of one unit of another. For example, if you travel 30 miles every two hours, a unit rate expresses this comparison in terms of one hour: in one hour, you travel 15 miles, so your unit rate is 15 miles per hour. Other examples are how much one ounce of food costs (price per ounce), or figuring out how much one egg costs out of the dozen (price per 1 egg, instead of price per 12 eggs). The denominator of a unit rate is always 1.

Unit rates are used to compare different situations to solve problems. For example, to make sure you get the best deal when deciding which kind of soda to buy, you can find the unit rate of each. If Soda #1 costs $1.50 for a 1-liter bottle, and soda #2 costs $2.75 for a 2-liter bottle, it would be a better deal to buy Soda #2, because its unit rate is only $1.375 per 1-liter, which is cheaper than Soda #1. Unit rates can also help determine the length of time a given event will take. For example, if you can paint 2 rooms in 4.5 hours, you can determine how long it will take you to paint 5 rooms by solving for the unit rate per room and then multiplying that by 5.

> **Review Video: Rates and Unit Rates**
> Visit mometrix.com/academy and enter code: 185363

TYPES OF QUESTIONS – RATIOS, RATES, PROPORTIONAL RELATIONSHIPS

You should expect three types of questions in this category. First, you may be asked to use a proportional relationship between two quantities to solve a multistep problem or to find a ratio or rate. Proportional relationships can be direct relationships (as *x* increases, *y* increases) or inverse relationships (as *x* increases, *y* decreases). Remember, units can be cancelled just like factors. You may be expected to use some basic knowledge such as *distance = rate × time*. Second, you might be asked to calculate a ratio or rate and to use that rate or ratio to solve a multistep problem. Third, you might be given a ratio or rate and be expected to solve a multistep problem. You may see a test question that says, "The ratio of boys to girls in the children's choir is 2:3. If there are eight boys in the choir, how many total children are in the choir?" You may be given a mixture problem in the form of a ratio and be expected to determine how much of a component is needed. You may be asked to determine a ratio associated with a geometric relationship, such as the ratio of a circle's circumference to its radius. You may be given a scale drawing and be expected to find a ratio associated with that drawing.

TYPES OF QUESTIONS – PERCENTAGES

Questions involving percentages typically come in three basic forms. For example, "What is 10% of 50?" or "5 is what percentage of 50?" or "5 is 10% of what number?" Questions involving percentages may also include percentage increase or decrease. These questions may be worded using *percentage change*. For example, "If gasoline prices rose from $2.76 to $3.61, what is the percentage change?" More complicated questions may be asked, and you will need to have a solid understanding of percentages in order to approach such questions. You may be given a table of values or a pie chart and be expected to calculate percentages from the information given. You may be expected to use these calculations to answer a related question.

TYPES OF QUESTIONS – UNITS AND UNIT CONVERSION

You should expect to be asked to determine a unit rate and then use that rate to solve another problem. You may see a question that gives a conversion rate for an unfamiliar quantity to a familiar quantity, such as from a foreign currency to US dollars. You may be asked to solve a multistep unit problem using unfamiliar conversion rates along with other concepts, such as finding percentages. You may be asked to solve multistep problems to determine an item's density, or you may be asked to apply the concept of density. You may see a problem that says, "A bar of gold has dimensions of 5.0 cm by 5.0 cm by 10.0 cm. If gold has a density of 19,300 kg/m³, what is the mass of the gold bar in grams?"

SCATTER PLOT

Scatter plots show the relationship between two sets of data. The first step in creating a scatter plot is to collect data. Suppose you are analyzing the relationship between age and hours of sleep. You would collect a representative sample of the population using a list or chart to organize your data. Next, you would arrange the data in a table with the independent variable on the left-hand side and the dependent variable on the right-hand side. To graph your data, look at the range in the values. In this situation, the independent variable, or x-values, and the dependent variable, or y-values, all are positive so you only need to draw and label Quadrant I on the coordinate grid. Look at the data and find the most appropriate intervals to label the axes. Plot the points using (x, y), moving over x units on the horizontal axis and up y units on the vertical axis to see the relationship between the two data sets.

> **Review Video: Scatter Plot**
> Visit mometrix.com/academy and enter code: 596526

TYPES OF QUESTIONS – SCATTER PLOT

You should expect to be given a scatterplot in a real-world context. The scatterplot may already include a line of best fit, or you may be expected to select the equation of a line or curve of best fit. You may be expected to interpret the relationship between two variables based on the scatterplot. This relationship may be linear, quadratic, or exponential. You may be expected to use the line or curve of best fit to make a prediction about the situation. You may be given a scatter plot and asked, "Based on the line of best fit to the data shown, which of the following values is closest to the average yearly increase?." You must determine the slope of the line of best fit to answer the question. It is important to understand correlations shown by scatterplots. Make sure you do not try to apply a line of best fit to data that show no correlation. Make sure you do not try to apply a line to a curvilinear model. You probably will not have to actually find the equation of the line of best fit. You just need to be able to interpret the information that is given.

CORRELATIONS

A scatter plot is a way to represent the relationship between two data sets. The data can have one of three types of relationships, or correlations: a positive correlation, a negative correlation, or no correlation. A positive correlation is one in which the points increase from left to right. A negative correlation is one in which the points decrease from left to right. A scatter plot with no correlation is one in which the points show no relationship and neither rise nor fall. The correlation can help to determine the line of best fit. The line of best fit is a line drawn to best represent the data values. The line usually falls in the middle of the group of points and contains as many points as possible. When a graph has a positive or negative correlation, a line of regression can be drawn to determine an equation based on the relationship. When a graph has no correlation, a regression line cannot be drawn.

SUMMARIZE DATA IN TWO-WAY FREQUENCY TABLE

A two-way frequency table is a table that shows the number of data points falling into each combination of two categories in the form of a table, with one category on each axis. Creating a two-way frequency table is simply a matter of drawing a table with each axis labeled with the possibilities for the corresponding category, and then filling in the numbers in the appropriate cells. For instance, suppose you're told that at a given school, 30 male students take Spanish, 20 take French, and 25 German, while 26 female students take Spanish, 28 French, and 21 German. These data can be represented by the following two-way frequency table:

# of students	SPANISH	FRENCH	GERMAN
MALE	30	20	25
FEMALE	26	28	21

You should expect to see questions with categorical data summarized in two-way tables. You need to make comparisons among the data contained in the columns and rows of data. You may need to use proportions or calculate percentages. Two-way frequency tables typically include cells which total the data contained in the columns and rows, as well as an overall sum of data. These sums are used when calculating proportions and percentages. You may be asked to determine the relative frequencies of the data included in the rows or the columns. You may need to determine conditional probability, which is the probability of one event given the occurrence of another; additionally, you may be asked to compare conditional probabilities to determine the association between events. For example, consider a table with a row of data showing the number of students who study for a test more than and less than four hours a week and a row of data showing the number of students whose test grades are above and below 80%. The probability of a student making above 80% is calculated given a study time of more than four hours, and the probability of a student making below a 80% given a study time of more than four hours; if the probability of a student making above an 80% is much greater than the probability of making below an 80% given the same study time, there may be a correlation between study time and test score; alternatively, if the probabilities are approximately the same, there would appear to be no correlation.

TYPES OF QUESTIONS – INFERENCES ABOUT POPULATION PARAMETERS

You may be asked to estimate a population parameter given the results from a random sample of a population. A question might say, "In the survey of a random sample of 1,200 cell phone users aged 18-25 from a particular region, 420 used their phones exclusively to do their banking. If the region had 160,000 residents aged 18-25, approximately how many of those residents could be expected to use their cell phones exclusively to do their banking?" You are also expected to understand any confidence intervals and measurement errors included in the problem. You may see a question that says, "A researcher collected information from 1,000 randomly selected public high school science teachers in the United States and concluded that the median annual salary was between $52,400 and $63,800 with a 99% confidence level. Which of the following could represent the median annual salary for the same sample with a 95% confidence level?"

ESTIMATING A CONDITIONAL PROBABILITY FROM A TWO-WAY FREQUENCY TABLE

If we have a two-way frequency table, it is generally a straightforward matter to read off the probabilities of any two events A and B, as well as the joint probability of both events occurring, $P(A \cap B)$. We can then find the conditional probability P(A|B) by calculating $P(A|B) = \frac{P(A \cap B)}{P(B)}$.

For example, a certain store's recent T-shirt sales:

		Size			
		Small	Medium	Large	Total
Color	Blue	25	40	35	100
	White	27	25	22	74
	Black	8	23	15	26
	Total	60	88	72	220

Suppose we want to find the conditional probability that a customer buys a black shirt (event A), given that the shirt he buys is size small (event B). From the table, the probability P(A) that a customer buys a small shirt is $\frac{60}{220} = \frac{3}{11}$. The probability $P(A \cap B)$ that he buys a small, black shirt is $\frac{8}{220} = \frac{2}{55}$. The conditional probability P(A|B) that he buys a black shirt, given that he buys a small shirt, is therefore $P(A|B) = \frac{2/55}{3/11} = \frac{2}{15}$.

PROBABILITY

Probability is a branch of statistics that deals with the likelihood of something taking place. One classic example is a coin toss. There are only two possible results: heads or tails. The likelihood, or probability, that the coin will land as heads is 1 out of 2 (1/2, 0.5, 50%). Tails has the same probability. Another common example is a 6-sided die roll. There are six possible results from rolling a single die, each with an equal chance of happening, so the probability of any given number coming up is 1 out of 6.

Review Video: Intro to Probability
Visit mometrix.com/academy and enter code: 212374

Terms frequently used in probability:

- Event – a situation that produces results of some sort (a coin toss)
- Compound event – event that involves two or more independent events (rolling a pair of dice; taking the sum)
- Outcome – a possible result in an experiment or event (heads, tails)
- Desired outcome (or success) – an outcome that meets a particular set of criteria (a roll of 1 or 2 if we are looking for numbers less than 3)
- Independent events – two or more events whose outcomes do not affect one another (two coins tossed at the same time)
- Dependent events – two or more events whose outcomes affect one another (two cards drawn consecutively from the same deck)
- Certain outcome – probability of outcome is 100% or 1
- Impossible outcome – probability of outcome is 0% or 0
- Mutually exclusive outcomes – two or more outcomes whose criteria cannot all be satisfied in a single event (a coin coming up heads and tails on the same toss)

107

Probability is the likelihood of a certain outcome occurring for a given event. The theoretical probability can usually be determined without actually performing the event. The likelihood of a outcome occurring, or the probability of an outcome occurring, is given by the formula

$$P(A) = \frac{\text{Number of acceptable outcomes}}{\text{Number of possible outcomes}}$$

where $P(A)$ is the probability of an outcome A occurring, and each outcome is just as likely to occur as any other outcome. If each outcome has the same probability of occurring as every other possible outcome, the outcomes are said to be equally likely to occur. The total number of acceptable outcomes must be less than or equal to the total number of possible outcomes. If the two are equal, then the outcome is certain to occur and the probability is 1. If the number of acceptable outcomes is zero, then the outcome is impossible and the probability is 0.

Example:

There are 20 marbles in a bag and 5 are red. The theoretical probability of randomly selecting a red marble is 5 out of 20, (5/20 = 1/4, 0.25, or 25%).

When trying to calculate the probability of an event using the $\frac{desired\ outcomes}{total\ outcomes}$ formula, you may frequently find that there are too many outcomes to individually count them. Permutation and combination formulas offer a shortcut to counting outcomes. A permutation is an arrangement of a specific number of a set of objects in a specific order. The number of permutations of r items given a set of n items can be calculated as $_nP_r = \frac{n!}{(n-r)!}$. Combinations are similar to permutations, except there are no restrictions regarding the order of the elements. While ABC is considered a different permutation than BCA, ABC and BCA are considered the same combination. The number of **combinations** of r items given a set of n items can be calculated as $_nC_r = \frac{n!}{r!(n-r)!}$ or $_nC_r = \frac{_nP_r}{r!}$.

Example: Suppose you want to calculate how many different 5-card hands can be drawn from a deck of 52 cards. This is a combination since the order of the cards in a hand does not matter. There are 52 cards available, and 5 to be selected. Thus, the number of different hands is $_{52}C_5 = \frac{52!}{5!\times47!} = 2,598,960$.

Sometimes it may be easier to calculate the possibility of something not happening, or the complement of an event. Represented by the symbol $\bar{A}$, the complement of A is the probability that event A does not happen. When you know the probability of event A occurring, you can use the formula $P(\bar{A}) = 1 - P(A)$, where $P(\bar{A})$ is the probability of event A not occurring, and $P(A)$ is the probability of event A occurring.

The addition rule for probability is used for finding the probability of a compound event. Use the formula $P(A \text{ or } B) = P(A) + P(B) - P(A \text{ and } B)$, where $P(A \text{ and } B)$ is the probability of both events occurring to find the probability of a compound event. The probability of both events occurring at the same time must be subtracted to eliminate any overlap in the first two probabilities.

CONDITIONAL PROBABILITY
Conditional probability is the probability of an event occurring once another event has already occurred. Given event A and dependent event B, the probability of event B occurring when event A has already occurred is represented by the notation $P(A|B)$. To find the probability of event B occurring, take into account the fact that event A has already occurred and adjust the total number

Mometrix

of possible outcomes. For example, suppose you have ten balls numbered 1–10 and you want ball number 7 to be pulled in two pulls. On the first pull, the probability of getting the 7 is $\frac{1}{10}$ because there is one ball with a 7 on it and 10 balls to choose from. Assuming the first pull did not yield a 7, the probability of pulling a 7 on the second pull is now $\frac{1}{9}$ because there are only 9 balls remaining for the second pull.

The multiplication rule can be used to find the probability of two independent events occurring using the formula $P(A \text{ and } B) = P(A) \times P(B)$, where $P(A \text{ and } B)$ is the probability of two independent events occurring, $P(A)$ is the probability of the first event occurring, and $P(B)$ is the probability of the second event occurring.

The multiplication rule can also be used to find the probability of two dependent events occurring using the formula $P(A \text{ and } B) = P(A) \times P(B|A)$, where $P(A \text{ and } B)$ is the probability of two dependent events occurring and $P(B|A)$ is the probability of the second event occurring after the first event has already occurred.

Before using the multiplication rule, you MUST first determine whether the two events are dependent or independent.

Use a combination of the multiplication rule and the rule of complements to find the probability that at least one outcome of the element will occur. This given by the general formula $P(\text{at least one event occurring}) = 1 - P(\text{no outcomes occurring})$. For example, to find the probability that at least one even number will show when a pair of dice is rolled, find the probability that two odd numbers will be rolled (no even numbers) and subtract from one. You can always use a tree diagram or make a chart to list the possible outcomes when the sample space is small, such as in the dice-rolling example, but in most cases, it will be much faster to use the multiplication and complement formulas.

EXPECTED VALUE

Expected value is a method of determining expected outcome in a random situation. It is really a sum of the weighted probabilities of the possible outcomes. Multiply the probability of an event occurring by the weight assigned to that probability (such as the amount of money won or lost). A practical application of the expected value is to determine whether a game of chance is really fair. If the sum of the weighted probabilities is equal to zero, the game is generally considered fair because the player has a fair chance to at least to break even. If the expected value is less than zero, then players lose more than they win. For example, a lottery drawing might allow the player to choose any three-digit number, 000–999. The probability of choosing the winning number is 1:1000. If it costs \$1 to play, and a winning number receives \$500, the expected value is $\left(-\$1 \cdot \frac{999}{1,000}\right) + \left(\$500 \cdot \frac{1}{1,000}\right) = -0.499$ or $-\$0.50$. You can expect to lose on average 50 cents for every dollar you spend.

EMPIRICAL PROBABILITY

Most of the time, when we talk about probability, we mean theoretical probability. Empirical probability, or experimental probability or relative frequency, is the number of times an outcome occurs in a particular experiment or a certain number of observed events. While theoretical probability is based on what *should* happen, experimental probability is based on what *has* happened. Experimental probability is calculated in the same way as theoretical, except that actual outcomes are used instead of possible outcomes.

109

Theoretical and experimental probability do not always line up with one another. Theoretical probability says that out of 20 coin tosses, 10 should be heads. However, if we were to toss 20 coins, we might record just 5 heads. This doesn't mean that our theoretical probability is incorrect; it just means that this experiment had results that were different from what was predicted. A practical application of empirical probability is the insurance industry. There are no set functions that define life span, health, or safety. Insurance companies look at factors from hundreds of thousands of individuals to find patterns that they then use to set the formulas for insurance premiums.

MEASURES OF CENTRAL TENDENCY

The quantities of mean, median, and mode are all referred to as measures of central tendency. They can each give a picture of what the whole set of data looks like with just a single number. Knowing what each of these values represents is vital to making use of the information they provide.

The mean, also known as the arithmetic mean or average, of a data set is calculated by summing all the values in the set and dividing that sum by the number of values. For example, if a data set has 6 numbers and the sum of those 6 numbers is 30, the mean is calculated as 30/6 = 5.

The median is the middle value of a data set. The median can be found by putting the data set in numerical order, and locating the middle value. In the data set (1, 2, 3, 4, 5), the median is 3. If there is an even number of values in the set, the median is calculated by taking the average of the two middle values. In the data set, (1, 2, 3, 4, 5, 6), the median would be (3 + 4)/2 = 3.5.

The mode is the value that appears most frequently in the data set. In the data set (1, 2, 3, 4, 5, 5, 5), the mode would be 5 since the value 5 appears three times. If multiple values appear the same number of times, there are multiple values for the mode. If the data set were (1, 2, 2, 3, 4, 4, 5, 5), the modes would be 2, 4, and 5. If no value appears more than any other value in the data set, then there is no mode.

CONFIDENCE INTERVAL

A confidence interval gives a range of a values that is likely to include the parameter of interest. After a random sample, suppose a parameter, such as a median is estimated to be within a certain range with a 99% confidence level. This essentially means one time out of 100 times, the median value will not be in the specified interval. (You will not be asked to calculate the confidence levels; they will be given with the question.) For example, you may see a question that says, "A researcher collected information from 1,000 randomly selected public high school science teachers in the United States and concluded that the median annual salary was between $52,400 and $63,800 with a 99% confidence level. Which of the following could represent the median annual salary for the same sample with a 95% confidence level?" The key to answering this is to understand that a 95% confidence means that five out of 100 times the median value will not be in the specified interval. That means you are less confident that the median will be in that range. The range of salaries in the 95% confidence interval would be a subset of the range of salaries within the 99% confidence interval. The correct answer choice would show a narrower range of salaries, such as $55,000 to $60,000. This type of question can be answered without performing any calculations. You simply need to understand the meaning of confidence levels.

STANDARD DEVIATION

The standard deviation of a data set is a measurement of how much the data points vary from the mean. More precisely, it is equal to the square root of the average of the squares of the differences between each point and the mean: $s_x = \sqrt{\frac{\sum(X-\bar{X})^2}{N-1}}$.

The standard deviation is useful for determining the spread, or dispersion, of the data, or how far they vary from the mean. The smaller the standard deviation, the closer the values tend to be to the mean; the larger the standard deviation, the more they tend to be scattered far from the mean.

TYPES OF QUESTIONS – CENTER, SHAPE, AND SPREAD OF DATA

You may be given a data set and asked to calculate measures of center such as mean, median, and mode. You might be asked to determine spread, or range, for a given set of data. You may be asked to use given statistics to compare two separate sets of data. This comparison may involve mean, median, mode, range, and standard deviation, which are key topics in these types of questions. The mean is the numerical average of the data set. The median is the data point (or the average of two data points if there are an even number of data) when the data are ranked from least to greatest. The mode is the data point which occurs most often; there may be one mode, or there may be no mode or multiple modes. The range is the difference between the highest and lowest data points. The standard deviation is a measure of how much the data points differ from the mean. Basically, it describes how closely the data is clustered around the mean.

TYPES OF QUESTIONS – EVALUATE REPORTS TO MAKE INFERENCES

You should expect to be given tables, graphs, and/or text summaries and to be asked to make inferences, justify conclusions, and determine the appropriateness of the data collection methods. Data is often collected from a subset of a large population to draw conclusions about the population; the subset must be sufficiently large and randomly selected for the statistics to be reliable. Sometimes, data is collected over a period to determine possible trends, such as "x increases over time." Two variables may be compared and conclusions such as "As one variable increases, the other decreases," or "When one variable increases, the other variable increases" may be drawn. While you can make a statistical association, you cannot determine causal relationships. That means you cannot say that one variable increased or decreased because of the other variable increasing or decreasing. Another way to say this is that correlation does not imply causation. Correlation tells how strongly two variables are associated. However, just because two variables are strongly correlated does not mean that one causes the other.

DRAWING CONCLUSIONS FROM DATA TRENDS

You will be asked to determine if there is a correlation between two variables, but you cannot conclude that a change in one variable causes a change in the other. Ask yourself questions like, "Do both variables increase or decrease?" or "Does one increase as the other decreases?" Then, find the answer choice that makes the best statement explaining that correlation. If there is no correlation, look for a statement that reflects that. Avoid answer choices that say, "The increase of ___ caused the increase of ___" or "The increase of ___ caused the decrease of ___." Again, correlation does not imply causation. You may simply have to choose between answer choices that say, "There is a correlation between ___," or "There is no correlation between ___."

TYPES OF QUESTIONS – RELATING EQUATIONS TO GRAPHS

You need to be able to match a given graph to the type of equation it represents, whether it be linear, quadratic, or exponential. Questions about bacteria cultures and radioactive isotopes are modeled with exponential equations. Questions about initial fees plus rates associated with a variable are modeled with linear equations. The projectiles of arrows, rocks, balls, missiles or anything that is shot or thrown are modeled with quadratic equations. You should know the general shapes for linear equations (line), quadratic equations (parabola), and exponential equations (steep curve). Also, you should have a firm grasp of the slope-intercept from of a line. When you are working with a linear equation, it is important to avoid making quick, erroneous conclusions about the line. Often, the equation of the line will be written in a form to "hide" the true nature of the line. For example, you may be given an equation like $y - x = k(x + y)$ and asked to determine which is necessarily true of its graph: the graph is a line passing through the origin; the graph is a parabola; the graph is a line with a positive slope; or the graph is a line with a slope of k. At first glance, you might think this is a factored quadratic equation, or you might think it is a linear equation in point-slope form with a slope of k. However, if you rearrange the equation into the slope-intercept form $y = \frac{1+k}{1-k} x$, you can see that the graph of the equation is a line with a y-intercept of zero, which means that the line passes through the origin. Depending on the value of k, the slope of the line can be positive, negative, zero, or undefined.

LINEAR GROWTH VS. EXPONENTIAL GROWTH

Linear growth has a constant rate of growth. The growth over each interval is exactly the same. Linear growth is modeled by a line which has the growth rate as its slope. Exponential growth has a rate of growth that increases over time. The growth over each interval is not constant. This rate of growth is modeled by a steep curve. Linear growth can be modeled by an equation in the form slope-intercept form $y = mx + b$, in which m is the slope and b is the y-intercept. Exponential growth is modeled by an equation in the form $y = a(b^{kx}) + c$ in which b is the base such that $b > 0$ and $b \neq 1$. Exponential functions are used to model growth and decay. The values of b and k determine if the function models growth or decay. If you are given a table of values, linear growth is shown as an arithmetic sequence. The value of y increases (by addition) by a constant value over equal intervals of x. Exponential growth is shown as a geometric sequence. The value of y is multiplied by a fixed value over a set interval. Comparing tables for the linear equation $y = 2x$ and the exponential function $y = 2^x$ shows that y-values for the exponential function quickly surpasses those of the linear function.

x	-3	-2	-1	0	1	2	3	4
$y = 2x$	-6	-4	-2	0	2	4	6	8

x	-3	-2	-1	0	1	2	3	4
$y = 2^x$	$\frac{1}{8}$	$\frac{1}{4}$	$\frac{1}{2}$	1	2	4	8	16

Passport to Advanced Math

In this section the questions will deal with more advanced equations and expressions. Students need to be able to create quadratic and exponential equations that model a context. They also need to be able to solve these equations. Students should also be able to create equivalent expressions that involve radicals and rational exponents. Like the Heart of Algebra section this section will test systems of equations. These systems however will involve one linear and one quadratic equation in two variables. Finally, students should be able to perform operations such as addition, subtraction, and multiplication on polynomials.

SOLVING QUADRATIC EQUATIONS

The *Quadratic Formula* is used to solve quadratic equations when other methods are more difficult. To use the quadratic formula to solve a quadratic equation, begin by rewriting the equation in standard form $ax^2 + bx + c = 0$, where a, b, and c are coefficients. Once you have identified the values of the coefficients, substitute those values into the quadratic formula $x = \frac{-b \pm \sqrt{b^2 - 4ac}}{2a}$. Evaluate the equation and simplify the expression. Again, check each root by substituting into the original equation. In the quadratic formula, the portion of the formula under the radical ($b^2 - 4ac$) is called the *Discriminant*. If the discriminant is zero, there is only one root: zero. If the discriminant is positive, there are two different real roots. If the discriminant is negative, there are no real roots.

To solve a quadratic equation by *Factoring*, begin by rewriting the equation in standard form, if necessary. Factor the side with the variable then set each of the factors equal to zero and solve the resulting linear equations. Check your answers by substituting the roots you found into the original equation. If, when writing the equation in standard form, you have an equation in the form $x^2 + c = 0$ or $x^2 - c = 0$, set $x^2 = -c$ or $x^2 = c$ and take the square root of c. If $c = 0$, the only real root is zero. If c is positive, there are two real roots—the positive and negative square root values. If c is negative, there are no real roots because you cannot take the square root of a negative number.

> **Review Video: Factoring Quadratic Equations**
> Visit mometrix.com/academy and enter code: 336566

To solve a quadratic equation by *Completing the Square*, rewrite the equation so that all terms containing the variable are on the left side of the equal sign, and all the constants are on the right side of the equal sign. Make sure the coefficient of the squared term is 1. If there is a coefficient with the squared term, divide each term on both sides of the equal side by that number. Next, work with the coefficient of the single-variable term. Square half of this coefficient, and add that value to both sides. Now you can factor the left side (the side containing the variable) as the square of a binomial. $x^2 + 2ax + a^2 = C \Rightarrow (x + a)^2 = C$, where x is the variable, and a and C are constants. Take the square root of both sides and solve for the variable. Substitute the value of the variable in the original problem to check your work.

TYPES OF QUESTIONS – QUADRATIC FUNCTION WITH RATIONAL COEFFICIENTS

A quadratic function is a second-degree equation that graphs as a parabola. The general form for a quadratic function is $f(x) = ax^2 + bx + c$, where $f(x) = y$. If $a > 0$, the parabola is concave up. If $a < 0$, the parabola is concave down. The axis of symmetry for the parabola is given by $x = \frac{-b}{2a}$. The turning point of the parabola (the minimum value for a concave down and maximum for a concave up parabola) is given by $\left(\frac{-b}{2a}, f\left(\frac{-b}{2a}\right)\right)$. Quadratic functions are often used to model projectile motion. A rocket or other projectile launched from the ground will follow a parabolic trajectory.

113

You may be given a graph of a trajectory and asked to choose the function that best models that parabola. You must use the concavity, axis of symmetry, and turning point to work backwards to find the equation for the parabola.

EXPONENTIAL FUNCTION WITH RATIONAL COEFFICIENTS

An exponential function has the general form of $f(x) = a(b^{kx}) + c$, in which b is the base and $b > 0$ and $b \neq 1$. Exponential functions are used to model growth and decay. The values of b and k determine if the function models exponential growth or exponential decay. When graphed, an exponential function has a horizontal asymptote at $y = c$. The y-intercept of an exponential function is located at $(0, a + c)$.

Type	Values of b	Values of k	Example
Exponential Growth	$b > 1$	$k > 0$	$f(x) = 2^x$
Exponential Growth	$b < 1$	$k < 0$	$f(x) = \left(\frac{1}{2}\right)^{-x}$
Exponential Decay	$b > 1$	$k < 0$	$f(x) = 2^{-x}$
Exponential Decay	$b < 1$	$k > 0$	$f(x) = \left(\frac{1}{2}\right)^x$

You may be given the graph of an exponential function and asked to choose the correct equation. If y increases rapidly as x increases, the function models exponential growth. If y decreases rapidly as x increases, the function models exponential decay. You can determine c from the horizontal asymptote. Then, you can determine a from the y-intercept.

TYPES OF QUESTIONS – WRITING EXPRESSIONS

You must be able to translate verbal expressions into mathematical language. These may be simple or complex algebraic expressions (linear, quadratic, or exponential); you must be able to simplify these expressions using order of operations. You may be asked to determine an algebraic model involving costs or interest and then use that model to perform a calculation. You may be given a geometric situation involving area or perimeter in which you have to write and simplify an expression. These problems may be complex and require sketches in order to choose or produce a correct answer.

PRODUCE EXPRESSIONS OR EQUATIONS GIVEN A CONTEXT

Often, complex geometry problems involve writing a system of equations. For example, if the problem gives the area and perimeter of a rectangular garden and asks for its length and width, you can use the formulas $A = lw$ and $p = 2l + 2w$ to write a system of equations. Sometimes, geometry problems involve two shapes, one of which is inside another. For example, you may be given the inner dimensions of a picture frame and asked to find the outer dimensions; in this case, if you designate the length and width of frame's inner rectangle as l and w, respectively, then the length and width of the outer rectangle are respectively represented by $l + 2x$ and $w + 2x$, where x is the width of the picture frame.

CONSISTENT, INCONSISTENT, OR DEPENDENT SYSTEMS

If a system of equations set up to represent a real-world problem turns out to be consistent (having exactly one solution), that solution is the solution to the problem.

If the system turns out to be dependent (having infinitely many solutions), that means that the original information given was redundant, and was therefore not enough information to solve the problem. Practically speaking, this may mean that any of that infinite set of solutions will do, or it may mean that more information is needed.

If the system turns out to be inconsistent (having no solutions), that means the real-world situation described cannot be true. If the situation described was a hypothetical desired outcome, we now know that it is not possible to achieve that outcome; if the situation described was supposed to have really occurred, we can only conclude that it must have been described inaccurately.

Solve the rational equation: $\frac{2}{x} - 2 = x - 1$

To solve the rational equation, multiply each side of the equation by the LCD, which is x. This will transform the rational equation into a quadratic equation that can be solved by factoring:

$$\frac{2}{x} - 2 = x - 1$$
$$x\left(\frac{2}{x} - 2\right) = x(x - 1)$$
$$2 - 2x = x^2 - x$$
$$x^2 + x - 2 = 0$$
$$(x + 2)(x - 1) = 0$$
$$x = -2, x = 1$$

Both $x = -2$ and $x = 1$ check out in the original equation. The solution is $x = \{-2, 1\}$.

Solve the radical equation: $\sqrt{x - 1} + 3 = x$

To solve the radical equation, isolate the radical $\sqrt{x - 1}$ on one side of the equation. Then square both sides and solve the resulting quadratic equation:

$$\sqrt{x - 1} + 3 = x$$
$$\sqrt{x - 1} = x - 3$$
$$\left(\sqrt{x - 1}\right)^2 = (x - 3)^2$$
$$x - 1 = x^2 - 6x + 9$$
$$x^2 - 7x + 10 = 0$$
$$(x - 5)(x - 2) = 0$$
$$x = 2, x = 5$$

Only $x = 5$ checks out in the original equation; $\sqrt{2 - 1} + 3 \overset{?}{\Leftrightarrow} 2 \xrightarrow{yields} \sqrt{1} + 3 = 4 \neq 2!$

The solution, then, is just $x = \{5\}$.

EXTRANEOUS SOLUTION TO RATIONAL AND RADICAL EQUATION

An extraneous solution is the solution of an equation that arises during the process of solving an equation, which is not a solution of the original equation. When solving a rational equation, each side is often multiplied by x or an expression containing x. Since the value of x is unknown, this may mean multiplying by zero, which will make any equation the true statement 0 = 0. Similarly, when solving a radical expression, each side of the equation is often squared, or raised to some power.

This can also change the sign of unknown expressions. For example, the equation 3 = –3 is false, but squaring each side gives 9 = 9, which is true.

REWRITING RADICAL EXPRESSIONS

Radical expressions can be rewritten as equivalent expressions with rational exponents. In general $\sqrt[b]{n^a}$ is equivalent to $n^{\frac{a}{b}}$ and $\sqrt[b]{m^c n^a}$ is equivalent to $m^{\frac{c}{b}} n^{\frac{a}{b}}$. For example, $\sqrt{x}$ is equivalent to $x^{\frac{1}{2}}$ and $\sqrt[3]{x^2}$ is equivalent to $x^{\frac{2}{3}}$. The radical $\sqrt[5]{x-1}$ is equivalent to $(x-1)^{\frac{1}{5}}$. Another point to remember is that, while $n^{\frac{a}{b}}$ can be rewritten as $\sqrt[b]{n^a}$, it can also be rewritten as $(\sqrt[b]{n})^a$. It is also important to understand the concept of negative exponents. A negative exponent basically flips a term from the numerator to the denominator or from the denominator to the numerator. You may see a question that says, "Rewrite the expression $2x^{-\frac{3}{4}}$ in radical form" or "Rewrite the expression $(\sqrt[3]{2xy})^2$ with rational exponents."

EQUIVALENT EXPRESSIONS WITH RADICAL AND RATIONAL EXPONENTS

You may see questions asking you to simplify a radical expression or perform operations with radicals. You may see a question that says, "Simplify $\sqrt[3]{-27x^6 y^{15}}$," or "Simplify the expression $\sqrt{2}(3\sqrt{5}+\sqrt{20})$." You many see a question that says, "Which of the following expressions is equivalent to $\sqrt{(20)(4)+(12)(16)}$?" You should expect to be asked to simplify rational expressions. You may need to factor the numerator and the denominator and then cancel like factors, as in this example: "Simplify $\frac{x^2-4}{x^2-x-2}$." You may also be asked to change a rational expression from one form into another. For example, you may see a question that says, "If the expression $\frac{6x^2-5}{x-1}$ is written in the equivalent form $\frac{1}{x-1}+B$, what is B in terms of x?" You could equate the two expressions and solve for B, or you could use long division to simplify the first expression and compare the result to the equivalent expression to determine B.

SITUATIONS MODELED BY STATEMENTS THAT USE FUNCTION NOTATION

A statement using function notation can model any situation in which one quantity depends uniquely on one or more other quantities. For example, the area of a rectangle can be expressed as a function of its width and height. The maximum vertical distance a projectile travels can be expressed as a function of its initial vertical speed. An object's position, the amount of money in a bank account, or any other quantity that changes over time can be expressed as a function of time.

A relationship cannot be modeled with a function, however, if it involves two quantities neither of which is uniquely determined by the other—that is, if each quantity may have multiple values corresponding to the same value of the other. For example, we could not write a function to represent the relationship between peoples' height in inches and their weight in pounds. There are people of the same height with different weights, and people of the same weight but different heights.

USING STRUCTURE AND MATHEMATICAL OPERATIONS

You might be given an algebraic expression and asked which, if any, of several other expressions is equivalent, or you might be given several pairs of algebraic expressions and be asked to determine which pairs are equivalent. For example, you may see a question that says, "Which of following pairs of algebraic expressions are equivalent" and an answer choice such as "$(2x+3)(3x-4)$ and $6x^2+x+12$." You would determine that is an incorrect choice since these are not equivalent expressions. You might see a question that says, "Which of the following rational expressions is equivalent to $\frac{x+3}{x-5}$?" You may be given choices in which the numerators and denominators can factored and some of the factors canceled.

DETERMINING IF TWO EQUATIONS ARE EQUIVALENT

One way to check for equivalence is to evaluate each expression at a chosen value, say $x = 0$ or $x = 1$, and see if the results agree. If the expressions do not yield the same result, then they are not equivalent, but it is important to note that yielding the same result does not necessarily mean the expressions are equivalent. This is only a method to eliminate incorrect answers; as the choices are narrowed, you may continue to try other values until all but the correct choice have been eliminated. Another way to determine whether two algebraic expressions are equivalent is to choose the most complex expression and simplify it algebraically to see if you can produce the second expression. This may involve factoring and canceling like factors or distributing and combining like terms.

METHODS TO SOLVE QUADRATIC EQUATIONS

Quadratic equations may be solved by graphing, factoring, completing the square, or using the quadratic formula. Since these types of questions are in the no calculator section of the test, graphing is not your best choice due to time constraints. Set the equation equal to zero; if the quadratic expression is easily factored, factor it, and then solve the equation by setting each factor equal to zero. If the expression is not factorable and $a = 1$ when the equation is written in the general form $ax^2 + bx + c = 0$, you may choose to complete the square. Remember, if $a \neq 1$, you must divide the entire equation by a and work with resulting fractions. In these situations, it is easier to solve the equation using the quadratic formula $x = \frac{-b\pm\sqrt{b^2-4ac}}{2a}$. You may simply be asked to find the roots of a quadratic equation, or you may be asked to perform some operation with one of the roots once you have found the roots. Be careful to answer the question that is asked. For example, you may see a question that says, "If $3x^2 + 4x = 4$ and $x > 0$, what is the value of $x + \frac{1}{3}$?" First, you would write the equation in the form $3x^2 + 4x - 4 = 0$ and solve by factoring or by using the quadratic formula; then, you would use the positive root to find $x + \frac{1}{3}$.

PERFORMING ARITHMETIC OPERATIONS ON POLYNOMIALS

You should expect to add, subtract, and multiply polynomial expressions and simplify the results. These expressions will have rational coefficients. You may see a question that says, "Add $(2x^2 + 4y + 5xy)$, $(3x^2 - 3xy - x)$, and $(xy + 1)$" or "Subtract $(6x^2 + 6y - xy + 1)$ from $(2x^2 + 3xy - 2)$." You may see a question that says, "If $p = 3x^3 - 2x^2 + 5x - 7$ and $q = 2x^3 - 7x^2 - x + 3$, what is $p - 2q$?" You may see a question that says, "Multiply $(x + 2y)(4x - 3y + 1)$" or "What is the product of $(2x + 1)$, $(2x - 1)$, and $(2x^2 + 1)$?" In each of these types of questions, you should perform the operation, collecting like terms to simplify the result.

ADDING AND SUBTRACTING POLYNOMIALS

When adding or subtracting two polynomials, you should first identify the like terms. Like terms have the same base and the same exponent but not necessarily the same coefficient. When adding or subtracting polynomials, only like terms can be combined. For example, $2xy$ and $3xy$ are like terms, but $2x^2$ and $2x^3$ are not like terms. When finding a difference, make sure you have the polynomials written in the correct order. When removing parentheses from an expression which follows a minus sign, remember to change the sign of every term inside the parentheses. For example, when subtracting $(2x - y)$ from $(5x + 3y)$, the problem is written as $(5x + 3y) - (2x - y)$. Removing the parentheses yields $5x + 3y - 2x + y$, which is further simplified to $3x + 4y$. When multiplying two polynomials, you should multiply each term of one polynomial by each term of the

117

other and then simplify the result when necessary. Remember, when multiplying monomial terms, you should multiply coefficients but add the exponents of like bases.

SINGLE- VARIABLE EQUATION WITH RADICALS

To solve an equation with radicals, first, isolate the radical on one side of the equation. If there is more than one radical, isolate the most complex radical. Then, raise the equation to the appropriate power. For example, if the radical is a square root, you should square both sides. If there is still a radical in the equation, isolate the radical and repeat. Once the radicals are removed, solve for the unknown variable. Be sure to check every solution to determine if any are extraneous ones. You may see a question such as "What is one possible solution to the equation $\sqrt{x-1} = x - 7$?" You would need to solve for x and substitute each solution back into the original equation to see if the resulting statement is true. If the resulting statement is false, the solution is extraneous. (Note: if=f you are given choices for this type of question, you may simply plug each possible solution into the equation until you find one that works.) To solve an equation with a variable in the denominator of a fraction, multiply the equation by the least common denominator of every fraction included in the equation. This will clear the equation of fractions. Then, solve normally. Remember to check all solutions by substituting them back to the original equations. If any substituted value does not result in a true statement, it is an extraneous solution.

TYPES OF QUESTIONS – SOLVING SYSTEMS OF EQUATIONS

You may see a question with a graph of a line intersecting a circle or parabola. The question may ask about the number of solutions (which would be the number of times the line and circle or parabola intersect) or about the actual solutions (which would be the points of those intersections).

You may see a question with the equation of a line and the equation of a circle or parabola. In this case, you need to solve the linear equation for one variable and then substitute for that variable in the quadratic equation. If the question simply asks for the number of solutions, you may choose to make a quick sketch of the line and circle or parabola to see if you can see if they intersect and, if so, how many times.

One method to solve a system of equations is by graphing. A line with slope m and y-intercept b has the general form $y = mx + b$. A circle with radius r and center (h, k) has the general form $(x - h)^2 + (y - k)^2 = r^2$. A parabola has the general form $y = ax^2 + bx + c$. A line may intersect a circle or parabola at no point, one point, or two points. For example, if you are asked for the solutions to the system $\begin{cases} y = -x + 5 \\ x^2 + y^2 = 25 \end{cases}$, you would graph a line with a slope of -1 and a y-intercept of 5 and a circle centered at the origin with a radius of 5 units. You should be able to see even from a simple sketch that line intersects the circle at $(0, 5)$ and $(5, 0)$. More complicated systems of equations can be solved by substitution. For example, if you are asked for the solutions to the system $\begin{cases} 2x + 3y = 7 \\ (x - 4)^2 + y^2 = 10 \end{cases}$, it would be difficult to find the coordinates of the intersection points with a quick sketch. The quickest option is to solve the linear equation for one of the variables and then substitute the result for the corresponding variable in the quadratic equation.

ADDING OR SUBTRACTING RATIONAL EXPONENTS

You should expect questions asking you to add or subtract rational expressions. You may see a question that says, "Add $\frac{2a+3}{3ab} + \frac{3a-2}{2bc}$," or "Subtract $\frac{m-2}{m-3} - \frac{m-1}{m-2}$." The questions may have more than two terms and may combine addition and subtraction, such as "Simplify $\frac{1}{x} + \frac{2}{y} - \frac{3}{z}$." In order to be able to add or subtract rational expressions, the expressions must have the same denominator. Find the least common denominator (LCD) of the terms in the expression. Then, multiply each term of the expression by the ratio $\frac{LCD}{LCD}$. Simplify where possible and present your answer as one term over the LCD. Since these are rational expressions, not equations, you cannot clear the fractions as you do in an equation.

MULTIPLYING AND DIVIDING RATIONAL EXPRESSIONS

You should expect questions asking you to multiply or divide rational expressions. You may see a question that says, "Multiply $\frac{n^2+n-6}{4} \cdot \frac{8}{2n+6}$" or "Divide $\frac{m^2+6m+5}{m^2-2m-3} \div \frac{m^2+8m+15}{3m^2-9m}$." To multiply rational expressions, the numerators and the denominators of each expression must be factored. Always check for a common monomial factor first. Then, check for differences of squares or a perfect square trinomial. A difference of squares a^2-b^2 factors to $(a+b)(a-b)$. A perfect square trinomial factors to a binomial squared: $a^2 + 2ab + b^2$ factors to $(a+b)^2$, and $a^2 - 2ab + b^2$ factors to $(a-b)^2$. Also, check for other factorable trinomials. After factoring the numerators and denominators, cancel like factors and then multiply. To divide a rational expression, change the problem to a multiplication problem by multiplying the dividend by the reciprocal of the divisor, just like you would do if you were asked to divide two fractions containing no variables.

TYPES OF QUESTIONS – INTERPRETING NONLINEAR EXPRESSIONS

You should to be given a nonlinear expression that represents a real-life context. These nonlinear expressions may be rational expressions with a variable in the denominator. They may be exponential expressions or quadratic expressions or any other type of expression that is not linear. You should also expect to interpret non-linear functions. For example, if the nonlinear function is a quadratic function that models a projectile's trajectory, you may be given the equation and asked, "What are the values of x for which y is minimum?" You may be given a nonlinear function that models a scientific concept. For example, Newton's Universal Law of Gravitation states that the gravitational force (F) in Newtons is inversely proportional to the square of the distance (r) in meters between the centers of those two objects; this is represented by the relationship $F \propto \frac{1}{r^2}$. You may be asked a question like, "If the distance between two objects is doubled, what happens to the strength of the force between them?"

MODELING A PROJECTILE'S TRAJECTORY

Since quadratic equations graph as parabolas, they are often used to model trajectories. To find the values of x for which a quadratic equation is equal to zero, you should set the equation equal to zero and then solve by factoring or by using the quadratic equation. For a trajectory problem, usually one zero is at $x = 0$, representing the launch of the projectile, and the other zero represents the landing. Inverse square relationships model scientific concepts, such as the relationship between gravitational force and the distance between two objects, the electric force between two charges, and the magnetic force between two poles. In each of these laws, the force increases as the distance between the objects decreases, and the force decreases as the distance between the objects increase. More specifically, if the distance is doubled, the force is reduced to one fourth of the original value; if the distance is halved, the force quadruples. When working with exponential relationships, a common mistake is to handle the exponent incorrectly. If you are given an equation

119

and values to plug into that equation, be sure to apply the exponent to every factor inside the parenthesis under the exponent. Remember, when raising a power to a power, you should multiply exponents.

ZEROS AND FACTORS OF POLYNOMIALS

Zeros are roots or solutions of polynomials when the polynomials are set equal to zero. These zeros are the locations where the graph of the polynomial intersects the x-axis. If the polynomials are set equal to zero and then factored, each individual factor is set equal to zero and solved; this gives the root or zero associated with that factor. If a polynomial equation has a zero of -2, the polynomial has a factor of $(x + 2)$. The Factor Theorem can be used to determine whether a given value is a zero. The polynomial is divided (using synthetic division) by the value, and if there is no remainder, the given value is a zero of the polynomial; if remainder is not zero, the value is not a root. If you are given one or more factors or roots of a polynomial function, you can use these factors or roots to determine the remaining factors and roots of the polynomial by dividing the polynomial by the given factor.

TYPES OF QUESTIONS – ZEROS AND FACTORS OF POLYNOMIALS

You may be expected to factor a polynomial, or you may be given the factored form of a polynomial and asked to select the appropriate graph from a set of given graphs. You may see a question that says, "Which of the following graphs represents the polynomial $f(x) = (x-1)(x + 2)(x + 5)$?" or "Which of the following graphs represents the quadratic equation $y = x^2 + 4x - 5$?" You may be given a polynomial function with the ordered pairs of its zeros and be asked to solve for a missing coefficient or a missing coordinate. You may be given a function such as $f(x) = 2x^4 + 3x^2 - 5x + 7$ and be expected to use the Factor Theorem to find zeros or verify zeros. You may be given the zeros of a quadratic or cubic function and asked to write the function. You might see a question that says, "If the zeros of a cubic function are -2, 3, and 5 and the graph of that function passes through (1, 8), what is the equation of the function?"

TYPES OF QUESTIONS – NONLINEAR RELATIONSHIPS BETWEEN TWO VARIABLES

You may be asked to select a graph for a given nonlinear equation. You may be asked to select an equation given a nonlinear graph. You may be given a system of equations with both algebraic and graphical representations. You may be given a verbal description of the curve of a nonlinear relationship and asked to determine the equation of the function. You may be asked to determine key features of the graph of a nonlinear function from its equation. For example, you may see a question in which you are given a graph containing an intersecting circle, parabola, and line as well as the equations associated with them which says. "A system of equations and their graphs are shown above. How many solutions does the system have?" You may be given the equations of two exponential functions and asked if the graphs (which are not given) show that they are increasing or decreasing. You may see a question that says, "The functions $y_1 = 2\left(\frac{1}{2}\right)^x$ and $y_2 = 2\left(\frac{3}{2}\right)^x$ are graphed in the xy plane. Which of the following statements correctly describes whether each function is increasing or decreasing?"

FINDING A SOLUTION TO A SYSTEM OF THREE EQUATIONS

This test typically has one problem with a system of three equations. Usually the graphs as well as the equations are given. The key point is that the only solutions to this graph are the points at which all three graphs coincide or intersect. For example, the graph might include a circle, a parabola, and a line. There are no solutions to the given system if all three graphs do not intersect at one or more points. If the three graphs intersect at one point, then there is one solution to the given system, and that solution is the point of intersection. If the line intersects the circle at two points, and the line also intersects the parabola at the same exact two points, there are two solutions to the given system, and those solutions are the points of intersection. This system has at most two solutions.

TYPES OF QUESTIONS – USING FUNCTION NOTATION

You may be asked to evaluate a given function. For example, you may see a question that says, "If $f(x) = x^3 - 4x^2 + 3x - 1$, find $f(2)$." You should expect to be given two functions such as $f(x)$ and $g(x)$ and be asked to find $f(g(x))$ or $g(f(x))$. For example, you may see a question that says, "Let $f(x) = x^2 - 1$ and $g(x) = x + 1$. Which of the following describes $f(g(x))$?" Or you may be asked to work a similar problem given $f(x)$ and $g(f(x))$ and be asked to find $g(x)$. For example, you may see a question that says, "Let $f(x) = x^2 - 3$. If $g(f(x)) = \sqrt{x^2 + 1}$, which of the following describes $g(x)$?" You may be asked to evaluate composite functions, as in this example: "Two functions are defined as $f(t) = 4t^2 - t$ and $g(x) = -3x^2 - 2x - 1$. Find the value of $g(f(2))$."

TYPES OF QUESTIONS – ISOLATE OR IDENTIFY

You will be given a literal equation and be asked to be solve for one of the unknowns. Literal equations are equations often referred to as formulas. For example, in geometry, the formula for the area of a trapezoid is $A = \frac{h(b_1 + b_2)}{2}$, and in physics, the mirror equation is $\frac{1}{f} = \frac{1}{d_o} + \frac{1}{d_i}$. You may see a question that says, "The area of a trapezoid with bases b_1 and b_2 and height h can be found by $A = \frac{h(b_1 + b_2)}{2}$. Which of the following is the correct expression to find the height of a trapezoid given the area and lengths of the bases?" You may see a question that says, "The focal length f of a mirror can be determined from the object distance d_o and image distance d_i by the equation $\frac{1}{f} = \frac{1}{d_o} + \frac{1}{d_i}$. Which of the following is the correct expression to find the image distance of an image formed by a lens with a given object distance and focal length?"

Solving $A = \frac{h(b_1 + b_2)}{2}$

Literal equations can be solved for one of the unknown variables using basic algebraic operations. To solve $A = \frac{h(b_1 + b_2)}{2}$ for b_2, first multiply both sides of the equation by 2: $2A = h(b_1 + b_2)$. Then, divide by h: $\frac{2A}{h} = b_1 + b_2$. Then, subtract b_1: $\frac{2A}{h} - b_1 = b_2$. To solve $\frac{1}{f} = \frac{1}{d_o} + \frac{1}{d_i}$ for d_i, first subtract $\frac{1}{d_o}$ from both sides of the equation: $\frac{1}{f} - \frac{1}{d_o} = \frac{1}{d_i}$. Then, find a common denominator to combine the terms on the left-hand side of the equation: $\frac{d_o - f}{f d_o} = \frac{1}{d_i}$. Then, solve by taking the reciprocal of both sides: $\frac{f d_o}{d_o - f} = d_i$.

Additional Topics in Math

Questions in this section will test geometric and trigonometric concepts and the Pythagorean Theorem. The student should be familiar with geometric concepts such as volume, radius, diameter, chord length, angle, arc, and sector area. The questions will give certain information about a figure and require the student to solve for some missing information. Any required volume formulas will be provided on the test. The trigonometry questions will require students to use trigonometric ratios and the Pythagorean Theorem to solve problems dealing with right triangles. The student should be able to use these ratios and the Pythagorean Theorem to solve for missing lengths and angle measures in right triangles.

VOLUME FORMULAS

The formula for a prism or a cylinder is $V = Bh$, where B is the area of the base and h is the height of the solid. For a cylinder, the area of the circular base is determined by the formula $B = \pi r^2$. For a prism, the area of the base depends on the shape of the base; for example, a triangular base would have area $\frac{1}{2}bh$, while a rectangular base would have area bh.

For a pyramid or cone, the volume is $V = \frac{1}{3}Bh$, where B once again is the area of the base and h is the height. In other words, the volume of a pyramid or cone is one-third the volume of a prism or cylinder with the same base and the same height.

> **Review Video: Finding Volume in Geometry**
> Visit mometrix.com/academy and enter code: 754774

PYTHAGOREAN THEOREM

The side of a triangle opposite the right angle is called the hypotenuse. The other two sides are called the legs. The Pythagorean Theorem states a relationship among the legs and hypotenuse of a right triangle: $a^2 + b^2 = c^2$, where a and b are the lengths of the legs of a right triangle, and c is the length of the hypotenuse. Note that this formula will only work with right triangles.

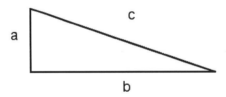

> **Review Video: Pythagorean Theorem**
> Visit mometrix.com/academy and enter code: 906576

TYPES OF QUESTIONS – VOLUME FORMULAS

You should expect to be asked questions concerning volumes of figures such as rectangular prisms and cylinders. You may be asked to use information such as length of a side, area of a face, or volume of a solid to calculate missing information. Area formulas for circles, rectangles, and triangles and volume formulas for rectangular prisms and cylinders are provided with the test. It is important to understand that the volume calculations may be more complicated than simply applying basic formulas. For example, you may be asked to find the volume of a hexagonal nut and given that the volume of a prism is $V = Bh$, where B is the area of the base and h is the height of the prism. Since you are not given the area formula for a regular hexagon, however, you must find the area by adding the areas of the six equilateral triangles which comprise the hexagon. Once you calculate the area of the base, you can find the volume of a hexagonal prism by multiplying the area of the base and the height; afterward, you must subtract the volume of the cylindrical hole from the volume of the hexagonal prism to find the volume of the hexagonal nut.

TYPES OF QUESTIONS – APPLIED PROBLEMS WITH RIGHT TRIANGLES

You should expect questions requiring you to use the Pythagorean Theorem and trigonometric ratios to find missing side lengths and angles of right triangles. The Pythagorean Theorem as well as the 30°-60°-90° and 45°-45°-90° special right triangles are provided on the test. You should be able to recognize situations in which the Pythagorean Theorem, trigonometry, and special right triangles can be applied. For example, a square can be divided by a diagonal into two 45°-45°-90° triangles. An equilateral triangle can be divided by an altitude into two 30°-60°-90° right triangles. Hexagons can be divided into six equilateral triangles, each of which can be further divided into two 30°-60°-90° triangles. You need to be able to apply the special right triangles to given triangles. For example, if you are given a 45°-45°-90° triangle with a side length of 5 cm, you should be able to determine that the hypotenuse has a length of $5\sqrt{2}$ cm. If you are given a 30°-60°-90° triangle with a short leg of length 3 inches, you should be able to determine that the hypotenuse has a length of 6 inches.

TRIGONOMETRIC RATIO SINE FOR AN ACUTE ANGLE USING RATIOS OF SIDES IN SIMILAR RIGHT TRIANGLES

Similar triangles have three pairs of congruent angles and three pairs of proportional sides. The proportion has the same value for all pairs of sides, so $\frac{a}{d} = \frac{c}{f}$ or (using cross multiplication and division to reorganize) $\frac{a}{c} = \frac{d}{f}$. The trigonometric ratio sine is opposite over hypotenuse. In $\triangle ABC$, $\sin A = \frac{a}{c}$ and in $\triangle DEF$, $\sin D = \frac{d}{f}$. So since $\frac{a}{c} = \frac{d}{f}$, $\sin A = \sin D$. This shows that the trigonometric ratio sine is a property of the angle because the ratio is the same in both triangles even though the triangles are different sizes.

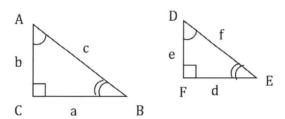

TRIGONOMETRIC RATIO TANGENT FOR AN ACUTE ANGLE USING RATIOS OF SIDES IN SIMILAR RIGHT TRIANGLES

Similar triangles have three pairs of congruent angles and three pairs of proportional sides. The proportion has the same value for all pairs of sides, so $\frac{a}{d} = \frac{b}{e}$ or (using cross multiplication and division to reorganize) $\frac{a}{b} = \frac{d}{e}$. The trigonometric ratio tangent is opposite over adjacent. In $\triangle ABC$, $\tan A = \frac{a}{b}$ and in $\triangle DEF$, $\tan D = \frac{d}{e}$. So since $\frac{a}{b} = \frac{d}{e}$, $\tan A = \tan D$. This shows that the trigonometric ratio tangent is a property of the angle because the ratio is the same in both triangles even though the triangles are different sizes.

COMPLEX NUMBERS

Complex numbers consist of a real component and an imaginary component. Complex numbers are expressed in the form $a + bi$ with real component a and imaginary component bi. The imaginary

123

unit i is equal to $\sqrt{-1}$. That means $i^2 = -1$. The imaginary unit provides a way to find the square root of a negative number. For example, $\sqrt{-25}$ is $5i$. You should expect questions asking you to add, subtract, multiply, divide, and simplify complex numbers. You may see a question that says, "Add $3 + 2i$ and $5 - 7i$" or "Subtract $4 + i\sqrt{5}$ from $2 + i\sqrt{5}$." Or you may see a question that says, "Multiply $6 + 2i$ by $8 - 4i$" or "Divide $1 - 3i$ by $9 - 7i$."

PERFORM OPERATIONS ON COMPLEX NUMBERS

Operations with complex numbers resemble operations with variables in algebra. Complex numbers are expressed in the form $a + bi$ with real component a and imaginary component bi. When adding or subtracting complex numbers, you can only combine like terms — real terms with real terms and imaginary terms with imaginary terms. For example, if you are asked to simplify $-2 + 4i - (-3 + 7i) - 5i$, you should first remove the parentheses to yield $-2 + 4i + 3 - 7i - 5i$. Combining likes terms yields $1 - 8i$. One interesting aspect with imaginary number is that if i has an exponent greater than 1, it can be simplified. For example, $i^2 = -1$, $i^3 = -i$, and $i^4 = 1$. When multiplying complex numbers, remember to simplify each i with an exponent greater than 1. For example, you might see a question that says, "Simplify $(2 - i)(3 + 2i)$." You need to distribute and multiply to get $6 + 4i - 3i - 2i^2$. This is further simplified to $6 + i - 2(-1)$, or $8 + i$.

SIMPLIFYING WITH I IN THE DENOMINATOR

If an expression contains an i in the denominator, it must be simplified. Remember, roots cannot be left in the denominator of a fraction. Since i is equivalent to $\sqrt{-1}$, i cannot be left in the denominator of a fraction. You must rationalize the denominator of a fraction that contains a complex denominator by multiplying the numerator and denominator by the conjugate of the denominator. The conjugate of the complex number $a + bi$ is $a - bi$. You can simplify $\frac{2}{5i}$ by simply multiplying $\frac{2}{5i} \cdot \frac{i}{i}$, which yields $-\frac{2}{5}i$. And you can simplify $\frac{5+3i}{2-4i}$ by multiplying $\frac{5+3i}{2-4i} \cdot \frac{2+4i}{2+4i}$. This yields $\frac{10+20i+6i-12}{4-8i+8i+16}$ which simplifies to $\frac{-2+26i}{20}$ or $\frac{-1+13i}{10}$, which can also be written as $-\frac{1}{10} + \frac{13}{10}i$.

CONVERTING BETWEEN DEGREES AND RADIANS

To convert from degrees to radians, multiply by $\frac{\pi \text{ rad}}{180°}$. For example, $60° \cdot \frac{\pi \text{ rad}}{180°}$ is $\frac{\pi}{3}$ radians. To convert from radians to degrees, multiply by $\frac{180°}{\pi \text{ rad}}$. For example, $\frac{\pi}{4}$ radians $\frac{180°}{\pi \text{ rad}}$ is $45°$. The equation to determine are length is $s = r\theta$, in which s is the arc length, r is the radius of the circle, and θ is the angular displacement or the angle subtended in radians. For example, if you are asked to find the length of the arc that subtends a $60°$ central angle in a circle with a radius of 10 cm, you would solve $s = (10 \text{ cm})(60°)\left(\frac{\pi \, rad}{180°}\right)$ to obtain an arc length in centimeters. You also need to be able to evaluate trigonometric functions of angles in radian measure without your calculator. You may see a question that involves finding the $\sin x$ in which $\frac{\pi}{2} < x < \pi$. It is important to be able recognize given intervals which indicate angle-containing quadrants, which are bound by 0, $\frac{\pi}{2}$, π, $\frac{3\pi}{2}$, and 2π. The statement "all students take calculus" or ASTC can help you to remember the signs of $\sin x$, $\cos x$, and $\tan x$ for an angle measuring $x°$ or x radians. In Quadrant I, the values of $\sin x$, $\cos x$, and $\tan x$ are all positive. In Quadrant II, only $\sin x$ is positive. In Quadrant III, only $\tan x$ is positive. In Quadrant IV, only $\cos x$ is positive.

AREA OF A SECTOR OF A CIRCLE AND ARC LENGTH OF A SECTOR OF A CIRCLE

The area of a sector of a circle is found by the formula, $A = \theta r^2$, where A is the area, θ is the measure of the central angle in radians, and r is the radius. To find the area when the central angle is in degrees, use the formula, $A = \theta\pi r^2$, where θ is the measure of the central angle in degrees and r is the radius. The arc length of a sector of a circle is found by the formula: arc length=$r\theta$, where r is the radius and θ is the measure of the central angle in radians. To find the arc length when the central angle is given in degrees, use the formula: arc length=$\theta 2\pi r$, where θ is the measure of the central angle in degrees and r is the radius.

CIRCLES

The center is the single point inside the circle that is equidistant from every point on the circle. (Point O in the diagram below.)

The radius is a line segment that joins the center of the circle and any one point on the circle. All radii of a circle are equal. (Segments OX, OY, and OZ in the diagram below.)

The diameter is a line segment that passes through the center of the circle and has both endpoints on the circle. The length of the diameter is exactly twice the length of the radius. (Segment XZ in the diagram below.)

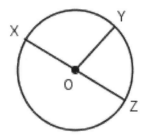

The area of a circle is found by the formula $A = \pi r^2$, where r is the length of the radius. If the diameter of the circle is given, remember to divide it in half to get the length of the radius before proceeding.

The circumference of a circle is found by the formula $C = 2\pi r$, where r is the radius. Again, remember to convert the diameter if you are given that measure rather than the radius.

Concentric circles are circles that have the same center, but not the same length of radii. A bulls-eye target is an example of concentric circles.

An arc is a portion of a circle. Specifically, an arc is the set of points between and including two points on a circle. An arc does not contain any points inside the circle. When a segment is drawn from the endpoints of an arc to the center of the circle, a sector is formed.

A central angle is an angle whose vertex is the center of a circle and whose legs intercept an arc of the circle. Angle XOY in the diagram above is a central angle. A minor arc is an arc that has a measure less than 180°. The measure of a central angle is equal to the measure of the minor arc it intercepts. A major arc is an arc having a measure of at least 180°. The measure of the major arc can be found by subtracting the measure of the central angle from 360°.

A semicircle is an arc whose endpoints are the endpoints of the diameter of a circle. A semicircle is exactly half of a circle.

An inscribed angle is an angle whose vertex lies on a circle and whose legs contain chords of that circle. The portion of the circle intercepted by the legs of the angle is called the intercepted arc. The measure of the intercepted arc is exactly twice the measure of the inscribed angle. In the following diagram, angle ABC is an inscribed angle. $\overset{\frown}{AC} = 2(m\angle ABC)$

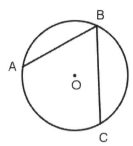

Any angle inscribed in a semicircle is a right angle. The intercepted arc is 180°, making the inscribed angle half that, or 90°. In the diagram below, angle ABC is inscribed in semicircle ABC, making angle ABC equal to 90°.

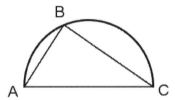

A chord is a line segment that has both endpoints on a circle. In the diagram below, $\overline{EB}$ is a chord.

Secant: A line that passes through a circle and contains a chord of that circle. In the diagram below, $\overleftrightarrow{EB}$ is a secant and contains chord $\overline{EB}$.

A tangent is a line in the same plane as a circle that touches the circle in exactly one point. While a line segment can be tangent to a circle as part of a line that is tangent, it is improper to say a tangent can be simply a line segment that touches the circle in exactly one point. In the diagram below, $\overleftrightarrow{CD}$ is tangent to circle A. Notice that $\overline{FB}$ is not tangent to the circle. $\overline{FB}$ is a line segment that touches the circle in exactly one point, but if the segment were extended, it would touch the circle in a second point. The point at which a tangent touches a circle is called the point of tangency. In the diagram below, point *B* is the point of tangency.

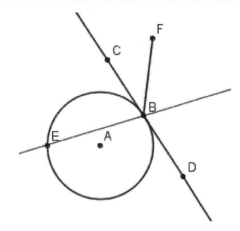

A secant is a line that intersects a circle in two points. Two secants may intersect inside the circle, on the circle, or outside the circle. When the two secants intersect on the circle, an inscribed angle is formed.

When two secants intersect inside a circle, the measure of each of two vertical angles is equal to half the sum of the two intercepted arcs. In the diagram below, m$\angle AEB = \frac{1}{2}(\widehat{AB} + \widehat{CD})$ and m$\angle BEC = \frac{1}{2}(\widehat{BC} + \widehat{AD})$.

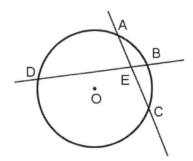

When two secants intersect outside a circle, the measure of the angle formed is equal to half the difference of the two arcs that lie between the two secants. In the diagram below, $m\angle E = \frac{1}{2}(\widehat{AB} - \widehat{CD})$.

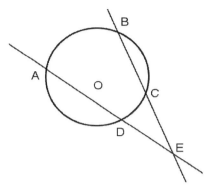

The arc length is the length of that portion of the circumference between two points on the circle. The formula for arc length is $s = \frac{\pi r\theta}{180°}$ where s is the arc length, r is the length of the radius, and θ is the angular measure of the arc in degrees, or $s = r\theta$, where θ is the angular measure of the arc in radians (2π radians = 360 degrees).

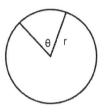

A sector is the portion of a circle formed by two radii and their intercepted arc. While the arc length is exclusively the points that are also on the circumference of the circle, the sector is the entire area bounded by the arc and the two radii.

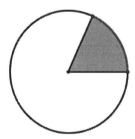

The area of a sector of a circle is found by the formula, $A = \frac{\theta r^2}{2}$, where A is the area, θ is the measure of the central angle in radians, and r is the radius. To find the area when the central angle is in degrees, use the formula, $A = \frac{\theta \pi r^2}{360}$, where θ is the measure of the central angle in degrees and r is the radius.

FORMULAS FOR CIRCLES

One formula for arc length is $s = r\theta$, in which s is the arc length, r is the radius of the circle, and θ is the angular displacement or the angle subtended in radians. Another formula for arc length involving the circumference is given by C is $\frac{s}{C} = \frac{\theta}{360°}$ when central angle θ is measured in degrees or $\frac{s}{C} = \frac{\theta}{2\pi}$ when θ is measured in radians. These formulas can be rearranged to solve for s, C, or θ; of course, if you know a circle's circumference, you can also determine its diameter d or radius r using the formula $C = \pi d$ or $C = 2\pi r$. The area of a sector is given by $\frac{A_{Sector}}{A_{Circle}} = \frac{\theta}{360°}$ when θ is measured in degrees or $\frac{A_{Sector}}{A_{Circle}} = \frac{\theta}{2\pi}$ when θ is measured in radians. Chord lengths are often found by drawing the perpendicular bisector of the chord through the center of the circle and then drawing line segments from the center of the circle to each of the chord's endpoints. This forms two congruent right triangles. The length of the chord can be found using a trigonometric function or the Pythagorean Theorem. On some questions, you may be expected to combine your knowledge of circles with your knowledge of other geometric concepts, such as properties of parallel lines. The formulas for the area and circumference of a circle and the Pythagorean Theorem are provided with the test.

SIMILARITY AND CONGRUENCE RULES

Similar triangles are triangles whose corresponding angles are equal and whose corresponding sides are proportional. Represented by AA. Similar triangles whose corresponding sides are congruent are also congruent triangles.

> **Review Video: Similar Triangles**
> Visit mometrix.com/academy and enter code: 398538

Three sides of one triangle are congruent to the three corresponding sides of the second triangle. Represented as SSS.

Two sides and the included angle (the angle formed by those two sides) of one triangle are congruent to the corresponding two sides and included angle of the second triangle. Represented by SAS.

Two angles and the included side (the side that joins the two angles) of one triangle are congruent to the corresponding two angles and included side of the second triangle. Represented by ASA.

Two angles and a non-included side of one triangle are congruent to the corresponding two angles and non-included side of the second triangle. Represented by AAS.

Note that AAA is not a form for congruent triangles. This would say that the three angles are congruent, but says nothing about the sides. This meets the requirements for similar triangles, but not congruent triangles.

SOLVING PROBLEMS WITH SIMILARITY AND CONGRUENCE

Congruent figures have the same size and same shape. Similar figures have the same shape but not the same size; their corresponding angles are congruent and their sides are proportional. All circles are similar. All squares are similar; likewise, all regular n-gons are similar to other regular n-gons. These concepts may appear in different types of test questions. For example, if a line is drawn through that triangle such that it is parallel to one side, a triangle similar to the original triangle is formed. The corresponding angles are congruent, and proportional relationships can be used to determine missing side lengths from the given information. Also, if parallel lines are cut by two transversals which intersect between or outside of parallel lines, two similar triangles are formed. If an altitude is drawn from the vertex of an isosceles triangle, two congruent triangles are formed.

M⊘metrix

If an altitude is drawn from the vertex of the right angle to the hypotenuse of a right triangle, the two triangles that are formed are similar to each other and to the original right triangle.

RELATIONSHIP BETWEEN SIMILARITY, RIGHT TRIANGLES, AND TRIGONOMETRIC RATIOS

An interesting relationship exists between similarity, right triangles, and the trigonometric ratios. If a line that is parallel to one of the legs of a right triangle is drawn through the right triangle, a right triangle is formed which is similar to the original triangle since the triangles share one acute angle and both contain a right angle. Therefore, the trigonometric ratios of similar right triangles are equal.

Complementary angles have a sum of 90°. The acute angles in a right triangle are complementary. In a right triangle, the sine of one of the acute angles equals the cosine of the other acute angle.

If an altitude is drawn from the vertex of the right angle to the hypotenuse of a right triangle as shown, the two triangles that are formed are similar to each other and to the original right triangle: $\Delta ACH \sim \Delta CBH$, $\Delta ACH \sim \Delta ABC$, and $\Delta CBH \sim \Delta ABC$.

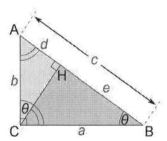

EQUATION OF A CIRCLE

A circle with radius r centered at the origin on the coordinate plane can be represented by the equation $x^2 + y^2 = r^2$. A circle with radius r and center (h, k) is represented by the equation $(x-h)^2 + (y-k)^2 = r^2$. For example, a circle at the origin with a radius of 5 units is represented by the equation $x^2 + y^2 = 25$. If this circle is shifted three units right and two units down, the translated circle is represented by the equation $(x-3)^2 + (y+2)^2 = 25$.

INTEGRATING INFORMATION FROM A CIRCLE INTO MORE COMPLEX QUESTIONS

A single question on this test may require knowledge of multiple geometric concepts. You may see a question about concentric circles or two intersecting circles; you might need to use information given about one circle to find information about the other. A question may provide the points of intersection of a line and a circle, and you may be asked to write and solve the system of equations, which would include both an equation for the line and an equation for the circle. You may be asked to convert between polar coordinates (r, θ) and rectangular (or Cartesian) coordinates (x, y). The relationship between polar and rectangular coordinates is shown below.

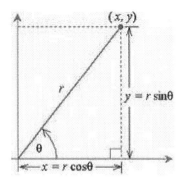

ANGLES

An angle is formed when two lines or line segments meet at a common point. It may be a common starting point for a pair of segments or rays, or it may be the intersection of lines. Angles are represented by the symbol $\angle$.

The vertex is the point at which two segments or rays meet to form an angle. If the angle is formed by intersecting rays, lines, and/or line segments, the vertex is the point at which four angles are formed. The pairs of angles opposite one another are called vertical angles, and their measures are equal.

An acute angle is an angle with a degree measure less than 90°.

A right angle is an angle with a degree measure of exactly 90°.

An obtuse angle is an angle with a degree measure greater than 90° but less than 180°.

A straight angle is an angle with a degree measure of exactly 180°. This is also a semicircle.

A reflex angle is an angle with a degree measure greater than 180° but less than 360°.

A full angle is an angle with a degree measure of exactly 360°.

Review Video: Geometric Symbols: Angles
Visit mometrix.com/academy and enter code: 452738

Two angles whose sum is exactly 90° are said to be complementary. The two angles may or may not be adjacent. In a right triangle, the two acute angles are complementary.

Two angles whose sum is exactly 180° are said to be supplementary. The two angles may or may not be adjacent. Two intersecting lines always form two pairs of supplementary angles. Adjacent supplementary angles will always form a straight line.

Two angles that have the same vertex and share a side are said to be adjacent. Vertical angles are not adjacent because they share a vertex but no common side.

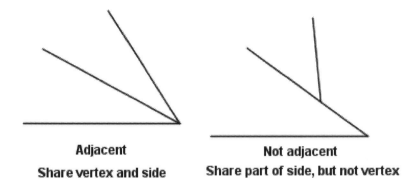

Adjacent
Share vertex and side

Not adjacent
Share part of side, but not vertex

When two parallel lines are cut by a transversal, the angles that are between the two parallel lines are interior angles. In the diagram below, angles 3, 4, 5, and 6 are interior angles.

When two parallel lines are cut by a transversal, the angles that are outside the parallel lines are exterior angles. In the diagram below, angles 1, 2, 7, and 8 are exterior angles.

When two parallel lines are cut by a transversal, the angles that are in the same position relative to the transversal and a parallel line are corresponding angles. The diagram below has four pairs of corresponding angles: angles 1 and 5; angles 2 and 6; angles 3 and 7; and angles 4 and 8. Corresponding angles formed by parallel lines are congruent.

When two parallel lines are cut by a transversal, the two interior angles that are on opposite sides of the transversal are called alternate interior angles. In the diagram below, there are two pairs of alternate interior angles: angles 3 and 6, and angles 4 and 5. Alternate interior angles formed by parallel lines are congruent.

When two parallel lines are cut by a transversal, the two exterior angles that are on opposite sides of the transversal are called alternate exterior angles.

In the diagram below, there are two pairs of alternate exterior angles: angles 1 and 8, and angles 2 and 7. Alternate exterior angles formed by parallel lines are congruent.

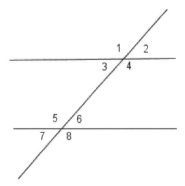

When two lines intersect, four angles are formed. The non-adjacent angles at this vertex are called vertical angles. Vertical angles are congruent. In the diagram, $\angle ABD \cong \angle CBE$ and $\angle ABC \cong \angle DBE$.

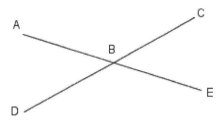

TRIANGLES

An equilateral triangle is a triangle with three congruent sides. An equilateral triangle will also have three congruent angles, each 60°. All equilateral triangles are also acute triangles.

An isosceles triangle is a triangle with two congruent sides. An isosceles triangle will also have two congruent angles opposite the two congruent sides.

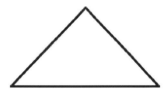

A scalene triangle is a triangle with no congruent sides. A scalene triangle will also have three angles of different measures. The angle with the largest measure is opposite the longest side, and the angle with the smallest measure is opposite the shortest side.

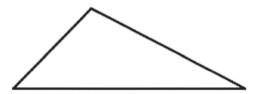

An acute triangle is a triangle whose three angles are all less than 90°. If two of the angles are equal, the acute triangle is also an isosceles triangle. If the three angles are all equal, the acute triangle is also an equilateral triangle.

A right triangle is a triangle with exactly one angle equal to 90°. All right triangles follow the Pythagorean Theorem. A right triangle can never be acute or obtuse.

An obtuse triangle is a triangle with exactly one angle greater than 90°. The other two angles may or may not be equal. If the two remaining angles are equal, the obtuse triangle is also an isosceles triangle.

TERMINOLOGY

Altitude of a Triangle: A line segment drawn from one vertex perpendicular to the opposite side. In the diagram below, $\overline{BE}$, $\overline{AD}$, and $\overline{CF}$ are altitudes. The three altitudes in a triangle are always concurrent.

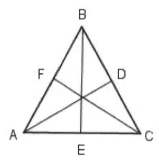

Height of a Triangle: The length of the altitude, although the two terms are often used interchangeably.

Orthocenter of a Triangle: The point of concurrency of the altitudes of a triangle. Note that in an obtuse triangle, the orthocenter will be outside the triangle, and in a right triangle, the orthocenter is the vertex of the right angle.

Median of a Triangle: A line segment drawn from one vertex to the midpoint of the opposite side. This is not the same as the altitude, except the altitude to the base of an isosceles triangle and all three altitudes of an equilateral triangle.

Centroid of a Triangle: The point of concurrency of the medians of a triangle. This is the same point as the orthocenter only in an equilateral triangle. Unlike the orthocenter, the centroid is always inside the triangle. The centroid can also be considered the exact center of the triangle. Any shape triangle can be perfectly balanced on a tip placed at the centroid. The centroid is also the point that is two-thirds the distance from the vertex to the opposite side.

Student-Produced Response

The SAT test includes some questions that are not multiple choice. Instead, they require you to solve the problem, then fill the exact number into a grid very similar to the one you used to enter your name and address on the form. The grid has a row of four boxes on top, with a column of numbers 0–9, a slash, and a decimal beneath each box.

To fill in the grid, write your answer in the boxes on top, then fill in the corresponding circle underneath. Use the slash to indicate fractions. It's a machine-scored test, so you don't get any credit for the number you write on top — that's strictly to help you fill in the circles correctly. If your answer doesn't fill up all four columns, that's okay. And it doesn't matter whether you left-justify or right-justify your answers. What does matter is that the circles be filled in correctly.

IF YOU CAN'T WRITE IT USING THE CHARACTERS PROVIDED, IT'S NOT RIGHT

No student-produced response will be a negative number or a percentage. If you get a negative number, you've made a mistake. Percentages should be expressed as a ratio or decimal; for example, 50% can be written as .50.

START ON THE LEFT

There are a few reasons to start with the first box every time. For one thing, it's faster. It will also help you be as precise as possible. If your answer is <1, though, don't use a leading 0 before the decimal. The SAT omits the 0 from column one to help you be as precise as possible. For decimals, use as many columns as you can. Don't round or truncate answers. If you calculate an answer to be .125, enter the full number, not .13.

REPEAT A REPEATING DECIMAL

Repeating decimals such as .666666 are only counted correct if you fill all the available columns. Either .666 or .667 will get credit. However, .66 will be counted as wrong.

DON'T USE MIXED NUMBERS

If you try to write 2 ½, the computer will think you've written 21/2 and count it wrong. Instead, use the improper fraction form of such numbers; for example, 2 ½ = 5/2.

USE YOUR CALCULATOR

You brought a calculator; use it. Work the problem twice to make sure you entered all the numbers correctly.

CHECK YOUR WORK

More than any other questions in the math section, student-produced responses need to be double-checked. Try working the problem backward, plugging answers back into the original equation.

IT'S OKAY TO GET MULTIPLE ANSWERS

Some questions may have more than one answer. In that case, any correct answer will do.

IN GENERAL

Approach the problem systematically. Take time to understand what is being asked for. In many cases, there is a drawing or graph that you can write on. Draw lines, jot notes, do whatever is necessary to create a visual picture and to allow you to understand what is being asked.

SAT Practice Test

Reading Test

Questions 1–10 are based on the following passage.

This passage is adapted from George Eliot, The Mill on the Floss. *Originally published in 1860.*

Now, good Mr. Glegg himself was stingy in the most amiable manner; his neighbors called him "near," which always means that the person in question is a lovable skinflint. If you expressed a preference for cheese-parings, Mr. Glegg would remember to save them for you, with a good-natured delight in gratifying your palate, and he was given to pet all animals which required no
5   appreciable keep.

There was no humbug or hypocrisy about Mr. Glegg; his eyes would have watered with true feeling over the sale of a widow's furniture, which a five-pound note from his side pocket would have prevented; but a donation of five pounds to a person "in a small way of life" would have seemed to him a mad kind of lavishness rather than "charity," which had always presented itself to
10 him as a contribution of small aids, not a neutralizing of misfortune. And Mr. Glegg was just as fond of saving other people's money as his own; he would have ridden as far round to avoid a turnpike when his expenses were to be paid for him, as when they were to come out of his own pocket, and was quite zealous in trying to induce indifferent acquaintances to adopt a cheap substitute for blacking.

15 This inalienable habit of saving, as an end in itself, belonged to the industrious men of business of a former generation, who made their fortunes slowly, almost as the tracking of the fox belongs to the harrier,—it constituted them a "race," which is nearly lost in these days of rapid money-getting, when lavishness comes close on the back of want. In old-fashioned times an "independence" was hardly ever made without a little miserliness as a condition, and you would have found that quality
20 in every provincial district, combined with characters as various as the fruits from which we can extract acid. The true Harpagons* were always marked and exceptional characters; not so the worthy tax-payers, who, having once pinched from real necessity, retained even in the midst of their comfortable retirement, with their wallfruit and wine-bins, the habit of regarding life as an ingenious process of nibbling out one's livelihood without leaving any perceptible deficit, and who
25 would have been as immediately prompted to give up a newly taxed luxury when they had had their clear five hundred a year, as when they had only five hundred pounds of capital.

Mr. Glegg, being of a reflective turn, and no longer occupied with wool, had much wondering meditation on the peculiar constitution of the female mind as unfolded to him in his domestic life; and yet he thought Mrs. Glegg's household ways a model for her sex. It struck him as a pitiable
30 irregularity in other women if they did not roll up their table-napkins with the same tightness and emphasis as Mrs. Glegg did, if their pastry had a less leathery consistence, and their damson cheese a less venerable hardness than hers; nay, even the peculiar combination of grocery and druglike odors in Mrs. Glegg's private cupboard impressed him as the only right thing in the way of cupboard smells. I am not sure that he would not have longed for the quarrelling again, if it had
35 ceased for an entire week; and it is certain that an acquiescent, mild wife would have left his meditations comparatively jejune and barren of mystery.

*A reference to Moliere's play *The Miser*, in which Harpagon is devoted to accumulating money.

1. Which choice best describes the tone of the passage?

A) carefully drawing a dark portrait of a selfish, morose man
B) humorously poking fun at a middle-aged man's eccentricities
C) romanticizing the thriftiness of a hard-working laborer
D) admiration of the longsuffering nature of a downtrodden husband

2. The word "near" in line 2 most nearly means

A) close by
B) dear
C) stingy
D) upcoming

3. What purpose does the hypothetical situation of the widow in paragraph 2 serve?

A) To illustrate Mr. Glegg's ruling passion of frugality.
B) To give a glimpse of the community in which the Gleggs lived.
C) To show that the Gleggs were well-to-do.
D) To show the value of money in the time period in which the book is set.

4. The examples in paragraph 3 show which of the following views of men like Mr. Glegg?

A) Scorn at the quick and easy way they made their money.
B) Appreciation for the hard work that led to their wealth.
C) Disdain for the way they hoarded their fortunes.
D) Confusion at the variety of personalities that are drawn to be miserly.

5. The term "independence" in line 18 refers to

A) political freedom
B) freedom from dependence on relatives
C) the state of making one's own decisions
D) sufficient savings to live on

6. What is the effect of using "pinched" instead of merely "saved" in line 22?

A) To show the physical suffering required to save money.
B) To show the miserly attitude that gave pain to others in order to save.
C) To show that people often stole to be able to save money.
D) To show that saving money was difficult and required giving up comforts.

7. What can be deduced about Mr. Glegg's character from his opinion of his wife's cooking and cupboard, described in paragraph 4?

A) His stinginess prevents him from appreciating any but the most economical housekeeping.
B) He has very fastidious tastes, and his wife has learned to cater to them specifically.
C) He finds comfort in the familiar, even when it would be considered unpleasant by others.
D) He is intimidated by his wife and has been brainwashed into thinking that everything she does is perfect.

8. Why might Mr. Glegg have "longed for the quarreling again" (line 34) in his marriage, if it ceased?

A) He was naturally cantankerous and enjoyed being at odds with others.
B) He had a great wit and enjoyed the battle of wordplay.
C) He was used to quarreling so life would seem strange without it.
D) He knew it was the way his wife showed love, so a lack of quarreling would be a sign of coldness.

9. The word "jejune" in line 36 most nearly means

A) dull
B) mysterious
C) quarrelsome
D) peaceful

10. Which of the following selections best illustrates Mr. Glegg's passion for frugality?

A) Lines 1-2 ("good Mr. Glegg ... lovable skinflint")
B) Lines 10-14, ("just as fond ... cheap substitute for blacking")
C) Lines 18-19 ("In old-fashioned times ... as a condition")
D) Lines 29-32 ("It struck him ... hardness than hers")

Questions 11–20 are based on the following passage.

This passage is adapted from Karen Hao, "A Radical New Neural Network Design Could Overcome Big Challenges in AI." ©2018 by MIT Technology Review.

An AI researcher at the University of Toronto, David Duvenaud wanted to build a deep-learning model that would predict a patient's health over time. But data from medical records is messy: throughout your life, you might visit the doctor at different times for different reasons, generating a smattering of measurements at arbitrary intervals. A traditional neural network struggles to handle
5   this. Its design requires it to learn from data with clear stages of observation. Thus, it is a poor tool for modeling continuous processes, especially ones that are measured irregularly over time.

The challenge led Duvenaud and his collaborators to redesign neural networks as we know them. Neural nets are the core machinery that make deep learning so powerful. A traditional neural net is made up of stacked layers of simple computational nodes that work together to find patterns
10   in data. The discrete layers are what keep it from effectively modeling continuous processes.

To understand this, we examine what the layers do in the first place. The most common process for training a neural network involves feeding it labeled data. Let's say you wanted to build a system that recognizes different animals. You'd feed a neural net animal pictures paired with corresponding animal names. Under the hood, it begins to solve a mathematical puzzle. It looks at
15   all the picture-name pairs and figures out a formula that reliably turns one (the image) into the other (the category). Once it cracks that puzzle, it can reuse the formula again and again to correctly categorize new animal photos.

But finding a single formula to describe the entire picture-to-name transformation would be overly broad and result in a low-accuracy model. It would be like trying to use a single rule to
20   differentiate cats and dogs. You could say dogs have floppy ears. But some dogs don't and some cats do, so you'd end up with a lot of false negatives and positives.

This is where a neural net's layers come in. They break up the transformation process into steps and let the network find a series of formulas that each describe a stage of the process. So the first layer might take in all the pixels and use a formula to pick out which ones are most relevant for cats
25   versus dogs. Each subsequent layer would identify increasingly complex features of the animal, until the final layer decides "dog" on the basis of the accumulated calculations. This step-by-step breakdown of the process allows a neural net to build more sophisticated models—which in turn should lead to more accurate predictions.

The layer approach has served the AI field well—but it also has a drawback. If you want to
30   model anything that transforms continuously over time, you also have to chunk it up into discrete steps. So, the best way to model reality as close as possible is to add more layers to increase the granularity. Taken to the extreme, this means the best neural network for this job would have an infinite number of layers to model infinitesimal step-changes.

If this is starting to sound familiar, that's because we have arrived at exactly the kind of problem
35   that calculus was invented to solve. Calculus gives you equations for how to calculate a series of changes across infinitesimal steps—in other words, it saves you from the nightmare of modeling continuous change in discrete units.

The result is really not even a network anymore; there are no more nodes and connections, just one continuous slab of computation. Nonetheless, sticking with convention, the researchers named
40   this design an "ODE net"—ODE for "ordinary differential equations."

Consider a continuous musical instrument like a violin, where you can slide your hand along the string to play any frequency you want; now consider a discrete one like a piano, where you have a distinct number of keys to play a limited number of frequencies. A traditional neural network is like a piano: try as you might, you won't be able to play a slide. Switching to an ODE net is like switching your piano to a violin.

45

Currently, the paper offers a proof of concept for the design, "but it's not ready for prime time yet," Duvenaud says. Like any initial technique proposed in the field, it still needs to fleshed out, experimented on, and improved until it can be put into production. But the method has the potential to shake up the field.

11. The main purpose of the passage is to
A) show the change in AI over the last few decades
B) encourage the reader to adopt a new technological trend
C) inform the reader of new developments in AI
D) express the current limitations of AI

12. Why is a traditional neural network insufficient for predicting patient health?
A) It computes too slowly, taking years to gather data and learn the individual needs of patients.
B) It needs clear data in regular steps, and most people's health history does not reflect that.
C) It requires more information than most people are comfortable sharing.
D) It is not able to handle the volume of information required for such predictions.

13. Why did Duvenaud seek to redesign neural networks?
A) They are not good at modeling continuous processes.
B) They have difficulty distinguishing between animals.
C) They take too long to accumulate the necessary data.
D) They cannot find patterns in data.

14. What does the example of the piano and violin in lines 41-45 illustrate?
A) A violin is more complicated than a piano, just as the ODE net is more complicated than a traditional neural network.
B) A violinist can move from note to note without moving to a different string, just as the ODE net moves seamlessly between layers.
C) The ability to slide from note to note on a violin, rather than taking steps between notes, symbolizes the ODE net's continuum that takes the place of layers.
D) The four strings of the violin symbolize the four layers of the ODE net.

15. What does the author mean in line 12 by "training" a neural network?
A) Feeding it images of animals until it learns what the different species look like.
B) Giving it a formula that enables it to discern patterns in data.
C) Teaching it to sort data into two categories with increasingly complex information.
D) Providing it with multiple data examples so that it can figure out patterns for categorization.

16. What does the article propose as the solution to the layer approach problem?
A) calculus
B) a violin
C) animal pictures
D) computational nodes

140

17. As used in line 19, "broad" most nearly means

A) expansive
B) spacious
C) open-minded
D) general

18. Which of the following can be inferred about neural net layers?

A) There are an infinite number of layers in a neural net.
B) Each layer is more complex than the one before it.
C) The layers make it challenging to create accurate models.
D) The layers are more user-friendly than an ODE net.

19. Which selection provides the best evidence for the answer to the previous question?

A) Lines 2-4 ("But data ... arbitrary intervals.")
B) Line 10 ("The discrete layers ... continuous processes.")
C) Lines 22-23 ("They break up ... stage of the process.")
D) Lines 31-32 ("So the best ... increase the granularity.")

20. What is the main idea of the final paragraph?

A) The ODE net is only a design concept as yet and has to pass through significant testing and tweaking.
B) The ODE net is not ready for prime time.
C) The ODE net needs more work before it will be ready, but could make a large difference in the AI field.
D) The ODE net will revolutionize business in the AI sector.

Questions 21–31 are based on the following passages.

Passage 1 is adapted from Edmund Burke, Reflections on the Revolution in France. *Originally published 1790.*

Passage 2 is adapted from Thomas Paine, Rights of Man. *Originally published 1791. Paine's work was written in response to Burke's, regarding the French Revolution.*

Passage 1

When I see the spirit of liberty in action, I see a strong principle at work; and this, for a while, is all I can possibly know of it. The wild gas, the fixed air, is plainly broke loose; but we ought to suspend our judgment until the first effervescence is a little subsided, till the liquor is cleared, and until we see something deeper than the agitation of a troubled and frothy surface. I must be
5   tolerably sure, before I venture publicly to congratulate men upon a blessing, that they have really received one.

Flattery corrupts both the receiver and the giver, and adulation is not of more service to the people than to kings. I should, therefore, suspend my congratulations on the new liberty of France until I was informed how it had been combined with government, with public force, with the
10   discipline and obedience of armies, with the collection of an effective and well-distributed revenue, with morality and religion, with the solidity of property, with peace and order, with civil and social manners. All these (in their way) are good things, too, and without them liberty is not a benefit whilst it lasts, and is not likely to continue long.

The effect of liberty to individuals is that they may do what they please; we ought to see what it
15   will please them to do, before we risk congratulations which may be soon turned into complaints. Prudence would dictate this in the case of separate, insulated, private men, but liberty, when men act in bodies, is power. Considerate people, before they declare themselves, will observe the use which is made of power and particularly of so trying a thing as new power in new persons of whose principles, tempers, and dispositions they have little or no experience, and in situations where
20   those who appear the most stirring in the scene may possibly not be the real movers.

Passage 2

It was not against Louis XVI, but against the despotic principles of the Government, that the nation revolted. These principles had not their origin in him, but in the original establishment, many centuries back: and they were become too deeply rooted to be removed, and the Augean stables of parasites and plunderers too abominably filthy to be cleansed by anything short of a
5   complete and universal Revolution.

When it becomes necessary to do anything, the whole heart and soul should go into the measure, or not attempt it. That crisis was then arrived, and there remained no choice but to act with determined vigor, or not to act at all. The king was known to be the friend of the nation, and this circumstance was favorable to the enterprise. Perhaps no man bred up in the style of an
10   absolute king, ever possessed a heart so little disposed to the exercise of that species of power as the present King of France.

But the principles of the Government itself still remained the same. The Monarch and the Monarchy were distinct and separate things; and it was against the established despotism of the latter, and not against the person or principles of the former, that the revolt commenced, and the
15   Revolution has been carried.

142

Mr. Burke does not attend to the distinction between men and principles, and, therefore, he does not see that a revolt may take place against the despotism of the latter, while there lies no charge of despotism against the former....

20 What Mr. Burke considers as a reproach to the French Revolution (that of bringing it forward under a reign more mild than the preceding ones) is one of its highest honors. The Revolutions that have taken place in other European countries, have been excited by personal hatred. The rage was against the man, and he became the victim. But, in the instance of France we see a Revolution generated in the rational contemplation of the Rights of Man, and distinguishing from the beginning between persons and principles. Lay then the axe to the root, and teach governments humanity.

21. In Passage 1, Burke indicates that it is important to

    A) admire the strong principle of liberty.
    B) wait to rejoice in freedom until it is certain that it will be good for the people.
    C) congratulate those who have received liberty on their blessing.
    D) avoid judging other cultures on their preferred freedoms until they are fully understood.

22. As used in line 3 of Passage 1, "liquor" most nearly means

    A) strong drink.
    B) celebratory champagne.
    C) obscuring darkness.
    D) haze of excitement.

23. In the first paragraph of Passage 2, how did Paine justify the French Revolution?

    A) The government had been corrupted beyond salvaging, and the only solution was a complete change.
    B) The aristocracy was a parasite that was sucking the life out of its people, and the nation would not survive without changing government.
    C) Louis XVI's rule was crippling the country and he needed to be replaced immediately with no chance of reinstatement.
    D) The laws were centuries old and were inappropriate for governing the French people.

24. Paine feels that Burke does not understand that

    A) liberty should be obtained at any cost.
    B) revolting against corrupt principles is not the same as rebelling against the rulers.
    C) the king of France actually loved his people.
    D) the nation of France was in crisis and it was necessary to act decisively before it was too late.

25. How would Burke most likely have responded to Paine's statement in lines 22-24 of Passage 2 that the revolution was "generated in the rational contemplation of the Rights of Man"?

    A) He would contend that human rights were actually violated by the revolution, not supported.
    B) He would point out that human rights cannot be rationally contemplated because they cannot be defined.
    C) He would argue that the revolution was not considered rationally, but emotionally.
    D) He would state that the people doing the contemplation were not the real movers, and thus their results were invalid.

26. Which of the following choices from Passage 1 provides the best evidence to answer the previous question?

    A) Lines 2-4 ("The wild gas ... frothy surface")
    B) Lines 4-6 ("I must ... received one")
    C) Lines 12-13 ("All these ... continue long")
    D) Lines 16-17 ("Prudence would ... is power")

27. How would Paine most likely have responded to Burke's statement in lines 12-13 of Passage 1 that liberty is "not likely to continue long" without the structure of government?

    A) He would argue that it was not the government, but the king, who was overthrown, and so the structure could remain stable, with modifications for more freedom.
    B) He would point out that removing the king was not the same as removing the governmental structure.
    C) He would contend that when men fight with such passion for liberty, they will not let it slip through their fingers.
    D) He would assert that the revolution was carefully thought through before action was taken.

28. Which of the following choices from Passage 2 provides the best evidence to answer the previous question?

    A) Lines 1-2 ("It was ... nation revolted")
    B) Lines 12-15 ("The monarch ... been carried")
    C) Lines 22-24 ("But, in ... and principles")
    D) Lines 24-25 ("Lay then ... governments humanity")

29. As used in line 21 of Passage 2, "excited" most nearly means

    A) giddy.
    B) instigated.
    C) enraged.
    D) invented.

30. Which of the following choices best represents the relationship between the two passages?

    A) Passage 2 provides a different angle to the argument in passage 1.
    B) Passage 2 is a rebuttal to the major claim of Passage 1.
    C) Passage 2 gives new evidence that refutes Passage 1.
    D) Passage 2 provides supporting evidence for Passage 1.

31. Paine and Burke would most likely agree that

    A) liberty is the highest gift a person can be given.
    B) while the king may love his people, he cannot change centuries of law and tradition.
    C) it is important to weigh options carefully before seeking freedom from a government.
    D) the original French government was corrupt and some kind of action was necessary.

Questions 32–41 are based on the following passage and supplementary material.

This passage is adapted from Christine A. Scheller, "Health Researchers Urge New Focus on Ancestry, Social Struggles." ©2019 by American Association for the Advancement of Science.

When medical professionals make appearance-based assumptions about patients without respect to genetic variation, it can lead to serious health consequences, said National Institutes of Health genetic epidemiologist Charles Rotimi at an 18 December 2018 discussion held at the American Association for the Advancement of Science headquarters, sponsored by the AAAS
5   Dialogue on Science, Ethics, and Religion.

Rotimi said that 97.3% of people have mixed genetic ancestry. "At the genome level, trying to use genetics to define what we call 'race' is like slicing soup," Rotimi said. "You can cut wherever you want, but the soup stays mixed. The ubiquity of mixed ancestry emphasizes the importance of accounting for ancestry in history, forensics, and health including drug labeling."

10   Rotimi described a "critically important" example from a 1996 study: An eight-year-old European boy was scheduled for unnecessary surgery because doctors failed to diagnose him with sickle cell anemia. His parents were from Grenada and of Indian, northern European, and Mediterranean ancestry. Rotimi noted that Greece has a higher population of sickle cell carriers than South Africa.

15   "If we trace our ancestry far back enough, we're going to end up somewhere on the continent of Africa," said Rotimi, who is director of the Center for Research on Genomics and Global Health at the NIH. "This common history is the reason why we share so much of our genetic inheritance," he said.

The human genome looks like a history book that captures the experiences of our ancestors,
20   Rotimi said. For instance, there is a high rate of kidney failure among African-Americans. Although they are 13% of the U.S. population, African Americans make up 32% of patients with kidney failure. Genetic variations associated with increased kidney disease risk likely rose to high population frequency in Africa because they confer resistance to trypanosomal parasite infection and protect against the lethal form of African sleeping sickness, which was historically a bigger
25   threat than kidney failure, Rotimi said.

"Individuals who don't look like Africans but have African ancestry carry this variant. So, you cannot use the concept of black or white to describe it," Rotimi said. "Ancestry is critically important, especially when talking about precision medicine or treating individuals. It's a whole lot more important than the way we see ourselves."

30   For these reasons, improving the lack of diversity in genomic research has long been Rotimi's passion. Although Rotimi said that the driving force behind health disparities is social structures, not genetics, he concluded, "The fact that we're not engaging different populations can actually lead us to wrong decisions."

Medical anthropologist Lesley Jo Weaver expanded on this idea, describing her research on how
35   structural inequalities shape the health outcomes of women with Type 2 Diabetes in northern India.

"Racial legacies of colonialism underpin many of the health inequalities that we see today in India and beyond," said Weaver, an assistant professor of international studies at the University of Oregon.

40   Weaver told the story of a New Delhi woman who found it difficult to properly manage her diabetes because her low caste, dark skin, and lack of education severely limited her opportunities.

    India has the second highest Type 2 Diabetes rate in the world, with 60 million people across all castes suffering from the condition, Weaver said. Systematic inequality is layered on top of systematic inequality to reinforce health disparities in the population, she said. "This is something that public health practitioners rarely think about."

45   The women in Weaver's study who used religious practice as a coping mechanism along with biomedical interventions were more successful at managing the stresses associated with their diabetes than were women who used biomedical interventions alone, but the best health outcomes were found among those who implemented both approaches, she said.

    "There is something in our cultural and spiritual heritage that is relevant for scientists and
50 other researchers doing precision medicine and analyzing the human genome," said Gay Byron, professor at the Howard University School of Divinity.

    Byron suggested, "It is only in telling our stories in the fullness of their particularity that we can begin to appreciate the full tapestry of health."

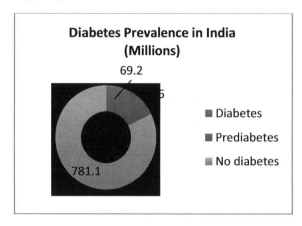

Data taken from hindustantimes.com.

32. The main purpose of the passage is to
    A) bring to light the difficulties of underprivileged people in obtaining healthcare.
    B) show the importance of race in one's health.
    C) describe the role of genetics and social background in health.
    D) show the differences in Eastern and Western medical practice.

33. As used in line 17, "inheritance" most nearly means
    A) a parent's estate, left in a will to offspring.
    B) a parent's genetics.
    C) the health habits that are passed down through the generations.
    D) the genetic combination of one's ancestors.

34. What does the "critically important" example in paragraph 3 indicate to support the author's premise?
- A) Mixed ancestry makes it more challenging to understand one's health tapestry.
- B) Sickle cell anemia is difficult to diagnose without knowledge of where one's ancestors lived.
- C) Knowing one's genetic background is critical to obtaining proper healthcare.
- D) Too many doctors are unaware of how to glean health information from one's family background.

35. The passage implies that
- A) with better understanding of genetic backgrounds, doctors can provide better treatment.
- B) as people understand their ancestry better, they can improve their health.
- C) combining spiritual and physical practices can be instrumental in finding a cure for disease.
- D) diabetes could be eliminated with proper study of genetics.

36. Which of the following choices best supports the answer to the previous question?
- A) Lines 10-12 ("An eight-year-old ... cell anemia")
- B) Lines 27-29 ("Ancestry is ... treating individuals")
- C) Lines 45-47 ("The women ... interventions alone")
- D) Lines 49-50 ("There is ... human genome")

37. As used in line 53, "tapestry" most nearly means
- A) a colorful textile.
- B) a depiction of how health is like a beautiful, intricate blanket.
- C) a picture made of multiple interwoven components.
- D) a combination of everything that leads to good health.

38. Paragraph 11 states that 60 million people in India have Type 2 diabetes, while the chart shows 69.2 million with diabetes. What is a logical explanation for this discrepancy?
- A) The author of the passage could have been rounding down for simplicity.
- B) The passage refers to Type 2 diabetes, while the chart could include Type 1 as well.
- C) The passage could have been referring to just the country of India, while the chart could have included small, surrounding nations.
- D) Either the passage or the chart could have used incorrect information.

39. Which of the following could be added to the chart to make it more relevant to the passage?
- A) whether the number of people with diabetes has increased or decreased in recent years
- B) the demographics of those with diabetes by gender and caste
- C) the percentage of people with diabetes in surrounding countries for comparison
- D) the percentage of people in India with sickle cell disease

40. Which of the following statements is best supported by the data in the chart?
- A) While nearly 70 million people in India currently have diabetes, an even greater number have prediabetes and may not even know it.
- B) The nation of India is in crisis, with nearly half of the country either diabetic or prediabetic.
- C) Despite the prevalence of diabetes in India, the outlook is improving due to a lower number with prediabetes.
- D) India's diabetes problem is poised to worsen, as the number of those with prediabetes is nearly double the number of those currently diagnosed with diabetes.

147

41. Which paragraph would be the best place to add an anecdote about a person who used her family's spiritual practices in disease treatment?

    A) Paragraph 11 (lines 41-44)
    B) Paragraph 12 (lines 45-48)
    C) Paragraph 13 (lines 49-51)
    D) Paragraph 14 (lines 52-53)

Questions 42–52 are based on the following passage and supplementary material.

This passage is adapted from Neil Howe, "America the Sleep-Deprived." ©2017 by Forbes.

Americans aren't spending enough time snoozing. In 2013 (the last year measured by Gallup), the average American slept 6.8 hours a night—with 40 percent banking less than six hours. The nation hasn't always been this sleep-deprived: Back in 1910, people slept an average of nine hours per night. Our culture of sleeplessness has been propelled by technologies like the
5   light bulb and the Internet, which have given us more opportunities to stay awake in an increasingly 24/7 world.

Most Americans are aware they aren't getting enough sleep, which has spurred the growth of an entire industry. In the mid-1980s, insomniacs were simply told to sleep more. The concept of sleep medicine didn't take off until the '90s and early '00s, when medical terms like "sleep disorder" and
10   "sleep aid" entered common parlance. Consumers spent $41 billion on sleep-related products in 2015, a figure that could rise to $52 billion by 2020.

This consumer category includes much more than prescription and over-the-counter sleep aids. Starting with the introduction of Select Comfort's Sleep Number bed in the 1980s, the $13 billion mattress industry has innovated to keep consumers from lying awake.

15   Sleep-deprived consumers are also turning to tech-enabled devices. Products use sensors that sit on or under mattresses to track movements, sounds, and breathing. Apps use smartphones to do the same—and also time alarms so users wake up during their lightest sleep phase.

Organizations of all types are adapting to America's need for shuteye. Silicon Valley has led the charge, implementing flexible work schedules and other sleep-supporting perks. Hubspot, a
20   marketing-software company, has a dedicated nap room—complete with a hammock and cloud-covered walls. It makes sense: Well-rested workers make better decisions, are less stressed, and are less prone to errors. Likewise, studies show that students whose schools start later have better impulse control, earn higher grades, and aren't involved in as many car accidents.

The nation's bad sleep habits are closely tied to generational attitudes. Boomers are the biggest
25   workaholics of any generation. In the '80s, Boomer yuppies eschewed traditional sleep patterns—choosing to wake up for a pre-dawn jog after a late night at the office. They may be buying state-of-the-art sound machines to lull them to sleep, but that doesn't mean they are trying to go to bed any earlier.

For Generation X, sleep has never been easy to come by. As kids, their parents were lax about
30   enforcing regular bedtimes. And now, according to Fitbit's sleep data, Americans in their 40s and early 50s get the least amount of sleep. Squeezed on all sides by the demands of everyday life (from work to family), Xers want proven practices—from drugs to "sleep hacks"—to help them cope.

Millennials are now at a crossroads between their need to sleep and their desire to stay awake. Unlike Boomers who took drugs to mellow out, Millennials are increasingly taking stimulants like
35   Ritalin, Adderall, and modafinil to stay focused both in the classroom and in the workplace. For this achievement-oriented generation, the pressure to be always on in order to earn the next gold star is pushing them toward drugs that keep them awake. At this point, a good night's rest is more of a dream than a reality.

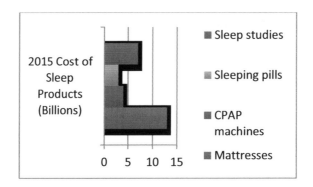

42. What does the author suggest as a leading reason that people are sleeping less than a hundred years ago?

A) technology
B) taking stimulants
C) better mattresses and other sleep aids
D) failure to enforce good bedtimes

43. Which generation sleeps the least, on average?

A) Millennials
B) Generation X
C) Boomers
D) Early 20th century

44. As used in line 4, "propelled" most nearly means

A) moved in circles
B) lifted off the ground
C) pushed uncomfortably
D) moved forward

45. The author indicates that each generation

A) has its own reasons for losing sleep.
B) is going to bed later.
C) is increasingly turning to drugs to help with their sleep problems.
D) is spending more on sleep-related products.

46. Which choice provides the best evidence for the answer to the previous question?

A) Lines 10-11 ("Consumers spent ... by 2020")
B) Line 24 ("The nation's ... generational attitudes")
C) Lines 30-31 ("And now ... amount of sleep")
D) Lines 34-35 ("Millennials are ... the workplace")

47. Another article claims that each successive generation for the past 60 years has slept less than the previous one. Which of the following statements in the passage supports or contradicts this claim?

A) Support: Lines 4-6 ("Our culture ... 24/7 world")
B) Support: Lines 10-11 ("Consumers spent ... by 2020")
C) Contradict: Lines 24-25 ("Boomers are ... any generation")
D) Contradict: Lines 30-31 ("And now ... amount of sleep")

48. As used in line 25, "eschewed" most nearly means

   A) lost hold of
   B) deliberately gave up
   C) slowly distanced from
   D) despised

49. Does the author's overall tone indicate that there is hope for better sleep habits in the future?

   A) Yes, because many schools and businesses are actively seeking to promote good sleep practices.
   B) Yes, because new, more effective sleep products are being developed.
   C) No, because despite the research and spending, the pressure of the modern lifestyle is not lessening.
   D) No, because spending on sleep-related products keeps rising.

50. Based on the chart, on which two products is the most money spent?

   A) sleep studies and sleeping pills
   B) sleep studies and CPAP machines
   C) CPAP machines and mattresses
   D) sleep studies and mattresses

51. Does the chart support the author's claim in lines 10-11 about the amount of consumer spending?

   A) Yes, because the amounts in the chart add up to $41 billion.
   B) Yes, because the mattress industry costs $13 billion.
   C) No, because the amounts in the chart do not add up to $41 billion.
   D) No, because the chart shows the wrong cost for the mattress industry.

52. Which consumer sleep products mentioned in the passage could be added to the chart?

   A) tech devices
   B) pillows
   C) nap rooms
   D) prescription sleep aids

Writing and Language Test

Questions 1–11 are based on the following passage.

Could the future of crops include planting without soil? The concept of hydroponics, or growing plants by directly exposing the roots to water and nutrients, [1] both conserving resources such as water and stimulating extra growth and food production.

While this concept sounds new and innovative—and [2] in fact has being extensively studied by NASA in recent years—the idea is not original to the past decade, or even the past century. [3] Books were published, as early as the 17th century, discussing the idea of growing plants without the traditional concept of planting them in the earth. The term "hydroponics" was first introduced in 1937 by William Gericke, who grew tomatoes in his back yard in a solution of minerals. Since this time, numerous experiments have been conducted and some large hydroponics farms have even been constructed.

1.
A) NO CHANGE
B) allows farmers to both conserve resources
C) aids in both conserving resources
D) both conserves resources

2.
A) NO CHANGE
B) has been
C) is been
D) having been

3.
A) NO CHANGE
B) Books, as early as the 17th century, were published:
C) As early as the 17th century, books were published
D) Books were published as early as the 17th century—

Rather than soil, plants are grown in a variety of [4] <u>substitutes; such</u> as rockwool, clay pellets, pumice, wood fiber, or even packing peanuts. These allow the roots easy access to both the nutrient-rich water and to oxygen.

There are many advantages to hydroponic farming. Due to the controlled greenhouse environment, crops can be [5] <u>grown and no</u> pesticides. There is also less waste of water because of no run-off. Furthermore, proponents of hydroponics claim that this method can lead to much greater yields. This is due not only to the better nutrition but [6] <u>additionally to</u> the protection from harsh weather conditions and pests. Additionally, hydroponics farmers are not limited to a single crop during the normal growing [7] <u>season, they</u> can produce year-round.

4.
   A) NO CHANGE
   B) substitutes, such
   C) substitutes: like
   D) substitutes, like

5.
   A) NO CHANGE
   B) grown without
   C) grown without no
   D) grown even with no

6.
   A) NO CHANGE
   B) in addition
   C) even to
   D) in also to

7.
   A) NO CHANGE
   B) season, or they
   C) season, then they
   D) season; they

1. [8] <u>In addition</u>, hydroponics does have disadvantages. *2.* Before beginning, a farmer must have a greenhouse with proper growing stations and temperature control. *3.* Soil replacement, nutrients, and specialized lighting must also be purchased. *4.* Finally, removing exposure to the outdoor environment means that the farmer must [9] <u>eliminate</u> needs such as pollination. *5.* [10] <u>The setup for growing without soil is costly.</u>

Despite the disadvantages, hydroponics is likely to become more popular in coming years. Not only can crops be grown year-round, but plants can also be much closer together, or even grown [11] <u>vertically,</u> allowing for a much greater yield per acre. Additionally, hydroponics may have implications in other areas. For example, NASA has done research with hydroponics to mimic a Martian environment. So while the work and expense of soil-less gardening is significant, this market, which is already in the hundreds of millions of dollars worldwide, may be a glimpse of the future of farming.

8.
- A) NO CHANGE
- B) Comparatively
- C) Moreover
- D) However

9.
- A) NO CHANGE
- B) track
- C) provide for
- D) remove

10. What is the most logical place for this sentence?
- A) NO CHANGE
- B) after sentence 1
- C) after sentence 2
- D) after sentence 3

11.
- A) NO CHANGE
- B) in a vertical manner
- C) vertical
- D) horizontal

Questions 12–22 are based on the following passage.

Throughout human history, mankind [12] sought to track the days and seasons. [13] Tracing back millennia, archaeologists have discovered calendars, showing the ancient views of the earth's movement and time's passage. Though most calendars are very similar in length, a few changes have been made as measurements have become more precise.

Some calendars have been used for much of recorded human history. For instance, the Assyrian calendar has been in use for over 6,750 years. Many communities still celebrate the Assyrian New Year every spring.

The earliest known calendar was discovered in Scotland—twelve pits with a corresponding arc. Researchers have categorized it as a lunar calendar, [14] the phases of the moon are the basis for this.

12.
A) NO CHANGE
B) seeks
C) has sought
D) is seeking

13.
A) NO CHANGE
B) Tracing back millennia, calendars were discovered,
C) Calendars tracing back millennia have been discovered by archaeologists
D) Archaeologists have discovered calendars tracing back millennia,

14.
A) NO CHANGE
B) based on the phases of the moon
C) using the phases of the moon as its basis
D) with its basis being the phases of the moon

155

[15] Although Scotland is home to the oldest calendar, most current ones are termed solar calendars. That is, they are based on the fact that the earth travels around the sun in a certain number of days. However, several cultures created lunisolar calendars, using [16] both solar and lunar measurements to determine the year and months. The Chinese calendar ([17] that is no longer the country's official calendar but is still used in many places) was originally a lunisolar calendar, with the length of the year based on the [18] sun, however the new year beginning on the new moon before the winter solstice. Lunisolar calendars use intercalary months (a technique similar to a leap day) to add sufficient days to make the lunar months add up to the solar year. Some years have 12 months, but every second or third year, an intercalary month is added to keep the months aligned with the seasons.

15. Which of the following best introduces this paragraph?
- A) NO CHANGE
- B) Because the earth travels around the sun
- C) While many of the oldest calendars were lunar
- D) Despite the phases of the moon used for many calendars

16.
- A) NO CHANGE
- B) either solar or lunar
- C) neither solar nor lunar
- D) solar and/or lunar

17.
- A) NO CHANGE
- B) which
- C) how
- D) what

18.
- A) NO CHANGE
- B) sun; however
- C) sun, although
- D) sun and

In 46 BCE, Julius Caesar instituted the Julian calendar, a solar calendar that became the predominant method of measurement in the Western world for over 1600 years. Before this, the Roman calendar was often [19] stabilized by political goals: years were lengthened or shortened to adjust terms of office (since many offices were held for a year), depending on who was in power. [20] To fix this political issue, Caesar consulted with an Egyptian astronomer, who advised him to adopt a solar calendar. This calendar brought stability, but after Caesar's assassination, the Roman priests mistakenly added too many leap days.

Because of this, Easter moved farther from the vernal equinox, so in 1582 CE Pope Gregory XIII introduced a revised calendar, [21] shifted the date forward ten days. Rather than adding an intercalary month every few years, this Gregorian calendar adds a leap day every four years (with a few exceptions), measuring the solar year as 365.2425 days. [22] Though still imprecise, this number is widely accepted worldwide and allows mankind to do what he has attempted throughout history: to keep the year in sync with the seasons.

19.
- A) NO CHANGE
- B) renamed
- C) skewed
- D) torn

20. Should this sentence be left, moved, or removed from the paragraph?
- A) It should be left where it is, as a response to the calendar's adjustment to further political goals.
- B) It should be moved to the end of the paragraph, as a response to the mistake of too many leap days.
- C) It should be removed from the paragraph because solar calendars have already been discussed in a previous paragraph.
- D) It should be removed from the paragraph because it does not add relevant information.

21.
- A) NO CHANGE
- B) therefore he shifted
- C) he shifted
- D) shifting

22. Which of the following is the best conclusion to this selection?
- A) NO CHANGE
- B) The Gregorian calendar is the most widely used throughout the world today, allowing for ease of communication and trade worldwide.
- C) After all the turmoil of finding an accurate calendar, the Gregorian calendar has finally provided for that need.
- D) Though not all cultures ascribe to the Gregorian calendar, it is the most accurate and has brought unity across countries as all can now agree on the date.

Mometrix

Questions 23–33 are based on the following passage and supplementary material.

The ever-changing technological world in which we live constantly offers new opportunities and perspectives on age-old traditions. Communication in particular has changed rapidly, with new ways of [23] <u>connectedness</u> constantly appearing. As we are increasingly able to communicate from any place and at any time, this has led to questions of how this ability could help in other areas.

[24] <u>Even if</u> technological advances in communication are often considered from a social standpoint, as people can connect more and more easily, one sector that has been immensely affected is the career sector. Many companies can now submit deliverables without appearing in person. Online meetings can [25] <u>conduct</u> from the comfort of each person's office. Instant communication allows for quick answers and increased productivity.

23.
- A) NO CHANGE
- B) being in connection
- C) connecting
- D) finding connection methods

24.
- A) NO CHANGE
- B) While
- C) However
- D) Consequently

25.
- A) NO CHANGE
- B) be conducted
- C) hold
- D) held

Not only are employees able to [26] more work from the corporate office, with less need to travel for meetings and site visits, but there is an increasing trend toward employees who work from a home office, [27] although checking in virtually throughout the day or even logging in remotely to a work computer. Telecommuting has many advantages both to the employee and the employer. The employee, obviously, can save time and money by staying home (studies estimate telecommuters save an average of $4,000 per year in travel and office-related costs), and may be able to have a more flexible schedule to work around children's school days or other responsibilities. Companies can also save money [28] with fewer overhead: [29] with off-site employees, they can avoid the cost of office space, lighting, heating/cooling, and other expenses, as well as improving employee retention, saving an estimated $11,000 per telecommuting employee each year. Ideally, telecommuting can lead to greater profit and efficiency, as employees are able to concentrate on work in their most comfortable environment.

26.
A) NO CHANGE
B) working more from the corporate office
C) perform work more from the corporate office
D) work from the corporate office more often

27.
A) NO CHANGE
B) but
C) even
D) DELETE the underlined portion.

28.
A) NO CHANGE
B) with lesser
C) by lowering
D) on smaller

29. What is the best way of rewriting this for clarity and meaning?
A) NO CHANGE
B) with off-site employees, they can avoid the cost of office space, lighting, heating/cooling, and other expenses. Additionally, they can improve employee retention. Overall, they save an estimated $11,000 per telecommuting employee per year.
C) with off-site employees, they can avoid the cost of office space, lighting, heating/cooling, and other expenses. This saves companies an estimated $11,000 per telecommuting employee each year.
D) with off-site employees, they can avoid the cost of office space. They also save on lighting, heating/cooling, and other expenses, saving an estimated $11,000 per telecommuting employee each year.

However, telecommuting comes with its drawbacks. Technological glitches (internet connection problems, faulty microphones, etc.) can make virtual meetings [30] an advantage. Security can be a concern when employees are working with sensitive information from their homes. Accountability is also more challenging when one is working from home with minimal supervision. [31] And in an increasingly isolated world, telecommuting keeps people farther apart, removing the social interaction that a job normally provides.

In response, some companies have reached a compromise. Employees may have a mixed schedule, telecommuting one or two days a week and coming in to the office on the others. A 2013 worldwide study shows that nearly half of business [32] managers' telecommute for much of the workweek, and over half are willing to manage remote workers. While telecommunication obviously is impractical for certain sectors, it appears to be a promising way for many companies to meet both individual needs and corporate goals.

30.
A) NO CHANGE
B) a challenge
C) a bore
D) humorous

31. Here the author is considering adding an example of an employee who was discovered to be away from home, handling personal business, while supposedly on the clock. Should the writer make this addition here?
A) Yes, because it explains the vague point on accountability in the previous sentence.
B) Yes, because it is the most pressing concern related to telecommuting.
C) No, because it breaks the flow of thought to add an example for one item from the list in this paragraph and gives it undue emphasis.
D) No, because accountability is not the greatest concern related to telecommuting.

32.
A) NO CHANGE
B) manager's
C) managers
D) manager

Number of US employees working from office vs. home (millions)

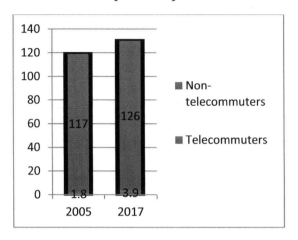

33. What can be deduced about the number of telecommuters in relation to the total number of workers?

A) The number of telecommuters has increased, while the number of non-telecommuters has decreased.

B) Both telecommuters and non-telecommuters have increased proportionally.

C) The percentage of non-telecommuters is increasing faster than the percentage of telecommuters.

D) The percentage of telecommuters is increasing faster than the percentage of non-telecommuters.

Questions 34–44 are based on the following passage.

Anyone who has participated in a humanities class or museum [34] visit, has doubtless seen classical paintings depicting bowls of fruit. Why is that clusters of grapes and piles of apples were so intriguing to artists?

A glance through ancient history shows that this was not merely a Renaissance theme. Ancient Egyptian paintings of fruit have been discovered in most of the tombs, [35] eliciting a belief that they would become real food for the dead to eat in the afterlife. They could also symbolize rebirth, fertility, and abundance.

Fruit is meaningful in many other religions and cultures as well, [36] from Greek mythology to Islam to Christianity. Pomegranates, figs, and apples figure into ancient Greek and Roman myths, symbolic of fertility, temptation, and prosperity. Both Islam and Christianity link fruit with temptation and sin, [37] even with joy and abundance. Ancient Chinese beliefs hold pears as signs of immortality.

34.
- A) NO CHANGE
- B) visit; has
- C) visit—has
- D) visit has

35.
- A) NO CHANGE
- B) mentioning
- C) signifying
- D) harboring

36.
- A) NO CHANGE
- B) from Greek mythology, Islam, and Christianity
- C) among Greek mythology, Islam, and Christianity
- D) including Greek mythology, to Islam, to Christianity

37.
- A) NO CHANGE
- B) as well as
- C) including
- D) also

162

So why did each of these separate cultures find significance in fruit? Many scholars believe this is because fruit is a natural allegory for human life. At its peak, fruit is rich, sweet, and desirable. Inevitably, though, it withers and decays, a reminder of the [38] transiency of life.

Some ancient cultures such as the Romans found particular meaning in life's brevity. Roman mosaics in dining areas often depicted food, symbolizing abundance and pleasure in [39] feasting. Along with skulls to remind viewers that death was imminent and inescapable, even as they ate and drank.

In the 1600s, artists [40] reflected from these ancient cultures for inspiration. At the same time, there was an emphasis on the natural world. Since fruit played an important role in both of these, it became a popular subject for the paintbrush. Both secular and religious art found beauty and symbolism in various fruits, so a painted cluster of grapes was a common [41] site in many homes.

38.
   A) NO CHANGE
   B) joy
   C) longevity
   D) sorrow

39.
   A) NO CHANGE
   B) feasting. This came along
   C) feasting, this was along
   D) feasting, along

40.
   A) NO CHANGE
   B) referred back on
   C) drew upon
   D) recalled from

41.
   A) NO CHANGE
   B) sight in
   C) cite to
   D) sight to

Even in more modern work, fruit remains a common theme. Picasso painted numerous pieces that included fruit (though it was certainly a departure from the classical style). [42] For his representations of repeating fruits, Andy Warhol is also well known. While it may not hold the same symbolism today, fruit is still a visual representation of one of humanity's most basic needs—[43] nourishment. It also evokes imagery of fragility and both perfection and flaw, all of which are common themes explored in today's culture.

1. From ancient tomb paintings to Renaissance masterpieces to contemporary art, fruit as art has stood the test of time. *2.* Fruit is thus a reminder of humanity's nature, and though much has changed throughout history, mankind still finds meaning and beauty in the same things...even if for different reasons. [44]

42.
A) NO CHANGE
B) Additionally, Andy Warhol, for his representations of repeating fruits, is well known.
C) Andy Warhol is also well known for his representations of repeating fruits.
D) For representing fruits through repetition, Andy Warhol is also well known.

43.
A) NO CHANGE
B) nourishing
C) to be nourished
D) being nourished

44. The author wishes to add the following sentence to the concluding paragraph:

There are numerous varieties of fruit, but all follow a cycle of death and rebirth.

Which of the following is the best location for this sentence?
A) before sentence 1
B) before sentence 2
C) after sentence 2
D) DELETE, because this sentence does not fit in this paragraph.

Math – No Calculator

Questions 1–15 are multiple choice. Questions 16–20 are grid-in.

1. If $3x - 4 = -1$, what is the value of $12x + 3$?
   A) 18
   B) 15
   C) 6
   D) 1

2. In the function below, b is a constant. If $f(-2) = 0$, what is the value of $f(3)$?
$$f(x) = \frac{1}{2}x + b$$

   A) $-\frac{5}{2}$
   B) -1
   C) $\frac{1}{2}$
   D) $\frac{1}{2}$

3. If (x, y) is the solution to the following system of equations, what is the value of $x - y$?
$$4x - y = 11$$
$$x = 3y$$

   A) 0
   B) 1
   C) 2
   D) 3

4. Which of the following is equivalent to the expression: $2(2x - 3)^2 - (3x + 5)$
   A) $8x^2 - 21x + 13$
   B) $8x^2 - 27x + 13$
   C) $8x^2 - 21x + 23$
   D) $8x^2 - 27x + 23$

5. Jan has six pairs of socks for every pair of shoes she owns. If she has 12 pairs of shoes and s pairs of socks, which of the following equations is true?
   A) $12s = 6$
   B) $6s = 12$
   C) $\frac{s}{6} = 12$
   D) $s + 6 = 12$

6. What is the perimeter of a 45-45-90 triangle if the hypotenuse is 4 inches?
   A) 4 inches
   B) 8 inches
   C) $4 + 4\sqrt{2}$ inches
   D) $4 + 2\sqrt{2}$ inches

7. The function f is defined by a polynomial. The table below gives values for x and $f(x)$. Which of the following must be a factor of $f(x)$?

x	$f(x)$
0	4
1	2
2	0

A) x
B) $x - 1$
C) $x + 2$
D) $x - 2$

8. In the system of equations below, a is a constant and x and y are variables. For which of the following values of a will the system have no solution?

$$x + 3y = -7$$
$$ax - 2y = 6$$

A) $-\dfrac{2}{3}$
B) $-\dfrac{1}{3}$
C) 0
D) $\dfrac{7}{3}$

9. In the graph below, lines h and k are perpendicular, and they intersect at point $(3, a)$ as shown. What is the value of a?

A) $\dfrac{3}{2}$
B) 2
C) $\dfrac{5}{2}$
D) 4

10. For $f(x)$ below, m is a constant and $f(-2) = 4$. What is the value of $f(6)$?

$$f(x) = x^2 + mx - 3$$

$36 + m6 - 3$

$f(6) = 33 + m6$

A) $-\frac{3}{2}$
B) 12
C) 21
D) 24

11. In the equations below, i refers to the amount of money (in dollars) invested in production of x products and p refers to the profits. What is the "break even" number of products, where investments are equal to profits?

$$i = 15,200 + 0.75x$$
$$p = 5.5x$$

A) 2,432
B) 3,075
C) 3,200
D) 17,600

12. The equation below calculates the growth of an apple tree, where h is the height in feet and y is the number of years since the tree was planted. How many inches does the tree grow each year?

$$h = 2.5 + 0.75y$$

A) 0.75
B) 2.5
C) 9
D) 30

13. If $2x - y = 4$, what is the value of $\frac{4^x}{2^y}$?

A) 8
B) 16
C) 32
D) Cannot be determined

14. If $2(mx - 2)(nx + 5) = 8x^2 + px - 20$, and $m + n = 5$, what are the two possible values of p?

A) −6 and 36
B) 1 and 4
C) 4 and 5
D) 6 and 20

15. What is the sum of all values of x that satisfy the following equation?

$$3x^2 - 3x - 34 = 2$$

A) −3
B) 0
C) 1
D) 4

167

16. A number of cash prizes were awarded for the top salespeople at ABC Communications, each in the amount of $100, $200, or $400. If the prizes totaled $1,600 and there were 7 total prizes awarded, what is the greatest possible number of $100 prizes awarded?

Grid your answer.

17. If $x > 0$ and $x^2 - 7 = 9$, what is the value of x?

Grid your answer.

18. In the figure below (not drawn to scale), $\triangle ABC$ is similar to $\triangle EDC$. What is the length of AB?

Grid your answer.

19. In right triangle MNP below, angle M measures $a°$ and $\cos a° = \frac{3}{5}$. What is $\cos(90 - a°)$?

Grid your answer.

20. The y-intercept of a line is $y = -3$. The line goes through the point (3, 1). What is the slope of the line?

Grid your answer.

Math – Calculator

Questions 1–30 are multiple choice. Questions 31–38 are gridded.

1. The table below shows the breakdown of soup orders at a restaurant. There were two kinds of soup (chicken and veggie) and two sizes (cup and bowl). If a person among those who ordered soup is chosen at random, what is the probability that this person ordered a cup of veggie soup?

	Chicken	Veggie	Total
Cup	7	8	15
Bowl	15	12	27
Total	22	20	42

A) $\frac{8}{15}$

B) $\frac{1}{6}$

C) $\frac{2}{5}$

D) $\frac{4}{21}$

2. Which of the following is equivalent to the expression: $(x + 2)^2 - (-2x^2 + 4)$

A) $3x^2 + 4x$

B) $3x^2 + 4x + 8$

C) $x^2 + 4x + 8$

D) $x^2 + 4x$

3. A researcher surveyed 350 people at a grocery store, offering them a sample of a well-known juice along with a new brand of juice. 85% of those who tasted the two juices preferred the new brand. Which of the following inferences is a logical conclusion?

A) 85% of shoppers will prefer the new brand of juice.

B) 15% of shoppers will prefer the new brand of juice.

C) The majority of shoppers will prefer the new brand of juice.

D) The majority of shoppers will prefer the well-known juice.

4. If $\frac{2}{3}a = -\frac{6}{7}$, what is the value of a?

A) $-\frac{18}{7}$

B) $-\frac{9}{7}$

C) $-\frac{4}{7}$

D) $-\frac{32}{21}$

5. If Nick can run 3 miles in 24 minutes, how many miles can he run in 3 hours?

A) 11.25 miles

B) 17.6 miles

C) 21.8 miles

D) 22.5 miles

169

6. It rained every day last week except Friday. If it rained twice as much on Monday as it did on Thursday, which of the following graphs could model the week's rainfall in inches?

A)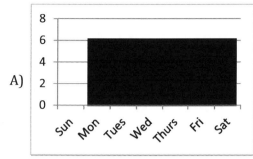

C)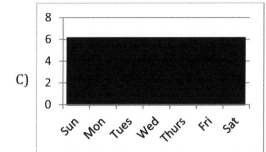

B)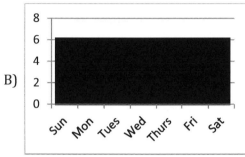

D)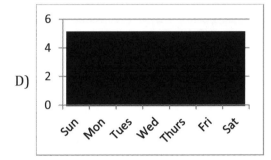

7. If 3 times the square of a positive number is 48, what is the result when twice the number is subtracted from 15?

- A) −1
- B) 4
- C) 7
- D) 11

8. A shipping container can hold up to 240 boxes or a maximum of 10,000 pounds. The boxes are all the same size, but some weigh 35 pounds and some weigh 50 pounds. If a is the number of 35-pound boxes and b is the number of 50-pound boxes, which of the following systems of inequalities represents this relationship?

- A) $a + b \leq 10,000$
  $35a + 50b \leq 240$
- B) $a + b \leq 240$
  $35a + 50b \leq 10,000$
- C) $\frac{a}{35} + \frac{b}{50} \leq 10,000$
  $a + b \leq 240$
- D) $a + b = 240$
  $35a + 50b = 10,000$

9. Based on the below equation, what is the value of $ax - b$?

$$6ax + 14 - 6b = 2$$

- A) −12
- B) −2
- C) 2
- D) 12

Questions 10 and 11 refer to the following information.

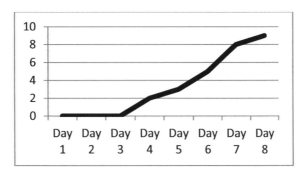

Beth plants a number of sunflower seeds and checks daily to see if any have sprouted. The graph above shows how many seedlings are growing each day when she checks.

10. Which day did the first seedling appear?

A) Day 1
B) Day 2
C) Day 3
D) Day 4

11. How many seeds sprouted on Day 8?

A) 0
B) 1
C) 4
D) 9

12. If $x^{-\frac{1}{2}} = m$, what is x?

A) m^2
B) $1 - m^2$
C) $\frac{1}{m^2}$
D) $\frac{1}{m}$

13. The equation below is used to solve for the distance, d (meters), that an object travels in a certain amount of time, t (seconds), with an initial velocity of v meters per second. Which of the following equations gives a in terms of d, v, and t?

$$d = vt + \frac{1}{2}at^2$$

A) $\frac{2d-2vt}{t}$.
B) $\frac{2dvt}{t^2}$
C) $\frac{2d}{t^2} - \frac{2v}{t}$
D) $\frac{2d}{t^2} - 2vt$

14. If the solution for the system of equations below is (x, y), what is the value of $x^2 - 3y$?

$$5x - 6y = 12$$
$$-2x + 3y = -5$$

  A) –3
  B) –1
  C) 3
  D) 5

Questions 15 and 16 refer to the following information.

The table below represents the test scores on a chemistry final, as well as the lab grades for the semester.

Final Exam	78	85	91	77	94	83	87
Lab Grade	84	86	98	90	97	85	90

15. What is the difference of the mean and median of the lab grades?

  A) 0
  B) 1.5
  C) 3
  D) 4.5

16. Which of the following is the most logical explanation for the difference between the lab grades and final exam grades?

  A) The lab grade included all lab scores for the semester while the final was a single exam.
  B) The final exam was more challenging than the labs.
  C) The maximum score on the final exam was 105 instead of 100.
  D) Half of the students in the class were graded by a different teacher.

17. Kasie is filling glasses with water. Each glass is cylindrical with a radius of 1.25 inches and a height of 6 inches. If she fills them to a height of 5 inches, how many glasses can she fill with 3 quarts of water (1 gallon = 231 cubic inches).

  A) 3
  B) 5
  C) 7
  D) 9

Questions 18–20 refer to the following information.

Elise, Max, and Rylie are each offering lawn care services. Their prices for each service are listed in the table below. Prices are per square foot.

	Elise	Max	Rylie
Mowing	$0.0025	$0.002	$0.003
Edging	$0.0015	$0.0015	$0.002
Weeding	$0.055	$0.065	$0.05

18. Ms. Lin wants to have her 7,500 square foot lawn mowed and edged, and also has a flower bed of x square feet to be weeded. Which of the following inequalities represents x if Elise's services are a better deal than Max's?

A) $x < 250$
B) $x < 375$
C) $x > 250$
D) $x > 375$

19. Rylie was asked to mow and edge a lawn as well as weeding a 1,000 square foot garden. If she will spend $12 on gas and other overhead costs, how large of a lawn does she need to be able to make a $75 profit?

A) $2{,}600 \text{ ft}^2$
B) $5{,}000 \text{ ft}^2$
C) $6{,}875 \text{ ft}^2$
D) $7{,}400 \text{ ft}^2$

20. If $4a + 3 \leq 1$, what is the greatest possible value of $6a - 2$?

A) -5
B) -3
C) $-\dfrac{1}{2}$
D) 1

21. The scatterplot below shows Julio's time (in hours) on the y-axis spent practicing his trumpet on the days (x-axis) leading up to a band concert. What is the difference in the amount of time he spent on the final day versus the amount predicted by the line of best fit?

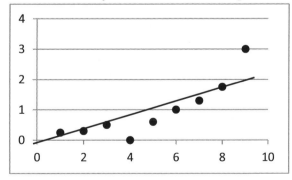

A) 0.5 hours
B) 1 hour
C) 2 hours
D) 3 hours

22. The sum of three numbers is 420. If one of the numbers, *m*, is 25% less than the sum of the other two numbers, what is *m*?

A) 144
B) 180
C) 220
D) 324

23. Angles *m* and *n* are acute angles (measured in degrees) in two different triangles. The sine of *m* is equal to the cosine of *n*. If $m = 3x + 12$ and $n = -x + 32$, what is *x*?

A) 2.5
B) 9
C) 23
D) 81

24. The equation of a circle is shown below. What is the circle's diameter?

$$x^2 + y^2 - 4x + 2y = 4$$

A) 2
B) 3
C) 5
D) 6

25. The intercepts of a linear function *f* are at $(k, 0)$ and $(0, m)$. If $k > m > 0$, which of the following describes the slope of *f*?

A) It is positive.
B) It is negative.
C) It is undefined.
D) It is zero.

26. Given the following graph, where *CD* is a perpendicular bisector of *AB*, point *A* is at (–3,1), and point *B* is at (4,0), what is the equation of line *CD*?

A) $y = 7x - 3$
B) $y = -\frac{1}{7}x - 3$
C) $y = \frac{10}{3}x - 3$
D) $y = 7x - \frac{20}{7}$

27. *XYZ* Industries made 20% greater profit this year than last, and expects to increase profit margins by another 20% next year. If their profit was $55,000 last year, what is their projected profit for next year?

    A) $66,000
    B) $73,920
    C) $77,000
    D) $79,200

28. The graph of the system of inequalities $y \leq \frac{2}{3}x - \frac{3}{2}$ and $y \geq -2x - \frac{5}{2}$ has solutions in which quadrants on the *xy*-plane below?

    A) Quadrants I and IV
    B) Quadrants II and III
    C) Quadrants I, II, and IV
    D) Quadrants I, III, and IV

29. If x is the mean of a and 12, y is the mean of $3a$ and 5, and z is the mean of $5a$ and -2, what is the mean of x, y, and z in terms of a?

    A) $9a + 15$
    B) $3a + 5$
    C) $\frac{3a+5}{2}$
    D) $\frac{9a+15}{2}$

30. In the equation below, m is a positive constant and the equation describes the graph of a parabola in the *xy*-plane. Which of the following equations is an equivalent form?

$$2y = 2x^2 - 8m$$

    A) $y = (x - 2m)^2$
    B) $y = (x + \frac{m}{2})(x - \frac{m}{2})$
    C) $y = (x + 2\sqrt{m})(x - 2\sqrt{m})$
    D) $y = (x + 2m)(x - 2m)$

31. If rate and time are inversely proportional, and rate is 24 m/s when time is 120 s, what is the rate, in m/s, when time is 200 s?

    Grid your answer.

32. On line *AD* below, *AC* = *BD*. What is the length of *BC*?

Grid your answer.

33. Meg is creating a scaled drawing of her house. If her bedroom wall is 12 feet long and is represented as 3 inches on the drawing, how many feet long is her living room if it is represented as 4.5 inches on the drawing?

Grid your answer.

34. Ben bought a bag of assorted rubber balls and measured each one. Each had a diameter between 1.2 and 1.5 inches. What is a possible volume, rounded to the nearest cubic inch, of one of the balls?

Grid your answer.

35. The graph of $y = 2x^2 + 3x$ intersects the graph of $y = -x$ at (0, 0) and (*a*, *b*). What is the value of *b*?

Grid your answer.

36. Jules and Zack were filling baskets with berries for their fruit stand. Jules' baskets of strawberries held 14, 13, 16, 15, 13, 14, 14, and 13 berries. Zack's baskets of raspberries held 26, 25, 23, 27, 28, 30, 29, and *x* berries. If the mean number of strawberries per basket is 13 less than the mean number of raspberries, what is the value of *x*?

Grid your answer.

37. What is the *y*-coordinate of the center of the circle defined in the equation below?

$$x^2 + y^2 - y - 6x = -\frac{21}{4}$$

Grid your answer.

38. A population of bacteria tripled every day. After 5 days, there were 2,430 bacteria. How many were there originally?

Grid your answer.

Answer Key and Explanations

Reading Test

1. Choice B is the best answer. The tone of this passage is light-hearted as it describes Mr. Glegg's extreme thriftiness, to the point of absurdity. Along with thriftiness, the passage points out Mr. Glegg's view of his marriage—he is so used to the "leathery" pastry that he considers it the standard for cooking, and has come to expect frequent quarrels as a normal part of life. While his actions may be characterized at times as selfish or morose (A), the tone is not dark. And while Mr. Glegg is described as thrifty (C), the author does not romanticize his efforts. Finally, while he could possibly be considered downtrodden as a result of the quarrels and questionable housekeeping, the author writes with satire rather than admiration, to provoke laughter rather than sympathy.

2. Choice C is the best answer. The word "near" is used to describe Mr. Glegg's character as a miserly or stingy man. It is not the literal meaning of being physically close (A) or being "near and dear" (B), or of being about to appear on the scene (D).

3. Choice A is the best answer. The situation of the widow, in which Mr. Glegg expresses "true feeling" but is unwilling to make a small donation to help, shows that frugality is the ruling virtue of his life. The story does not give much insight into the Gleggs' community (B), as it is merely a hypothetical situation. It shows that the Gleggs have enough money to help a destitute widow, but does not give a clear picture of their monetary worth (C). And while we may gain some insight into the value of money at a time when five pounds would settle a widow's small debt, it does not give us an accurate idea of monetary value in this time period (D).

4. Choice B is the best answer. While the author pokes fun at Mr. Glegg for his eccentricities, in paragraph 3 she describes men like him as "industrious" and "marked and exceptional." She points out his lack of generosity in paragraph 2, but in this paragraph, she notes the hard work that went into slowly accumulating wealth by diligent industry and self-denial. The mention of quickly making money (A) is referring to a different set of people. The author does not show disdain (in this paragraph) for the hoarding of hard-won fortunes (C). And though she mentions the variety of characters that fall into this category, she does not appear to be confused by this (D).

5. Choice D is the best answer. Paragraph 3 is referring to those who carefully save to build up a sufficient amount to live comfortably, by their various standards. It is not referring to independence in a political or legal sense (A), or to being free from dependence on relatives (B), though that would be a natural side effect. Nor does it refer to independently making choices for oneself (C).

6. Choice D is the best answer. The use of "pinched" illustrates the challenges and self-denial involved in saving money. This could possibly have caused physical suffering with some of the sacrifices (A), but that is not the intended meaning. Pinched does not refer to pain caused to others by saving (B), though this doubtless happened on occasion, as in the hypothetical widow's situation in paragraph 2. The term "pinched" has been used as slang for "stole" (C), but that is not the intent here.

7. Choice C is the best answer. The entire selection shows that Mr. Glegg is a man of habit, whether of saving money or his household routine. The passage points out that although Mrs. Glegg's cooking is less than excellent (leathery pastry and hard damson cheese), Mr. Glegg prefers it to any other because he has grown accustomed to it. The passage does not state whether Mrs. Glegg's housekeeping is economical (A), nor does it give any indication that his wife tailors her cooking and housekeeping to Mr. Glegg's tastes (B). Finally, there is no evidence from this passage that Mr. Glegg has been brainwashed into thinking that his wife's housekeeping is perfect (D).

8. Choice C is the best answer. As mentioned in the previous question, Mr. Glegg clung to what was familiar, however uncomfortable or unconventional. While Mr. Glegg is stingy, he is also described as "amiable" (paragraph 1), so it is unlikely that he enjoys being at odds with others (A). There is no evidence that he has a quick wit and enjoys verbal sparring (B). Although Mr. Glegg may have missed the quarreling, it is not because the quarrels prove his wife's love (D), but simply because it seemed right and normal.

9. Choice A is the best answer. From context, we can infer that the word "jejune" means dull or uninteresting. This best goes along with "barren of mystery" and describes the hypothetical situation if Mrs. Glegg were no longer quarrelsome and therefore stimulating. It would be incorrect to say that this could be mysterious (B) since this contradicts "barren of mystery." "Quarrelsome" (C) is also incorrect because the word is referring to an atmosphere devoid of quarreling. And while this could be considered peaceful (D), the connotation is negative, so "dull" is the best fit.

10. Choice B is the best answer. The anecdote in paragraph 2, in which Mr. Glegg not only tries to save his own money but is "quite zealous" in helping others live more cheaply, illustrates how passionate he is about frugality. Calling him a "lovable skinflint" (A) refers to his frugality but does not illustrate it. The selection from paragraph 3 (C) makes a general statement about miserliness but does not give a specific illustration of Mr. Glegg's frugality. His admiration for his wife's housekeeping (D) is not directly linked to frugality.

11. Choice C is the best answer. The passage discusses the development of a new network design that has the potential to change the AI industry. It doesn't focus on how AI has changed (A), though it predicts change with the new development. It does not encourage the reader to adopt this trend (B), as it is not currently available. And while it mentions the current limitations of AI (D), the point is that a solution may have been found for these limitations.

12. Choice B is the best answer. The first paragraph states that a traditional neural network requires "data with clear stages of observation." Most people do not have enough regularly spaced, uniform doctor visits to meet this need. Years of data are needed, but the network itself does not take years to compute (A). There is no mention of sensitive information needed (C) or the inability to handle the amount of information available (D).

13. Choice A is the best answer. A traditional neural network is "a poor tool for modeling continuous processes," according to the first paragraph. While the third paragraph gives an example of distinguishing between animals (B), this is not the main problem. The networks themselves do not take too long to accumulate data (C), though it can be years before sufficient data is available for modeling. And they do find patterns in data (D), though the process needs improvement.

14. Choice C is the best answer. Unlike a piano, which has defined notes in regular steps like the layers of a traditional neural network, a violin string offers a continuous increase in pitch. As a finger slides from one note to the next, it crosses an infinite number of slight variations in pitch. In the same way, the ODE net offers a continuous calculation of data rather than a series of steps, or layers. This may seem more complicated (A), but that is not the point of the illustration (rather, it is shown as a way to simplify a complicated process). A violinist can move from one note to another without changing strings (B), but the point is not about moving seamlessly between layers but creating a continuum that takes the place of layers. The ODE net does not have four layers (D), but replaces layers.

15. Choice D is the best answer. The author speaks of training a neural network by inputting labeled data, such as a picture of an animal along with the name of the animal (cat, dog, etc.). Because not all cats and dogs look alike, it is important to provide multiple examples so the network can figure out the patterns and create a formula to distinguish categories. The example given in the article is using images of animals (A), but a neural network can be used for much more than categorizing animals. The user does not give the formula to the network (B), but gives the network sufficient data to create its own formula. While the network does learn to sort data into categories (C), it is not limited to two, nor is the information necessarily increasing in complexity.

16. Choice A is the best answer. Paragraph 6 introduces the problems of the layer approach, and paragraph 7 states that calculus can solve this kind of problem. A violin (B) is used as an illustration of continuous modeling, but not as a solution. Animal pictures (C) are an example of a method of teaching neural networks. And computational nodes (D) are what work to find patterns and create the layers.

17. Choice D is the best answer. Paragraph 4 points out that using a single formula to classify data is too "broad." In other words, it is not specific or detailed enough to make accurate decisions. While "broad" can mean expansive (A), spacious (B), or open-minded (C) in different contexts, the emphasis here is that it is too general.

18. Choice C is the best answer. Duvenaud and his colleagues created the ODE net because the layers made it hard to use given data to model continuous processes. The number of layers in a neural net is not infinite (A); in fact, this is largely why they do not work smoothly. Paragraph 5 notes that each layer may identify a more complex feature (B) as it seeks to identify an animal, but does not say that the layers themselves become more complex as they go. The layers are not seen as more user-friendly than the ODE-net (D). Rather, the ODE-net eases the burden of creating multiple layers.

19. Choice B is the best answer. The answer to the previous question is C, "The layers make it challenging to create accurate models." The best evidence for this comes in Paragraph 2: "The discrete layers are what keep it from effectively modeling continuous processes." The sentence from Paragraph 1 (A) gives an example of why data collection is difficult, but does not specifically address the issue of layers. The sentence from Paragraph 5 (C) explains what the layers do, but not why they are a problem. The sentence from Paragraph 6 (D) explains that more layers are needed for better modeling, but still does not clearly state that the layers get in the way of accurate models.

20. Choice C is the best answer. The last paragraph makes two points: caution, because the ODE net is not ready for implementation and has several hurdles to clear first, and hope, because once it is ready it could "shake up" the AI field. Only answer choice C includes both of these points. Each of the other answer choices focuses on just one.

21. Choice B is the best answer. In the opening paragraph, Burke cautions the reader to wait to congratulate people on their freedom until he or she can see beyond the turmoil and emotions and judge whether this freedom is actually "a blessing." While he does call liberty a strong principle (A), he advises caution on admiring it. He also advises caution in congratulating those who have just found liberty (C). His reference to avoiding judgment was not in reference to different cultures and their preferred freedoms (D), but a general statement about understanding what newly-won freedom really was.

22. Choice D is the best answer. Burke uses the analogy of liquor to explain how people could not think rationally in the early excitement of liberty. He was not referring to literal liquor (A, B). While it did have the connotation of obscuring the truth, there is no reference to darkness (C).

23. Choice A is the best answer. Paine advocates the overthrow of the government rather than its reform, claiming that its despotic principles were "too deeply rooted to be removed" except by revolution. Answer choice B is similar, but Paine does not claim that the nation would not survive without change. Paine specifically states that the revolution is **not** against Louis XVI, so answer choice C is incorrect. Paine refers to the principles that are centuries old, but makes no reference to laws that may be inappropriate for the current generation of French people (D).

24. Choice B is the best answer. In paragraph 4 of Passage 2, Paine states that Burke does not "attend to the distinction between men and principles." In other words, he does not understand that revolting against a corrupt government is not synonymous with rejecting a king. Paine does not argue that liberty should be obtained at any cost (A). Rather, he comments that many other revolutions were inspired by hatred rather than good motives. Paine does refer to the king's regard for his people (C), but does not indicate that Burke is unaware of this. And while Paine does urge acting "with determined vigor" in the crisis, he again does not indicate that Burke is unaware.

25. Choice C is the best answer. Burke argues in the first paragraph of Passage 1 that the emotions of the revolution make it difficult to judge rationally. He does not make any mention of human rights (A, B). He mentions that the real movers are not always the ones who "appear the most stirring" (D), but does not imply that those who contemplated the revolution were not the movers.

26. Choice A is the best answer. The answer to the previous question is C. The best evidence to support Burke's idea of using emotions over rational thought is in paragraph 1, where he likens the heightened emotions associated with the revolution to drinking alcohol, making it difficult to think clearly. In answer choice B, Burke cautions people on rejoicing over liberty before they are sure it will be for the best. In answer choice C, Burke warns that liberty will not last without the structure of government. In answer choice D, Burke explains that liberty is power, when people act together. None of these statements address the idea of rationale and emotions.

27. Choice D is the best answer. Paine responded to Burke's criticism that liberty was too hastily celebrated by stating that it was the product of "rational contemplation." He argued that it was the government, not the king, that needed to be overthrown, so answer choice A is incorrect. Paine also did point out that removing the king was not the same as removing the governmental structure, but he did advocate the removal of that structure, so answer choice B is incorrect. He did discuss that people were fighting passionately for liberty, but did not say that this passion would preserve liberty, so answer choice C is wrong.

28. Choice C is the best answer. The answer to the previous question is that Paine asserts that the revolution was carefully considered before action. Answer choice C reflects this "rational contemplation." Paine's call to "teach governments humanity" (D) is not in reference to this. Answer choices A and B are in relation to the difference between the monarchy and the government, which refer to incorrect answer choices from the previous question.

29. Choice B is the best answer. Paine uses the word "excited" to describe how hatred has instigated revolutions in many countries. He is not referring to feelings of excitement or giddiness (A). Though he is discussing rage, it would not be correct to say that the revolutions themselves were enraged (C). "Invented" (D) does not give the correct connotation; revolutions were encouraged by hatred, but hatred did not invent them.

30. Choice B is the best answer. Paine rebuts Burke's work by pointing out what he believed to be a flaw in Burke's reasoning. This evidence is not new (C), nor merely looking at it from a different angle (A). Finally, Paine is not supporting Burke's premise (D).

31. Choice C is the best answer. Burke spends the entire passage warning against revolting without a clear idea of what victory would look like, and Paine also mentions the importance of careful forethought rather than being led by emotions. Neither indicates that liberty is the highest gift a person can be given (A), though Paine does consider it very important. Paine makes the point that the king may love his people while the laws are still corrupt (B), but Burke makes no mention of this. Paine also indicates that the French government was corrupt and action was necessary (D), but Burke does not concede that anything was necessary other than caution before action.

32. Choice C is the best answer. The passage highlights how one's genetic makeup can affect health, along with one's social background (hint: a glance at the article title often helps to deduce the main idea). It mentions the difficulties of underprivileged people (A), but that is not the main point. The article discusses race, but mentions that it's not a matter of "black or white," but the complex genetic makeup that matters. The passage does discuss health practices in India, but does not use this article to contrast Eastern and Western practices.

33. Choice D is the best answer. The author is referring to a person's genetic makeup that has been combined and passed down over generations. It is not referring to a legal inheritance (A) or simply one parent's genetics (B). It is referring to physical makeup rather than adapted health habits (C).

34. Choice C is the best answer. The author uses the example of the young boy whose doctors failed to diagnose sickle cell disease to show how one's genetic background can hold valuable clues regarding healthcare. The boy's mixed ancestry may have made it more challenging (A), but that was not the author's point. Sickle cell anemia may be more easily diagnosed with knowledge of where one's ancestors lived (B), but this is only the illustration, not the main point. The author decries the fact that doctors do not take genetic background into account, but does not indicate that they are unaware (D).

35. Choice A is the best answer. The passage implies that if doctors were aware of the genetic backgrounds of their patients, they would be better able to give treatment tailored to their specific needs. It does not state that the patients themselves could improve their health through knowledge of their ancestry (B). The passage mentions combining religious practices and biomedical interventions (C) to cope with stress, but does not claim that this can cure disease. Nor does the passage claim that greater knowledge of genetics could be used to eliminate diabetes (D), but rather to provide better treatment.

36. Choice B is the best answer. The answer to the previous question is that with better understanding of genetic backgrounds, doctors can provide better treatment. Paragraph 6 gives the best evidence for this: "Ancestry is critically important, especially when talking about precision medicine or treating individuals." The sentence from paragraph 3 (B) gives an example that the author uses to show the importance of genetics, but does not clearly state the idea. Paragraph 12 (C) is about diabetes and could also be linked to an incorrect answer choice from the previous question. Paragraph 13 (D) discusses the importance of cultural and spiritual heritage, not genetics, and could be used as evidence for one of the incorrect answer choices from the previous question.

37. Choice C is the best answer. The author uses the word "tapestry" in the final sentence as an illustration of how a person's health is affected by genetic makeup, social setting, and religious practices, all woven together into a single picture. She is not referring to a literal tapestry (A), nor is she calling health a blanket (B). While "tapestry" is a combination of health-related topics, it is not only the parts that lead to good health (D).

38. Choice B is the best answer. The most likely explanation is that the chart includes both Type 1 and Type 2, since it does not specify. While the author could have rounded the number, it is very unlikely that she would have rounded down from 69.2 to 60, rather than up to 70, so answer choice A is incorrect. There is no reason to believe that the chart includes data from countries outside India, so answer choice C is incorrect. There is always a possibility of misinformation, but it is unwise to presume this, with no other evidence, when finding a discrepancy, so answer choice D is incorrect.

39. Choice B is the best answer. The passage discusses diabetes in India, particularly noting how its effects are different based on gender and social standing. The increase or decrease in diabetes could be tied into the passage, but is not directly mentioned, so answer choice A is incorrect. Statistics about the surrounding countries would be useful only if the passage mentioned differences in genetics or culture in those countries, so answer choice C is incorrect. While the passage mentions sickle cell disease in paragraph 3, there is no mention of it in relation to India, so answer choice D is incorrect.

40. Choice A is the best answer. The chart shows that 69.2 million people in India have diabetes and 97.6 million have prediabetes. Since 97.6 million is greater than 69.2, answer choice A is supported. Answer choice B states that nearly half of India's population is either diabetic or prediabetic, but it is clear from the chart that these two categories take up much less than half of the doughnut chart, so this answer choice is incorrect. The number of those with prediabetes is greater than the number with diabetes, so answer choice C is incorrect because it states the opposite. And while the number with prediabetes is larger than the number with diabetes, it is not close to double the number, so answer choice D is incorrect.

41. Choice C is the best answer. Paragraphs 12 and 13 directly mention spiritual practices, while paragraph 14 alludes to the "full tapestry of human health," which could include spiritual practices. But the most appropriate place is paragraph 13, which discusses cultural and spiritual heritage and hints at their influence on physical health.

42. Choice A is the best answer. In the first paragraph, the author mentions that technology, such as light bulbs and the Internet, are encouraging people to sleep less. Paragraph 8 mentions that many millennials are taking stimulants to stay awake (B), but this is one demographic rather than a leading problem worldwide. Access to better mattresses and other sleep aids (C) should help people to sleep *more*, not less. In paragraph 7, the author mentions failure to enforce good bedtimes (D), but this again is a single generation and only one factor in that generation's sleep problems.

43. Choice B is the best answer. The author notes in paragraph 7 that members of Generation X "get the least amount of sleep." While Millennials (A) and Boomers (C) both tend to get less than is healthy, they are not as sleep-deprived. The statistic from 1910, mentioned in the first paragraph, shows that people in the early 20th century (D) slept much more than people today.

44. Choice D is the best answer. This sentence is discussing how technology has encouraged or moved forward our "culture of sleeplessness." Moving in circles (A) or lifting off the ground (B) are too literal of interpretations (the culture is not physically being moved). Stating that the push forward is uncomfortable (D) is a matter of conjecture.

45. Choice A is the best answer. The author states that sleep habits are related to generational attitudes and explains why each generation is losing sleep for different reasons. The passage does not specify times that different generations are going to bed (B). While the passage mentions that Gen Xers and Millennials are taking drugs because of their sleep problems (C), it does not indicate that later generations use more. And while paragraph 2 discusses the growing spending on sleep-related products (D), it does not indicate that later generations are spending more.

46. Choice B is the best answer. Paragraph 6 states that each generation had unique "generational attitudes" that shaped their sleep problems. The sentence on consumer spending (A) relates to one of the incorrect answers from the previous question. The sentences from paragraph 7 (C) and 8 (D) each refer to a specific generation rather than the general statement made in the previous question.

47. Choice D is the best answer. Paragraph 7 states that Generation X sleeps less than any others, including the younger Millennials, which contradicts the other article's claim. Paragraph 1 (A) points out that we live in "an increasingly 24/7 world," but this does not prove that each successive generation sleeps less. Paragraph 2 (B) notes the increasing spending on sleep-related products, but again this does not confirm the increasing lack of sleep. Paragraph 6 (C) discusses the Boomer generation, the "biggest workaholics of any generation." However, this does not directly address amount of sleep.

48. Choice B is the best answer. Paragraph 6 discusses how Boomers gave up traditional sleep patterns by working late and rising early. It was a deliberate choice, not a loss (A) or a slow distancing (C). While "eschewed" sometimes has the connotation of despising, the author does not suggest disdain for sleep (D), but simply prioritizing other things.

49. Choice C is the best answer. The author's overall tone is concerned rather than optimistic, as evidenced in multiple places such as the closing statement: "a good night's rest is more of a dream than a reality." The author does mention that some schools and businesses are helping to address the problem (A) and that more sleep products are being developed (B) but indicates that these can only do so much when people aren't spending enough time in bed. The author also mentions that spending on sleep-related products is rising (D), but does not indicate whether this has an effect on America's sleep problems.

50. Choice D is the best answer. Looking at the chart, we can see that sleep studies cost approximately $7 billion, sleeping pills cost approximately $3 billion, CPAP machines cost approximately $4 billion, and mattresses cost approximately $13 billion. Thus, sleep studies and mattresses are the top two items in terms of cost.

51. Choice C is the best answer. Paragraph 2 mentions that consumer spending on sleep-related products was $41 billion in 2015. If we add up the approximate amounts in the chart (approximately $7, $3, $4, and $13 billion), we can see that this is nowhere close to $41 billion. Paragraph 3 mentions the $13 billion mattress industry, which is accurately portrayed in the graph, but the question specifically refers to the information in paragraph 2, so the mattress data is irrelevant. There could be several reasons for the seeming discrepancy; for example, the chart could have chosen only four of many possible categories of sleep products.

52. Choice A is the best answer. The passage mentions tech devices, nap rooms, and prescription sleep aids. Pillows (B) are not mentioned. Nap rooms (C) are not sleep products purchased by consumers, but are provided by some businesses. Prescription sleep aids (D) are already represented in the chart, so we would not add them.

Writing and Language

1. Choice C is the best answer. This clause needs a present-tense verb for the sentence to be complete. Answer choice A is incorrect because it does not include a present-tense verb ("conserving" and "stimulating" are participles). Choices B and D are incorrect because they change the participle "conserving" to the present-tense verb "conserve(s)" without adjusting "stimulating," so the parts of speech do not match. Choice C correctly adds a verb (aids) and leaves "conserving" to match "stimulating."

2. Choice B is the best answer. The correct present perfect phrase is "has been." To use "being" (A), the verb needs to be "is" instead of "has" (although this would not fit logically with the sentence, referring to past research rather than an ongoing process). "Is been" (C) incorrectly combines present tense and present perfect. "Having been" (D) is a correct pairing but does not flow logically with this clause because of the "and" before the underlined portion.

3. Choice C is the best answer. Answer choice C is both straightforward and clear. Choice A places the clauses in a less clear order and adds unnecessary commas. Choice B also creates an awkward order and adds an incorrect colon, since the part of the sentence after the colon does not define the first or give a list. Choice D removes the unnecessary commas but adds an incorrect em-dash, since it does not set off a parenthetical statement or provide a necessary pause.

4. Choice B is the best answer. The phrase "such as" begins a nonrestrictive clause (a clause that can be removed from the sentence without altering the meaning). Nonrestrictive clauses must be preceded by commas. Using a semicolon (A) is incorrect. Changing "such" to "like" (C, D) is incorrect because this causes the sentence to read "like as," which is incorrect.

5. Choice B is the best answer. "No pesticides" refers to the manner in which crops are grown. It is not two separate actions, so "and" (A) is incorrect. Using "without no" (C) is a double negative, which is incorrect. Choice D could be correct without the word "even."

6. Choice A is the best answer. This sentence uses a form of "not only ... but also," substituting "additionally" for "also." To use "in addition" (B) is incorrect because it lacks the "to." "Even to" (C) is incorrect because it does not go with "not only." "In also to" (D) is incorrect because of the added "in."

7. Choice D is the best answer. Both the part of the sentence before the punctuation and after it are independent clauses (stand-alone sentences). They can either be separated with a period or joined by a semicolon. Joining them with a comma (A) creates a comma-splice sentence. Using a conjunction such as "and" would be grammatically correct with a comma, but "or" (B) does not make sense. Adding "then" (C) creates another independent clause, again needing a semicolon or period rather than a comma.

8. Choice D is the best answer. This paragraph is written in contrast to the previous one, showing the disadvantages rather than the advantages. So the introduction needs to reflect that. Choices A, B, and C each use a term that shows agreement rather than contrast.

9. Choice C is the best answer. Because the plants are not exposed to the open air, they are not pollinated by insects (unless introduced by the farmer). It is the farmer's responsibility to provide for these needs. He/she cannot eliminate (A) or remove (D) natural needs, and simply tracking them (B) is not sufficient.

10. Choice B is the best answer. This sentence gives an introduction to the subject of cost, which is discussed in sentences 2 and 3. So the best place for this sentence would be immediately preceding them. After sentence 2 or 3 (C, D) would be awkward positioning. Finally, its current position (A) is incorrect because it does not summarize the entire set of disadvantages, but only some of them.

11. Choice A is the best answer. The term is modifying the verb "grown" so it must be an adverb. Although "in a vertical manner" (B) is technically correct, it is unnecessarily verbose and therefore not the best answer. Answer choices C and D are adjectives rather than adverbs.

12. Choice C is the best answer. We can see from the other sentences in this paragraph that each is written in present perfect tense. To match these, we need to choose a term with "has" or "have." Choice A is past tense and Choices B and C are present tense, so they are incorrect.

13. Choice D is the best answer. As written (A) the sentence has a dangling modifier (because the subject of "tracing back millennia" should be "calendars," but the way the sentence is written the subject is, incorrectly, "archaeologists"). Choice B has the correct subject, but is written in passive voice. Additionally, it is written in past tense rather than present perfect, which does not fit with the rest of the paragraph. Choice C is also written in passive voice, and it does not end with a comma, which indicates that the archaeologists, not the calendars, are showing the ancient views of movement and time. Only choice D is straightforward and grammatically correct.

14. Choice B is the best answer. As written (A), the sentence is a comma-splice because each clause is a complete sentence and needs to be joined by a semicolon. Choices C and D are convoluted and potentially confusing. Only answer choice B is both grammatically correct and clear.

15. Choice C is the best answer. This paragraph discusses solar and lunisolar calendars. It is transitioning from the previous paragraph, which discussed the ancient lunar calendar found in Scotland, so the introduction should acknowledge the old subject while introducing the new one. Answer choice A refers to the previous paragraph, but the detail used (Scotland) is not relevant to the subject of solar calendars. Answer choice B introduces the idea of solar calendars but does not transition from the previous paragraph. Answer choice D refers to the previous paragraph but the wording is awkward and confusing. Choice C refers back to the previous paragraph while setting up the contrast for the current paragraph.

16. Choice A is the best answer. The word "lunisolar" indicates a combination of lunar and solar, and by reading the following sentence we can confirm this combination. Answer choice B is incorrect because it indicates only one, choice C is incorrect because it indicates zero, and choice D is incorrect because it leaves the possibility of only one.

17. Choice B is the best answer. The parenthetical phrase is a nonrestrictive clause. In other words, the sentence is complete and makes sense without it. "Which" is the proper word to use with nonrestrictive clauses. A restrictive clause, on the other hand, would use "that" (A). Neither "how" (C) nor "what" (D) make grammatical sense in this context.

18. Choice D is the best answer. The sentence is referring to the lunisolar calendar, which is based on both solar and lunar measurements. Using "however" (A, B) or "although" (C) provides contradiction rather than agreement.

19. Choice C is the best answer. This sentence discusses the way Roman politicians adjusted the calendar to reflect political goals. The best term for this is "skewed." To say that it was stabilized (A) would reflect the opposite. The Romans did not rename (B) or tear (D) the calendar.

20. Choice D is the best answer. This story about the Egyptian astronomer adds an interesting fact, but does not contribute meaningful information, providing supporting details to the main points. It is true that this is the best position in the paragraph, following up on the political problem (A), but this does not warrant keeping it in the paragraph. This sentence is not a response to the priests' mistake of too many leap days, so the end of the paragraph would not be the best position (B). The fact that solar calendars have been previously discussed is not a reason to remove it (C), as the solar calendar is one of the main ideas and is mentioned multiple times.

21. Choice D is the best answer. Because this clause is preceded by a comma rather than a semicolon, it cannot be an independent clause. So, answer choices B and C are incorrect since they create independent clauses (stand-alone sentences) and therefore lead to comma-splice sentences. Answer A is incorrect because it is missing verbiage to make the sentence grammatically correct: it either needs a subject or a conjunction. The participle form provides a grammatically correct opening to the clause.

22. Choice A is the best answer. The conclusion should reflect back on the selection as a whole, providing summation and closure. As written (A), the conclusion gives closure by stating that the Gregorian calendar is widely accepted throughout the world. It also refers back to the opening paragraph, recalling mankind's desire to track the seasons. Answer choice B does a good job of summing this paragraph, but does not reflect on the passage as a whole. Answer choice C reflects back only on the turmoil of finding an accurate calendar, which misses the main point, and gives a simplistic solution. Answer choice D makes the unfounded claim that the Gregorian calendar is the most accurate and that all people agree on the date.

23. Choice C is the best answer. The simplest, most straightforward choice is the participle "connecting." Answer choice A is incorrect because it uses a noun. Answer choices B and D are incorrect because they are convoluted and unclear.

24. Choice B is the best answer. The first clause in this sentence sets up a point that will be contrasted later in the sentence, so the proper term is "while." "Even if" (A) is incorrect because it changes the first part of the sentence to hypothetical rather than fact, which does not make sense in this sentence. "However" (C) and "consequently" (D) are both grammatically incorrect because they are not followed by commas, but they also do not make sense because both refer back to the previous paragraph rather than setting up a contrast for later.

25. Choice B is the best answer. A helping verb is necessary in this sentence since it utilizes passive voice (rather than stating a direct subject who conducts the meetings). Since answer choices A, C, and D do not include a form of "to be," they are incorrect.

26. Choice D is the best answer. The point of the sentence is that because employees do not need to travel as often, they spend more time working from the corporate office. This is best communicated by answer choice D. Answer choice A is missing a verb. Answer choice C provides a verb but the construction is awkward and confusing. Answer choice B uses an incorrect verb form ("working" instead of "work") to match the "to" that precedes the underlined portion.

27. Choice D is the best answer. The part of the sentence after the underlined portion is a present participle clause, adding details to the previous clause. Adding an adverb or conjunctive adverb such as "although" (A), "but" (B), or "even" (C) makes the sentence grammatically incorrect as well as potentially creating confusion.

28. Choice C is the best answer. This sentence states how companies can save money by lessening their overhead costs. Answer choice A is incorrect because "overhead" is singular and "fewer" refers to multiple items. Answer choice B is incorrect because of the improper use of "lesser" (which should be used in comparison of two items). Choice D is incorrect because "smaller" is used to compare physical size rather than cost.

29. Choice C is the best answer. As written (A), this is a very long sentence, which makes comprehension more difficult. Additionally, the clause on improving employee retention, though relevant to the paragraph, does not belong in a sentence about lowering overhead because it is not a direct overhead cost. So we can rule out answer choices A and B, which include this clause. Answer choice D divides the list of cost between two sentences, which leaves the conclusion slightly ambiguous (Is it a total savings of $11,000, including office space cost, or does the $11,000 refer only to the expenses listed in this sentence?). Answer choice C provides the most clarity, listing the ways of saving in one sentence and providing the results in the next.

30. Choice B is the best answer. This paragraph is discussing the drawbacks of telecommuting, so we can expect that this sentence has a negative point. "A challenge" fits this expectation. Thus "an advantage" (A) and "humorous" (D) are incorrect because they suggest the opposite. These meetings may be boring at times (C), but that is would be a trivial drawback, not serious enough for this paragraph.

31. Choice C is the best answer. This paragraph lists four drawbacks to telecommuting: technological glitches, security, accountability, and isolation. To interpose an example of one of these drawbacks breaks the flow of thought, making the list more difficult to distinguish. It also adds emphasis, creating the impression that accountability is the most serious of the disadvantages (which the rest of the passage gives no evidence to support).

32. Choice C is the best answer. This term is plural, not possessive. Answer choices A and B are incorrect because they are possessive, and answer choice D is incorrect because it is singular.

33. Choice D is the best answer. We can see from the graph that the numbers of both telecommuters and non-telecommuters increased from 2005 to 2017, so answer choice A is incorrect. The number of telecommuters more than doubled, from 1.8 million to 3.9 million, while the number of non-telecommuters only increased by 9 million, a less than 10% increase. So we can rule out a proportional increase (B) and that the percentage of non-telecommuters is increasing faster than the percentage of telecommuters (C).

34. Choice D is the best answer. "Has" is part of the main verb of the sentence ("has seen"). As such it is closely linked to the main subject, "anyone." There is no punctuation between subject and verb except in cases such as a clause that is set off with commas to come between subject and verb. Since answer choices A, B, and C all separate subject and verb with punctuation, they are incorrect.

35. Choice C is the best answer. The paintings of fruit that have been discovered give archaeologists clues as to the ancient Egyptians' beliefs. The fruit does not elicit (A) belief, or cause either the archaeologists or ancient Egyptians to believe. Neither does the fruit actually mention (B) or harbor (D) belief. It is simply a symbol signifying, or pointing out, what the Egyptians believed.

36. Choice A is the best answer. When comparing different items, the "from ... to" construction, with no commas, is correct. Answer choices B and C are incorrect because of the words "from" and "among," which cannot be used in this way, although a word such as "including" would make them correct. However, "including" cannot be used in place of the "from" in the "from ... to" construction (D).

37. Choice B is the best answer. The clause beginning with the underlined term is adding another item to the list begun earlier in the sentence, although a contrasting item. It is not explaining part of the previous clause, as "even" (A) or "including" (C) would indicate. It simply needs a conjunction such as "and" to join the clauses. "As well as" is the best term for this. "Also" (D) has a similar meaning, but is grammatically incorrect without a conjunction ("and also" would be correct).

38. Choice A is the best answer. This sentence describes how fruit ages and withers, just as human life also ages and withers. "Transiency" refers to something that only lasts a short time, which fits with the intent of the sentence. "Joy" (B) does not fit with withering and decaying. "Longevity" (C) is the opposite of transiency, suggesting long life. "Sorrow" (D) is not an exact fit because it conveys an emotion that might go along with aging and death, but does not give the full connotation.

39. Choice D is the best answer. As written (A), the sentence beginning with "along" is a fragment, lacking a subject and verb. Answer choice B corrects this but is ambiguous, as it is unclear what "this" refers to. Answer choice C creates a comma splice by joining two complete sentences with a comma. Answer choice D correctly connects the dependent clause to the main sentence with a comma.

40. Choice C is the best answer. These answer choices all give the right meaning, but only one is grammatically correct. Answer choice A is incorrect because one reflects **on** things, not **from** them. Answer choice B is incorrect because one refers back **to** things, not **on** them. Answer choice D is incorrect because one recalls things, but does not recall **from** them.

41. Choice B is the best answer. This is referring to something seen with the eyes, so "sight" is the correct spelling. "Site" (A) refers to a physical or virtual location, such as a jobsite or website, and "cite" (C) is a verb used in referring to a source. The sentence refers to paintings that are found **in** homes, not **to** them, so choice D is incorrect.

42. Choice C is the best answer. For clarity and understanding, it is often best to begin with the subject, followed by the verb and direct object. Answer choices A and D separate the phrase "known for" by the entire sentence. Answer choice B breaks up the sentence into short, choppy chunks in an odd order. Only answer choice C is straightforward and clear.

43. Choice A is the best answer. The underlined portion is defining "one of humanity's most basic needs" from earlier in the sentence. While answer choices C and D fit grammatically, they are less clear and concise than choice A. Answer choice B does not fit grammatically since it is a verb rather than a noun.

44. Choice B is the best answer. This sentence provides a sense of unity, which is useful in a closing paragraph, so answer choice D is incorrect. It also sets up for the final statement on humanity's nature, so the best place for it is before sentence 2. It does not make the best opening sentence for the paragraph, because it does not refer to the previous paragraphs, as sentence 1 does, so answer choice A is incorrect. It is also not a good closing sentence because it does not make a major point or summarize the points of the passage, so answer choice C is incorrect.

Math – No Calculator

1. Choice B is correct. We first solve for x in the first equation. We add 4 to each side to obtain $3x = 3$, and then divide each side by 3 to obtain $x = 1$ (be careful not to mistakenly select answer choice D rather than finishing the problem). Then we can plug this value of x into the second equation: $12(1) + 3 = 15$.

2. Choice A is correct. We first need to solve for the constant by using in the ordered pair $(-2, 0)$:

$$0 = -\frac{1}{2}(-2) + b$$

We simplify to $0 = 1 + b$ and then solve for b by subtracting 1 from each side: $-1 = b$. Now we can complete our equation:

$$f(x) = -\frac{1}{2}x - 1$$

Finally, we plug in 3 for x and solve:

$$f(3) = -\frac{1}{2}(3) - 1 = -\frac{3}{2} - \frac{2}{2} = -\frac{5}{2}$$

Answer choice B is incorrect because it is the value of b rather than the function required. Choice C is incorrect because it uses 1 for b rather than -1. Choice D is incorrect because it leaves off the negative value when multiplying by x.

3. Choice C is correct. We can solve the system of equations by using substitution. We can plug in $3y$ for x in the top equation:

$$4(3y) - y = 11$$

This simplifies to $11y = 11$, and dividing each side by 11 yields $y = 1$. Then we can solve for x with the bottom equation:

$$x = 3(1) = 3$$

Finally, we can calculate $x - y = 3 - 1 = 2$. Choice B is incorrect because it is the value of y. Choice D is incorrect because it is the value of x.

4. Choice B is correct. We follow PEMDAS (parentheses, exponents, multiplication/division, addition/subtraction) for the order of operations. Nothing inside the parentheses can be further simplified, so we begin by squaring $2x - 3$. We use FOIL to obtain:

$$(2x - 3)^2 = 4x^2 - 6x - 6x + 9 = 4x^2 - 12x + 9$$

We then multiply this by 2 to obtain $8x^2 - 24x + 18$. Finally, we subtract $3x + 5$:

$$8x^2 - 24x + 18 - 3x + 5$$

Combining like terms yields $8x^2 - 27x + 13$. Choice A is incorrect because it adds the $3x$ instead of subtracting. Choice C is incorrect because it adds the $3x$ instead of subtracting and adds the 5 instead of subtracting it. Choice D is incorrect because it adds the 5 instead of subtracting it.

5. Choice C is correct. If Jan has 6 pairs of socks for each pair of shoes, we can write that socks = 6(shoes). We can then substitute 12 for the shoes and s for the socks: $s = 6(12)$. We look through the answer choices to see which matches this. Answer choice A can be rewritten as $s = \frac{6}{12}$. Answer choice B can be rewritten as $s = \frac{12}{6}$. Answer choice C can be rewritten as $s = 6(12)$. Answer choice D can be rewritten as $s = 12 - 6$. So only answer choice C matches.

6. Choice C is correct. In a 45-45-90 triangle, the legs can be found by dividing the hypotenuse by $\sqrt{2}$, so one leg is $\frac{4}{\sqrt{2}}$. We simplify $\frac{4}{\sqrt{2}}$ by multiplying by $\frac{\sqrt{2}}{\sqrt{2}}$. This yields:

$$\frac{4\sqrt{2}}{\sqrt{2}\sqrt{2}} = \frac{4\sqrt{2}}{2} = 2\sqrt{2}$$

Therefore, the three sides of the triangle are $2\sqrt{2}$, $2\sqrt{2}$, and 4. We add these sides together to obtain the perimeter: $4 + 4\sqrt{2}$. Answer choice A is incorrect because it is the area rather than the perimeter. Answer choice B is incorrect because it is the area without the last step of dividing by 2. Answer choice D is incorrect because it is only two of the three sides.

7. Choice D is correct. We look for a value at which $f(x) = 0$ to determine a factor, because the graph of the equation crosses the y-axis at this point. The table shows that $f(x) = 0$ when $x = 2$, so the point is $(2, 0)$. This means that if we were to factor the original equation, one of the factors would be $(x - 2)$, as $y = x - 2$ goes through the point $(2, 0)$. Answer choices A, B, and C are incorrect because none of them give a result of 0 when $x = 2$.

8. Choice A is correct. The solution(s) to a system of equations is the point or points at which the graphs of the two equations cross. If a system has no solution, this means that the graphs never cross. In other words, the two graphs are parallel. In the system here, we know the lines will be parallel if the slopes are identical. We can look at the first equation to find the slope by moving the x-value to the right and solving for y:

$$y = -\frac{1}{3}x - \frac{7}{3}$$

Thus, the slope of the second equation needs to also be $-\frac{1}{3}$. We again move the x-value to the right and solve for y:

$$y = \frac{-a}{-2}x + \frac{6}{-2}$$

Therefore, the slope here is $\frac{a}{2}$. We can set the slopes equal to each other to solve for a:

$$\frac{a}{2} = -\frac{1}{3}$$

Then we cross-multiply:

$$3a = -2$$

Finally, we divide both sides by 3 to find that $a = -\frac{2}{3}$. Answer choice A is incorrect because it is the value of the slope.

9. Choice B is correct. To find the missing point, we must use what we know about the slopes of the two lines. We are told that the two lines are perpendicular, so we know that their slopes must be negative inverses:

$$m_h = -\frac{1}{m_k}$$

First, find the value of the two slopes in terms of a:

$$m_h = \frac{a - 0}{3 - (-1)} = \frac{a}{4}$$

$$m_k = \frac{a - 0}{3 - 4} = \frac{a}{-1} = -a$$

Next, set these two values up as negative inverses:

$$m_h = -\frac{1}{m_k} = \frac{a}{4} = -\frac{1}{-a}$$

$$\frac{a}{4} = \frac{1}{a}$$

Finally, cross-multiply and solve for a:

$$a^2 = 4$$

$$a = 2$$

10. Choice D is correct. With the point given, we can solve for m in the equation:

$$(-2)^2 + m(-2) - 3 = 4$$

We simplify this to $4 - 2m - 3 = 4$. This can be further simplified to $-2m = 3$, or $m = -\frac{3}{2}$ (be careful not to stop here and mistakenly select answer choice A). So, our equation is:

$$f(x) = x^2 - \frac{3}{2}x - 3$$

We can plug in 6 for x to yield $6^2 - \frac{3}{2}(6) - 3 = 36 - 9 - 3 = 24$.

11. Choice C is correct. We need to find the point at which i is equal to p, so we set the two equations equal to each other: $5.5x = 15{,}200 + 0.75x$. We subtract $0.75x$ from each side to yield $4.75x = 15{,}200$. Dividing each side by 4.75 yields $x = 3{,}200$. Answer choice A is incorrect because it is obtained by adding $0.75x$ to each side of the equation rather than subtracting. Answer choice D is incorrect because it is the value of i or p rather than x.

Mometrix

12. Choice C is correct. The equation can be translated:

$$\text{height} = (\text{original height when planted}) + 0.75(\text{number of years since planted})$$

In other words, it grows 0.75 feet every year. The question asks for the number of inches, so we multiply 0.75 by 12 to obtain 9 inches per year. Answer choice A is incorrect because it is the number of feet rather than inches.

13. Choice B is correct. We first need to simplify $\frac{4^x}{2^y}$. Since 4 is equal to 2^2, we can write it as

$$\frac{4^x}{2^y} = \frac{(2^2)^x}{2^y} = \frac{2^{2x}}{2^y}$$

Now both numerator and denominator have a base of 2, so we can simplify to 2^{2x-y}. We know from the first equation that $2x - y = 4$, so $2^{2x-y} = 2^4$, or 16. Choice A is incorrect because it is 2^3 and choice D is incorrect because it is 2^5.

14. Choice A is correct. We can expand the left side of the equation:

$$2mnx^2 + 10mx - 4nx - 20$$

Since this is equal to $8x^2 + px - 20$, we know that $2mn = 8$, or $mn = 4$. If $m + n = 5$, we can rewrite this as $m = 5 - n$. We can substitute this into $mn = 4$:

$$(5 - n)n = 4$$

$$5n - n^2 = 4$$

Rearrange terms and factor:

$$n^2 - 5n + 4 = 0$$

$$(n - 4)(n - 1) = 0$$

We can set each factored term equal to 0: $n - 4 = 0$ and $n - 1 = 0$. These simplify to $n = 4$ and $n = 1$. So, either $m = 4$ and $n = 1$, or $m = 1$ and $n = 4$ (be careful not to stop here and select answer choice B). We can plug in these values to find the possible values of p. If $m = 4$ and $n = 1$:

$$2(4)(1)x^2 + 10(4)x - 4(1)x - 20 = 8x^2 + 36x - 20$$

If $m = 1$ and $n = 4$:

$$2(1)(4)x^2 + 10(1)x - 4(4)x - 20 = 8x^2 - 6x - 20$$

Thus, p can be either 36 or –6.

15. Choice C is correct. We need to simplify the equation so we can factor it. First, we subtract 2 from each side: $3x^2 - 3x - 36 = 0$. Then we can divide each term by 3: $x^2 - x - 12 = 0$. Finally, we can factor: $(x + 3)(x - 4) = 0$. Setting each factored term equal to 0 yields $x + 3 = 0$ and $x - 4 = 0$, or $x = -3$ and $x = 4$. The sum of –3 and 4 is 1. Answer choices A and D are incorrect because they are possible values of x rather than the sum.

16. The correct answer is 4. Since the total is an even number of hundreds (16) and the $100 prize is the only prize that is an odd number of hundreds, we can conclude that there must be an even number of $100 prizes awarded. Since we are looking for the greatest number, we should begin at the top and check each number to see if it is possible.

If there are six $100 prizes awarded, this leaves only one other prize to make up the difference:

$$\$1600 - 6(\$100) = \$1000$$

Since there is not a $1000 prize, there cannot be six $100 prizes.

If there are four $100 prizes awarded, this leaves three other prizes to make up the difference:

$$\$1600 - 4(\$100) = \$1200$$

Note that $1200 divided by 3 is $400, so a combination of four $100 prizes and three $400 prizes satisfies all the parameters.

17. The correct answer is 4. We solve for x in the second equation by first adding 7 to each side: $x^2 = 16$. We then solve by taking the square root of each side to yield $x = \pm 4$. Since $x > 0$, this means that $x = 4$.

18. The correct answer is 6. If the two triangles are similar, corresponding sides are also similar. We can set up a ratio: $\frac{AB}{4} = \frac{9}{6}$. We then cross-multiply: $6AB = 9(4)$, or $6AB = 36$. We divide both sides by 6 to find that $AB = 6$.

19. The correct answer is $\frac{4}{5}$ or 0.8. The cosine of an angle can be calculated as the adjacent side (3) divided by the opposite side (5). If angle M measures $a°$, then angle N measures $(90 - a)°$, so we are looking for the cosine of angle N. We begin by solving for the remaining side of the triangle. If the hypotenuse of a right triangle is 5 and one leg is 3, the other leg can be found with the Pythagorean theorem:

$$3^2 + NP^2 = 5^2$$
$$9 + NP^2 = 25$$

We subtract 9 from each side to yield $NP^2 = 16$. Taking the root of each side yields $NP = 4$. So, we can find the cosine of angle N by taking the adjacent side (4) and dividing by the hypotenuse (5). So, the answer is $\frac{4}{5}$ or 0.8.

20. The correct answer is $\frac{4}{3}$. We can find the slope of a line from two points. If the y-intercept is $y = -3$, the line goes through the point (0, –3). Then we calculate the slope by dividing the difference in the y-values by the difference in the x-values: $\frac{1-(-3)}{3-0}$. This simplifies to $\frac{4}{3}$.

Math – Calculator

1. Choice D is correct. We can see from the table that 8 people ordered a cup of veggie soup, and that a total of 42 orders were placed. So, the probability is 8 out of 42, or $\frac{8}{42}$. We can divide both numerator and denominator by 2 to reduce the fraction to $\frac{4}{21}$. Choice A is the probability of choosing veggie soup given that a cup was selected (not the overall probability). Choice B is the probability of choosing a cup of chicken soup ($\frac{7}{42}$ reduces to $\frac{1}{6}$). Choice C is the probability of choosing a cup, given that veggie soup was selected ($\frac{8}{20}$ reduces to $\frac{2}{5}$).

2. Choice A is correct. We simplify the expression by first squaring the first parenthetical term:

$$(x + 2)(x + 2) = x^2 + 4x + 4$$

We then subtract the second parenthetical term:

$$x^2 + 4x + 4 + 2x^2 - 4$$

Combining like terms yields $3x^2 + 4x$. Choice B is incorrect because it is obtained by adding 4 instead of subtracting it. Choice C is incorrect because it is obtained by mistakenly subtracting $2x^2$ instead of adding it and by adding $4x$ instead of subtracting. Choice D is incorrect because it is obtained by mistakenly subtracting $2x^2$ instead of adding.

3. Choice C is correct. If 85% of the sample group prefer the new brand of juice, we can infer that the majority of shoppers will likely prefer it. We cannot say that 85% of all shoppers will prefer it (A), because that would require testing all shoppers, but we can make a generalization that most shoppers seem to prefer the new brand. Choice B is incorrect because 15% is the number of the surveyed shoppers who did NOT prefer the new brand. Choice D is incorrect because it implies the opposite of the correct answer.

4. Choice B is correct. We solve for a by dividing each side by $\frac{2}{3}$. We do this by multiplying each side by $\frac{3}{2}$:

$$a = -\frac{6}{7} \times \frac{3}{2} = -\frac{18}{14}$$

We divide numerator and denominator by 2 to find that $a = -\frac{9}{7}$. Choice A is incorrect because only the denominator is reduced. Choice C is incorrect because it involves multiplying $\frac{2}{3}$ instead of dividing. Choice D is incorrect because it involves subtracting $\frac{2}{3}$ from each side instead of dividing.

5. Choice D is correct. If Nick runs 3 miles in 24 minutes, his rate is $\frac{24}{3} = 8$ minutes per mile. Now we need to find how many miles he can run in 3 hours, or $3(60) = 180$ minutes. We can set up a ratio:

$$\frac{8 \text{ min}}{1 \text{ mi}} = \frac{180 \text{ min}}{x \text{ mi}}$$

Now we cross-multiply: $8x = 180(1)$. Dividing each side by 8 yields $x = 22.5$ miles.

6. Choice C is correct. We are looking for a graph with two key pieces of information: rainfall every day except Friday, and an amount of rain on Monday double the rain on Thursday. Answer choice A is incorrect because it shows no rain on Sunday. Answer choice B is incorrect because it shows rain on Friday. Answer choice D is incorrect because the amount of rain on Monday is equal to the amount of rain on Thursday. Only answer choice C is correct because it shows no rain on Friday, 6 inches on Monday, and 3 inches on Thursday.

7. Choice C is correct. We write the first part of the sentence as an equation: $3x^2 = 48$. We then divide each side by 3 to yield $x^2 = 16$. We take the root of each side to find that $x = \pm 4$. Since we are told that it is a positive number, we know the answer is 4. Finally, we multiply the number by 2 and subtract from 15: $15 - 2(4) = 7$. Choice A is incorrect because it is obtained by subtracting 15 from 8 rather than vice versa. Choice B is incorrect because it is the value of x, not the final answer. Choice D is incorrect because it is obtained by subtracting x from 15 without first doubling x.

8. Choice B is correct. The number of boxes adds up to 240 or less. We can write this as $a + b \leq 240$. Also, the total weight adds up to 10,000 pounds or less. Since the a boxes weigh 35 pounds each and the b boxes weigh 50 pounds each, we can write this as $35a + 50b \leq 10,000$. Choice A is incorrect because it lists the number of boxes as less than or equal to 10,000 and the total weight as less than or equal to 240. Choice C is incorrect because it sets up a ratio, which would make a and b much too large. Choice D is incorrect because it sets the values equal to the maximum amounts rather than recognizing that the values are "up to" those amounts.

9. Choice B is correct. To solve, we first isolate the terms with ax and b in them. We subtract 14 from both sides to obtain $6ax - 6b = -12$. Then we divide each term by 6 to obtain $ax - b = -2$. Choice A is incorrect because it leaves off the final step of dividing by 6. Choice C is incorrect because it leaves off the negative sign (it would be equal to $b - ax$). Choice D is incorrect because it leaves off the negative sign and the final step of dividing by 6.

10. Choice D is correct. For Days 1, 2, and 3 (choices A, B, and C) on the chart, the number of seedlings is 0. Day 4 is the first time we see the line move away from 0, showing that 2 seedlings sprouted that day.

11. Choice B is correct. The graph shows the number of seedlings that are growing at any given time. On Day 8, 9 seedlings were growing (though this is answer choice D, be careful not to stop here). On Day 7, 8 seedlings were growing, so 1 seed sprouted on Day 8.

12. Choice C is correct. To solve, we raise each side to the –2 power. This yields $(x^{-\frac{1}{2}})^{-2} = m^{-2}$. We can simplify to $x = \frac{1}{m^2}$. Answer choice A is incorrect because it raises m to the power of 2, not – 2. Answer choice B is incorrect because it adds in a constant (1) and does not raise m to the power of –2. Answer choice D is incorrect because it raises m to the power of –1, not –2.

13. Choice C is correct. We solve for a by rearranging the equation to isolate a. We subtract vt from both sides:

$$d - vt = \frac{1}{2}at^2$$

We then multiply each side by $\frac{2}{t^2}$:

$$a = \frac{2d - 2vt}{t^2}$$

Finally, we break it into two fractions and simplify:

$$\frac{2d}{t^2} - \frac{2v}{t}$$

Choice A is incorrect because it is missing one t in the denominator. Choice B is incorrect because it multiples the d and vt terms instead of subtracting them. Choice D is incorrect because it leaves off the denominator of t^2 in the second term.

14. Choice D is correct. We solve for x and y by using elimination. We can multiply the second equation by 2 to eliminate the y-terms:

$$\begin{aligned} 5x - 6y &= 12 \\ -4x + 6y &= -10 \\ \hline x &= 2 \end{aligned}$$

If $x = 2$, we can solve for y by plugging the x-value back into one of the equations. Using the second equation, this yields:

$$-2(2) + 3y = -5$$

We simplify and add 4 to each side: $3y = -1$. Dividing each side by 3 yields: $y = -\frac{1}{3}$. So, the solution is $(2, -\frac{1}{3})$. Now we can use these values to find $x^2 - 3y$: $2^2 - 3\left(-\frac{1}{3}\right) = 4 + 1 = 5$. Choice C is incorrect because it involves adding the negative term instead of subtracting it.

15. Choice A is correct. We first find the mean, or average, of the lab grades by adding them and dividing by the number of grades:

$$\frac{84 + 86 + 98 + 90 + 97 + 85 + 90}{7} = 90$$

Then we find the median by arranging the grades in increasing order and finding the middle value: 84, 85, 86, 90, 90, 97, 98. The middle number is 90. So the difference of the mean and median is $90 - 90 = 0$.

16. Choice B is correct. The most likely explanation is that the final exam was more difficult than the labs, leading to lower grades. While the lab grades may have been acquired over the course of the year, it does not necessarily follow that all students would score lower on the final for that reason (A). Having 105 points available on the final should lead to higher scores than on the labs, all else being equal (C). Having two groups of students graded by different teachers (D) would explain a difference between the two groups but not a difference between the lab and the final.

17. Choice C is correct. We first need to find the volume of water that Kasie is putting in each glass. The volume of a cylinder is $V = \pi r^2 h$. Since we know the radius is 1.25 and the height is 5 (ignore the actual height of the glass since it is not filled to the brim), we can write: $V = \pi(1.25)^2(5)$. We multiply to find that the volume is approximately 24.53 cubic inches. Now we need to find the number of cubic inches in 3 quarts:

$$\left(\frac{3\text{ qt}}{1}\right)\left(\frac{1\text{ gal}}{4\text{ qt}}\right)\left(\frac{231\text{ in}^3}{1\text{ gal}}\right) = 173.25\text{ in}^3$$

Finally, we divide 173.25 by 24.53 to find that Kasie could fill 7.06 glasses. In other words, she could completely fill 7 glasses. Choice B is incorrect because it is obtained by filling the glasses to the full 6 inches instead of 5. Choice D is incorrect because it is obtained by using a full gallon instead of 3 quarts.

18. Choice D is correct. We can calculate the cost of each person's mowing and edging. Elise's cost is:

$$0.0025(7500) + 0.0015(7500) = 18.75 + 11.25 = \$30$$

Max's cost is:

$$0.002(7500) + 0.0015(7500) = 15 + 11.25 = \$26.25$$

So, we can set up an inequality, letting x be the size of the flower bed. For Elise's services to be a better deal, they must cost less than Max's:

$$30 + 0.055x < 26.25 + 0.065x$$

We solve for x by subtracting 0.055x and 26.25 from each side:

$$3.75 < 0.01x$$

We rewrite this as $0.01x > 3.75$ and divide each side by 0.01 to obtain $x > 375$. It is important to remember to reverse the inequality sign when we move the x to the left so we don't end up with $x < 375$ (answer choice B).

19. Choice D is correct. For Rylie to make \$75 in profit, she needs to earn $75 + 12 = \$87$ to compensate for her overhead costs. We can calculate the amount she will earn by weeding the garden: $0.05(1000) = \$50$. We subtract this from \$87 to find that she needs to earn an additional \$37 from mowing and edging the lawn. Letting the size of the lawn be x, we can write out our equation: $0.003x + 0.002x = 37$. This simplifies to $0.005x = 37$. We divide each side by 0.005 to find that $x = 7400$. So, the lawn needs to be at least 7,400 square feet. Answer choice A is incorrect because it mistakenly subtracts the overhead rather than adding it to the \$75 to be earned. Choice B is incorrect because it does not take into account the overhead, simply using \$75 as the total to be earned.

20. Choice A is correct. We begin by solving the inequality for a. First, we subtract 3 from each side: $4a \leq -2$. Then we divide each side by 4 and reduce: $a \leq -\frac{1}{2}$. So, $-\frac{1}{2}$ is the greatest possible value for a. We plug this value into $6a - 2$ to yield $6\left(-\frac{1}{2}\right) - 2 = -3 - 2 = -5$. Answer choices B, C, and D are incorrect because they give impossibly high values.

21. Choice B is correct. The point marked on the scatterplot for the final day shows that Julio practiced for 3 hours, while the line of best fit crosses the 2-hour mark on the same day. The difference in 3 and 2 is 1 hour. Choice C is incorrect because it represents the amount predicted by the line of best fit rather than the difference. Choice D is incorrect because it represents the actual practice time rather than the difference.

22. Choice B is correct. We can let the other two numbers be n and p to solve the problem. We can now write:

$$m + n + p = 420$$

Since m is 25% less than $n + p$, we can say that:

$$m = 0.75(n + p) = \frac{3}{4}(n + p)$$

$$\frac{4}{3}m = n + p$$

So, we can substitute $\frac{4}{3}m$ for $n + p$ in the original equation:

$$m + \frac{4}{3}m = 420$$
$$\frac{7}{3}m = 420$$
$$m = 180$$

Choice C is incorrect because it is the sum of n and p rather than m.

23. Choice C is correct. If the sine of one angle is equal to the cosine of another, this means that the two angles are complementary. Complementary angles add up to 90°. So, $m + n = 90$, and therefore $(3x + 12) + (-x + 32) = 90$. We combine like terms to obtain $2x + 44 = 90$. We subtract 44 from each side: $2x = 46$. Finally, we divide each side by 2 to find that $x = 23$. Choice A is incorrect because it is obtained by setting m and n equal to each other. Choice B is incorrect because it is the value of n. Choice D is incorrect because it is the value of m.

24. Choice D is correct. The equation of a circle is $(x - h)^2 + (y - k)^2 = r^2$, where r is the radius. We need to put the equation in this form to solve for r. First, we separate the x- and y-terms and then we complete the square:

$$(x^2 - 4x) + (y^2 + 2y) = 4$$

$$(x^2 - 4x + 4) - 4 + (y^2 + 2y + 1) - 1 = 4$$

$$(x - 2)^2 + (y + 1)^2 - 5 = 4$$

$$(x - 2)^2 + (y + 1)^2 = 9$$

$$(x - 2)^2 + (y + 1)^2 = 3^2$$

Thus, we can see that the radius is 3 (be careful not to mistakenly choose answer choice B). Since the diameter is twice the radius, we multiply 3 by 2 to obtain 6.

25. Choice B is correct. If $k > 0$, the x-intercept is positive, lying on the x-axis between the 1st and 4th quadrants. If $m > 0$, the y-intercept is also positive, lying on the y-axis between the 1st and 2nd quadrants. For any value of k and m, the slope of the graph will be drawn downward from left to right, so it will be negative. Choice A is incorrect because it would require either k or m to be negative. Choice C is incorrect because it would require k to be 0. Choice D is incorrect because it would require m to be 0.

26. Choice A is correct. The perpendicular bisector of a line segment crosses the midpoint of the line segment at a 90° angle. We can find the midpoint of $(-3, 1)$ and $(4, 0)$ by adding the x-terms and dividing by 2, and doing the same with the y-terms. To find the x-coordinate: $\frac{-3+4}{2} = \frac{1}{2}$. To find the y-coordinate: $\frac{1+0}{2} = \frac{1}{2}$. So, point D is located at $(\frac{1}{2}, \frac{1}{2})$. The slope of the line that passes through A and B can be found by dividing the difference in the y-values by the difference in the x-values: $\frac{1-0}{-3-4} = -\frac{1}{7}$. Since CD is perpendicular to AB, the slope of CD is the negative reciprocal of AB's slope, or 7. Now that we have the slope and a point, we can solve for the equation of the line by plugging in the x- and y-values to the point-slope form of the equation: $y - \frac{1}{2} = 7(x - \frac{1}{2})$. We multiply through on the right side of the equation and add $\frac{1}{2}$ to each side: $y = 7x - \frac{7}{2} + \frac{1}{2}$. So, the equation of the line is $y = 7x - 3$.

27. Choice D is correct. Last year's profit was \$55,000, and this year's was 20% greater than that. We add 20% by multiplying by 0.2 and adding to the original number, or simply multiplying by 1.2. This gives us a current year profit of $55,000(1.2) = \$66,000$. We multiply by 1.2 again to project next year's profit: $66,000(1.2) = \$79,200$. Choice A is incorrect because it is equal to this year's projected profit. Choice B is incorrect because it applies the wrong multiplier to this year's profit. Choice C is incorrect because it adds 20% of last year's profit instead of 20% of this year's profit.

28. Choice D is correct. We can graph the two lines on a coordinate plane by plotting the y-intercept and then finding another point based on the slope. For the first equation, the y-intercept is $-\frac{3}{2}$, so we plot the point $(0, -\frac{3}{2})$. Then we use the slope $(\frac{2}{3})$ to plot another point by moving up 2 and 3 to the right, to $(3, \frac{1}{2})$. Now we can draw a line passing through the two points. It is a solid line because the solution is less than or equal to the equation. Next, we graph the second line. The y-intercept is $-\frac{5}{2}$, so we plot the point $(0, -\frac{5}{2})$. Then we use the slope (-2) to plot another point by moving down 2 and over 1, to $(1, -\frac{9}{2})$. Now we can draw a line passing through the two points. It is also a solid line because the solution is less than or equal to the equation. We shade the area that is both below the graph of the first line and above the graph of the second line. When we do this, we can see that the overlap of the shaded area in Quadrants I, III, and IV.

29. Choice C is correct. The mean, or average, can be found by adding all of the numbers and dividing by how many there are. So, $x = \frac{a+12}{2}$, $y = \frac{3a+5}{2}$, and $z = \frac{5a-2}{2}$. To find the mean of x, y, and z, we add x, y, and z and divide by 3. So, we first add the three fractions. Since they have a common denominator, we can add the numerators and divide by 2: $\frac{a+12+3a+5+5a-2}{2} = \frac{9a+15}{2}$. To divide by 3, we multiply by $\frac{1}{3}$:

$$\frac{9a+15}{2} \times \frac{1}{3} = \frac{9a+15}{6}$$

Finally, we divide each term by 3 to reduce: $\frac{3a+5}{2}$.

30. Choice C is correct. We first simplify by dividing each term by 2: $y = x^2 - 4m$. Now we check to see if the equation can be factored. The square root of x^2 is x, so we can factor into two x-terms, leaving one blank positive term and one blank negative term so that they will multiply to be a negative term: $(x+?)(x-?)$. Now we see if we can factor $-4m$. Since there are no "middle terms" in the equation, the two roots must be equal but opposite in sign so that they cancel out when they are added. The root of 4 is 2, and the root of m is $\sqrt{m}$, so one of the terms is $2\sqrt{m}$ and the other term is $-2\sqrt{m}$. So we can write the equation as $y = (x + 2\sqrt{m})(x - 2\sqrt{m})$. Choice A is incorrect because it gives equal positive roots and does not factor the $2m$. Choice B is incorrect because it does not correctly take the root of $2m$. Choice D is incorrect because it does not factor the $2m$.

31. The correct answer is 14.4 or $\frac{72}{5}$. When two numbers are inversely proportional, this means that one rises as the other falls, and they always multiply to equal the same amount. We can set up an equation: $r_1 t_1 = r_2 t_2$, where r = rate and t = time. Now we can plug in the values we know: $24(120) = r_2(200)$. We can then divide both sides by 200 to solve: $r_2 = \frac{24(120)}{200} = 14.4$ or $\frac{72}{5}$.

32. The correct answer is 12. If $AC = BD$, we can write $AB + BC = BC + CD$. We can eliminate the BC term from each side, simplifying to $AB = CD$. We then substitute the x-terms:

$$x - 1 = 2x - 9$$

Moving x-values to the left and numerical values to the right yields $-x = -8$, or $x = 8$. Now we can solve for BC:

$$3(8) - 12 = 24 - 12 = 12$$

33. The correct answer is 18. We can set up a ratio to solve:

$$\frac{12 \text{ ft}}{3 \text{ in}} = \frac{x \text{ ft}}{4.5 \text{ in}}$$

We note that the real measurements are in feet and the scale measurements are in inches. As long as we keep our ratios correct, the dimensions will not matter. We can cross-multiply:

$$3x = 12(4.5)$$
$$x = \frac{54}{3}$$
$$x = 18$$

So, the living room is 18 feet long.

34. The correct answer is 1 or 2. We can choose any value between 1.2 and 1.5 to use as our diameter. The formula for volume of a sphere is $V = \frac{4}{3}\pi r^3$, so the first step is to find the radius, dividing the diameter by 2. If we choose the smallest value, our diameter is $1.2 \div 2 = 0.6$. We then can calculate volume: $\frac{4}{3}\pi(0.6)^3$, which is approximately equal to 0.9. Rounding to the nearest cubic inch gives us 1 in³. If we choose the largest value, our diameter is $1.5 \div 2 = 0.75$. We then can calculate volume: $\frac{4}{3}\pi(0.75)^3$, which is approximately equal to 1.8. Rounding to the nearest cubic inch gives us 2 in³. Since any possible answer will be between these two values, either 1 or 2 is a correct answer.

35. The correct answer is 2. We can find the points of intersection by setting the two equations equal to each other:

$$2x^2 + 3x = -x$$

We combine like terms by adding x to each side:

$$2x^2 + 4x = 0$$

We can factor into:

$$(2x)(x + 2) = 0$$

Setting the first term equal to 0 yields: $2x = 0$. Thus, $x = 0$. This corresponds with the point we were given, (0, 0). Now we set the second term equal to 0: $x + 2 = 0$. We subtract 2 from each side to yield $x = -2$. This is a. To find b, we plug in –2 for x to either of the two equations and solve for y. Using the second equation: $y = -(-2)$, or $y = 2$. So, our point is (–2, 2) and $b = 2$.

36. The correct answer is 28. First, we find the mean of the strawberries since we have all of the necessary information. We add the number of strawberries in each basket and divide by 8, since there are 8 baskets:

$$\frac{14 + 13 + 16 + 15 + 13 + 14 + 14 + 13}{8} = \frac{112}{8} = 14$$

If 14 is 13 less than the mean of the raspberries, we add 13 to 14 to find that the mean of the raspberries is 27. Now we can solve for x:

$$\frac{26 + 25 + 23 + 27 + 28 + 30 + 29 + x}{8} = 27$$

We add the numbers in the numerator and multiply both sides by 8 to obtain: $188 + x = 216$

Finally, we subtract 188 from each side to find that $x = 28$.

37. The correct answer is $\frac{1}{2}$. We need to rewrite the equation to be in circle form:

$$(x - h)^2 + (y - k)^2 = r^2$$

First, we isolate the x- and y-terms:

$$(x^2 - 6x) + (y^2 - y) = -\frac{21}{4}$$

Next, we can complete the square to simplify the equation:

$$(x^2 - 6x + 9) - 9 + \left(y^2 - y + \frac{1}{4}\right) - \frac{1}{4} = -\frac{21}{4}$$

$$(x - 3)^2 + \left(y - \frac{1}{2}\right)^2 - \frac{37}{4} = -\frac{21}{4}$$

$$(x - 3)^2 + \left(y - \frac{1}{2}\right)^2 = \frac{16}{4} = 4$$

Now we can solve for the center point of the circle by setting the parts of the equations in parentheses equal to 0:

$$x - 3 = 0 \text{ becomes } x = 3$$

$$y - \frac{1}{2} = 0 \text{ becomes } y = \frac{1}{2}$$

So, the coordinates of the center are $(3, \frac{1}{2})$, meaning that the y-coordinate is $\frac{1}{2}$.

38. The correct answer is 10. Since the population is multiplied by 3 for 5 days, we can write $x(3^5) = 2430$, where x is the original population. We calculate 3^5 and simplify the equation to: $243x = 2430$. Dividing each side by 243 yields $x = 10$. So the original population was 10.

How to Overcome Test Anxiety

Just the thought of taking a test is enough to make most people a little nervous. A test is an important event that can have a long-term impact on your future, so it's important to take it seriously and it's natural to feel anxious about performing well. But just because anxiety is normal, that doesn't mean that it's helpful in test taking, or that you should simply accept it as part of your life. Anxiety can have a variety of effects. These effects can be mild, like making you feel slightly nervous, or severe, like blocking your ability to focus or remember even a simple detail.

If you experience test anxiety—whether severe or mild—it's important to know how to beat it. To discover this, first you need to understand what causes test anxiety.

Causes of Test Anxiety

While we often think of anxiety as an uncontrollable emotional state, it can actually be caused by simple, practical things. One of the most common causes of test anxiety is that a person does not feel adequately prepared for their test. This feeling can be the result of many different issues such as poor study habits or lack of organization, but the most common culprit is time management. Starting to study too late, failing to organize your study time to cover all of the material, or being distracted while you study will mean that you're not well prepared for the test. This may lead to cramming the night before, which will cause you to be physically and mentally exhausted for the test. Poor time management also contributes to feelings of stress, fear, and hopelessness as you realize you are not well prepared but don't know what to do about it.

Other times, test anxiety is not related to your preparation for the test but comes from unresolved fear. This may be a past failure on a test, or poor performance on tests in general. It may come from comparing yourself to others who seem to be performing better or from the stress of living up to expectations. Anxiety may be driven by fears of the future—how failure on this test would affect your educational and career goals. These fears are often completely irrational, but they can still negatively impact your test performance.

> **Review Video: <u>3 Reasons You Have Test Anxiety</u>**
> Visit mometrix.com/academy and enter code: 428468

Elements of Test Anxiety

As mentioned earlier, test anxiety is considered to be an emotional state, but it has physical and mental components as well. Sometimes you may not even realize that you are suffering from test anxiety until you notice the physical symptoms. These can include trembling hands, rapid heartbeat, sweating, nausea, and tense muscles. Extreme anxiety may lead to fainting or vomiting. Obviously, any of these symptoms can have a negative impact on testing. It is important to recognize them as soon as they begin to occur so that you can address the problem before it damages your performance.

> **Review Video: 3 Ways to Tell You Have Test Anxiety**
> Visit mometrix.com/academy and enter code: 927847

The mental components of test anxiety include trouble focusing and inability to remember learned information. During a test, your mind is on high alert, which can help you recall information and stay focused for an extended period of time. However, anxiety interferes with your mind's natural processes, causing you to blank out, even on the questions you know well. The strain of testing during anxiety makes it difficult to stay focused, especially on a test that may take several hours. Extreme anxiety can take a huge mental toll, making it difficult not only to recall test information but even to understand the test questions or pull your thoughts together.

> **Review Video: How Test Anxiety Affects Memory**
> Visit mometrix.com/academy and enter code: 609003

Effects of Test Anxiety

Test anxiety is like a disease—if left untreated, it will get progressively worse. Anxiety leads to poor performance, and this reinforces the feelings of fear and failure, which in turn lead to poor performances on subsequent tests. It can grow from a mild nervousness to a crippling condition. If allowed to progress, test anxiety can have a big impact on your schooling, and consequently on your future.

Test anxiety can spread to other parts of your life. Anxiety on tests can become anxiety in any stressful situation, and blanking on a test can turn into panicking in a job situation. But fortunately, you don't have to let anxiety rule your testing and determine your grades. There are a number of relatively simple steps you can take to move past anxiety and function normally on a test and in the rest of life.

> **Review Video: How Test Anxiety Impacts Your Grades**
> Visit mometrix.com/academy and enter code: 939819

Physical Steps for Beating Test Anxiety

While test anxiety is a serious problem, the good news is that it can be overcome. It doesn't have to control your ability to think and remember information. While it may take time, you can begin taking steps today to beat anxiety.

Just as your first hint that you may be struggling with anxiety comes from the physical symptoms, the first step to treating it is also physical. Rest is crucial for having a clear, strong mind. If you are tired, it is much easier to give in to anxiety. But if you establish good sleep habits, your body and mind will be ready to perform optimally, without the strain of exhaustion. Additionally, sleeping well helps you to retain information better, so you're more likely to recall the answers when you see the test questions.

Getting good sleep means more than going to bed on time. It's important to allow your brain time to relax. Take study breaks from time to time so it doesn't get overworked, and don't study right before bed. Take time to rest your mind before trying to rest your body, or you may find it difficult to fall asleep.

Review Video: The Importance of Sleep for Your Brain
Visit mometrix.com/academy and enter code: 319338

Along with sleep, other aspects of physical health are important in preparing for a test. Good nutrition is vital for good brain function. Sugary foods and drinks may give a burst of energy but this burst is followed by a crash, both physically and emotionally. Instead, fuel your body with protein and vitamin-rich foods.

Also, drink plenty of water. Dehydration can lead to headaches and exhaustion, especially if your brain is already under stress from the rigors of the test. Particularly if your test is a long one, drink water during the breaks. And if possible, take an energy-boosting snack to eat between sections.

Review Video: How Diet Can Affect your Mood
Visit mometrix.com/academy and enter code: 624317

Along with sleep and diet, a third important part of physical health is exercise. Maintaining a steady workout schedule is helpful, but even taking 5-minute study breaks to walk can help get your blood pumping faster and clear your head. Exercise also releases endorphins, which contribute to a positive feeling and can help combat test anxiety.

When you nurture your physical health, you are also contributing to your mental health. If your body is healthy, your mind is much more likely to be healthy as well. So take time to rest, nourish your body with healthy food and water, and get moving as much as possible. Taking these physical steps will make you stronger and more able to take the mental steps necessary to overcome test anxiety.

Review Video: How to Stay Healthy and Prevent Test Anxiety
Visit mometrix.com/academy and enter code: 877894

Mental Steps for Beating Test Anxiety

Working on the mental side of test anxiety can be more challenging, but as with the physical side, there are clear steps you can take to overcome it. As mentioned earlier, test anxiety often stems from lack of preparation, so the obvious solution is to prepare for the test. Effective studying may be the most important weapon you have for beating test anxiety, but you can and should employ several other mental tools to combat fear.

First, boost your confidence by reminding yourself of past success—tests or projects that you aced. If you're putting as much effort into preparing for this test as you did for those, there's no reason you should expect to fail here. Work hard to prepare; then trust your preparation.

Second, surround yourself with encouraging people. It can be helpful to find a study group, but be sure that the people you're around will encourage a positive attitude. If you spend time with others who are anxious or cynical, this will only contribute to your own anxiety. Look for others who are motivated to study hard from a desire to succeed, not from a fear of failure.

Third, reward yourself. A test is physically and mentally tiring, even without anxiety, and it can be helpful to have something to look forward to. Plan an activity following the test, regardless of the outcome, such as going to a movie or getting ice cream.

When you are taking the test, if you find yourself beginning to feel anxious, remind yourself that you know the material. Visualize successfully completing the test. Then take a few deep, relaxing breaths and return to it. Work through the questions carefully but with confidence, knowing that you are capable of succeeding.

Developing a healthy mental approach to test taking will also aid in other areas of life. Test anxiety affects more than just the actual test—it can be damaging to your mental health and even contribute to depression. It's important to beat test anxiety before it becomes a problem for more than testing.

Review Video: Test Anxiety and Depression
Visit mometrix.com/academy and enter code: 904704

Study Strategy

Being prepared for the test is necessary to combat anxiety, but what does being prepared look like? You may study for hours on end and still not feel prepared. What you need is a strategy for test prep. The next few pages outline our recommended steps to help you plan out and conquer the challenge of preparation.

STEP 1: SCOPE OUT THE TEST

Learn everything you can about the format (multiple choice, essay, etc.) and what will be on the test. Gather any study materials, course outlines, or sample exams that may be available. Not only will this help you to prepare, but knowing what to expect can help to alleviate test anxiety.

STEP 2: MAP OUT THE MATERIAL

Look through the textbook or study guide and make note of how many chapters or sections it has. Then divide these over the time you have. For example, if a book has 15 chapters and you have five days to study, you need to cover three chapters each day. Even better, if you have the time, leave an extra day at the end for overall review after you have gone through the material in depth.

If time is limited, you may need to prioritize the material. Look through it and make note of which sections you think you already have a good grasp on, and which need review. While you are studying, skim quickly through the familiar sections and take more time on the challenging parts. Write out your plan so you don't get lost as you go. Having a written plan also helps you feel more in control of the study, so anxiety is less likely to arise from feeling overwhelmed at the amount to cover.

STEP 3: GATHER YOUR TOOLS

Decide what study method works best for you. Do you prefer to highlight in the book as you study and then go back over the highlighted portions? Or do you type out notes of the important information? Or is it helpful to make flashcards that you can carry with you? Assemble the pens, index cards, highlighters, post-it notes, and any other materials you may need so you won't be distracted by getting up to find things while you study.

If you're having a hard time retaining the information or organizing your notes, experiment with different methods. For example, try color-coding by subject with colored pens, highlighters, or post-it notes. If you learn better by hearing, try recording yourself reading your notes so you can listen while in the car, working out, or simply sitting at your desk. Ask a friend to quiz you from your flashcards, or try teaching someone the material to solidify it in your mind.

STEP 4: CREATE YOUR ENVIRONMENT

It's important to avoid distractions while you study. This includes both the obvious distractions like visitors and the subtle distractions like an uncomfortable chair (or a too-comfortable couch that makes you want to fall asleep). Set up the best study environment possible: good lighting and a comfortable work area. If background music helps you focus, you may want to turn it on, but otherwise keep the room quiet. If you are using a computer to take notes, be sure you don't have any other windows open, especially applications like social media, games, or anything else that could distract you. Silence your phone and turn off notifications. Be sure to keep water close by so you stay hydrated while you study (but avoid unhealthy drinks and snacks).

Also, take into account the best time of day to study. Are you freshest first thing in the morning? Try to set aside some time then to work through the material. Is your mind clearer in the afternoon or evening? Schedule your study session then. Another method is to study at the same time of day that you will take the test, so that your brain gets used to working on the material at that time and will be ready to focus at test time.

STEP 5: STUDY!

Once you have done all the study preparation, it's time to settle into the actual studying. Sit down, take a few moments to settle your mind so you can focus, and begin to follow your study plan. Don't give in to distractions or let yourself procrastinate. This is your time to prepare so you'll be ready to fearlessly approach the test. Make the most of the time and stay focused.

Of course, you don't want to burn out. If you study too long you may find that you're not retaining the information very well. Take regular study breaks. For example, taking five minutes out of every hour to walk briskly, breathing deeply and swinging your arms, can help your mind stay fresh.

As you get to the end of each chapter or section, it's a good idea to do a quick review. Remind yourself of what you learned and work on any difficult parts. When you feel that you've mastered the material, move on to the next part. At the end of your study session, briefly skim through your notes again.

But while review is helpful, cramming last minute is NOT. If at all possible, work ahead so that you won't need to fit all your study into the last day. Cramming overloads your brain with more information than it can process and retain, and your tired mind may struggle to recall even previously learned information when it is overwhelmed with last-minute study. Also, the urgent nature of cramming and the stress placed on your brain contribute to anxiety. You'll be more likely to go to the test feeling unprepared and having trouble thinking clearly.

So don't cram, and don't stay up late before the test, even just to review your notes at a leisurely pace. Your brain needs rest more than it needs to go over the information again. In fact, plan to finish your studies by noon or early afternoon the day before the test. Give your brain the rest of the day to relax or focus on other things, and get a good night's sleep. Then you will be fresh for the test and better able to recall what you've studied.

STEP 6: TAKE A PRACTICE TEST

Many courses offer sample tests, either online or in the study materials. This is an excellent resource to check whether you have mastered the material, as well as to prepare for the test format and environment.

Check the test format ahead of time: the number of questions, the type (multiple choice, free response, etc.), and the time limit. Then create a plan for working through them. For example, if you have 30 minutes to take a 60-question test, your limit is 30 seconds per question. Spend less time on the questions you know well so that you can take more time on the difficult ones.

If you have time to take several practice tests, take the first one open book, with no time limit. Work through the questions at your own pace and make sure you fully understand them. Gradually work up to taking a test under test conditions: sit at a desk with all study materials put away and set a timer. Pace yourself to make sure you finish the test with time to spare and go back to check your answers if you have time.

After each test, check your answers. On the questions you missed, be sure you understand why you missed them. Did you misread the question (tests can use tricky wording)? Did you forget the information? Or was it something you hadn't learned? Go back and study any shaky areas that the practice tests reveal.

Taking these tests not only helps with your grade, but also aids in combating test anxiety. If you're already used to the test conditions, you're less likely to worry about it, and working through tests until you're scoring well gives you a confidence boost. Go through the practice tests until you feel comfortable, and then you can go into the test knowing that you're ready for it.

Test Tips

On test day, you should be confident, knowing that you've prepared well and are ready to answer the questions. But aside from preparation, there are several test day strategies you can employ to maximize your performance.

First, as stated before, get a good night's sleep the night before the test (and for several nights before that, if possible). Go into the test with a fresh, alert mind rather than staying up late to study.

Try not to change too much about your normal routine on the day of the test. It's important to eat a nutritious breakfast, but if you normally don't eat breakfast at all, consider eating just a protein bar. If you're a coffee drinker, go ahead and have your normal coffee. Just make sure you time it so that the caffeine doesn't wear off right in the middle of your test. Avoid sugary beverages, and drink enough water to stay hydrated but not so much that you need a restroom break 10 minutes into the test. If your test isn't first thing in the morning, consider going for a walk or doing a light workout before the test to get your blood flowing.

Allow yourself enough time to get ready, and leave for the test with plenty of time to spare so you won't have the anxiety of scrambling to arrive in time. Another reason to be early is to select a good seat. It's helpful to sit away from doors and windows, which can be distracting. Find a good seat, get out your supplies, and settle your mind before the test begins.

When the test begins, start by going over the instructions carefully, even if you already know what to expect. Make sure you avoid any careless mistakes by following the directions.

Then begin working through the questions, pacing yourself as you've practiced. If you're not sure on an answer, don't spend too much time on it, and don't let it shake your confidence. Either skip it and come back later, or eliminate as many wrong answers as possible and guess among the remaining ones. Don't dwell on these questions as you continue—put them out of your mind and focus on what lies ahead.

Be sure to read all of the answer choices, even if you're sure the first one is the right answer. Sometimes you'll find a better one if you keep reading. But don't second-guess yourself if you do immediately know the answer. Your gut instinct is usually right. Don't let test anxiety rob you of the information you know.

If you have time at the end of the test (and if the test format allows), go back and review your answers. Be cautious about changing any, since your first instinct tends to be correct, but make sure you didn't misread any of the questions or accidentally mark the wrong answer choice. Look over any you skipped and make an educated guess.

At the end, leave the test feeling confident. You've done your best, so don't waste time worrying about your performance or wishing you could change anything. Instead, celebrate the successful

completion of this test. And finally, use this test to learn how to deal with anxiety even better next time.

> **Review Video: 5 Tips to Beat Test Anxiety**
> Visit mometrix.com/academy and enter code: 570656

Important Qualification

Not all anxiety is created equal. If your test anxiety is causing major issues in your life beyond the classroom or testing center, or if you are experiencing troubling physical symptoms related to your anxiety, it may be a sign of a serious physiological or psychological condition. If this sounds like your situation, we strongly encourage you to seek professional help.

How to Overcome Your Fear of Math

The word *math* is enough to strike fear into most hearts. How many of us have memories of sitting through confusing lectures, wrestling over mind-numbing homework, or taking tests that still seem incomprehensible even after hours of study? Years after graduation, many still shudder at these memories.

The fact is, math is not just a classroom subject. It has real-world implications that you face every day, whether you realize it or not. This may be balancing your monthly budget, deciding how many supplies to buy for a project, or simply splitting a meal check with friends. The idea of daily confrontations with math can be so paralyzing that some develop a condition known as *math anxiety*.

But you do NOT need to be paralyzed by this anxiety! In fact, while you may have thought all your life that you're not good at math, or that your brain isn't wired to understand it, the truth is that you may have been conditioned to think this way. From your earliest school days, the way you were taught affected the way you viewed different subjects. And the way math has been taught has changed.

Several decades ago, there was a shift in American math classrooms. The focus changed from traditional problem-solving to a conceptual view of topics, de-emphasizing the importance of learning the basics and building on them. The solid foundation necessary for math progression and confidence was undermined. Math became more of a vague concept than a concrete idea. Today, it is common to think of math, not as a straightforward system, but as a mysterious, complicated method that can't be fully understood unless you're a genius.

This is why you may still have nightmares about being called on to answer a difficult problem in front of the class. Math anxiety is a very real, though unnecessary, fear.

Math anxiety may begin with a single class period. Let's say you missed a day in 6th grade math and never quite understood the concept that was taught while you were gone. Since math is cumulative, with each new concept building on past ones, this could very well affect the rest of your math career. Without that one day's knowledge, it will be difficult to understand any other concepts that link to it. Rather than realizing that you're just missing one key piece, you may begin to believe that you're simply not capable of understanding math.

This belief can change the way you approach other classes, career options, and everyday life experiences, if you become anxious at the thought that math might be required. A student who loves science may choose a different path of study upon realizing that multiple math classes will be required for a degree. An aspiring medical student may hesitate at the thought of going through the necessary math classes. For some this anxiety escalates into a more extreme state known as *math phobia*.

Math anxiety is challenging to address because it is rooted deeply and may come from a variety of causes: an embarrassing moment in class, a teacher who did not explain concepts well and contributed to a shaky foundation, or a failed test that contributed to the belief of math failure.

These causes add up over time, encouraged by society's popular view that math is hard and unpleasant. Eventually a person comes to firmly believe that he or she is simply bad at math. This belief makes it difficult to grasp new concepts or even remember old ones. Homework and test

Copyright © Mometrix Media. You have been licensed one copy of this document for personal use only. Any other reproduction or redistribution is strictly prohibited. All rights reserved.

grades begin to slip, which only confirms the belief. The poor performance is not due to lack of ability but is caused by math anxiety.

Math anxiety is an emotional issue, not a lack of intelligence. But when it becomes deeply rooted, it can become more than just an emotional problem. Physical symptoms appear. Blood pressure may rise and heartbeat may quicken at the sight of a math problem – or even the thought of math! This fear leads to a mental block. When someone with math anxiety is asked to perform a calculation, even a basic problem can seem overwhelming and impossible. The emotional and physical response to the thought of math prevents the brain from working through it logically.

The more this happens, the more a person's confidence drops, and the more math anxiety is generated. This vicious cycle must be broken!

The first step in breaking the cycle is to go back to very beginning and make sure you really understand the basics of how math works and why it works. It is not enough to memorize rules for multiplication and division. If you don't know WHY these rules work, your foundation will be shaky and you will be at risk of developing a phobia. Understanding mathematical concepts not only promotes confidence and security, but allows you to build on this understanding for new concepts. Additionally, you can solve unfamiliar problems using familiar concepts and processes.

Why is it that students in other countries regularly outperform American students in math? The answer likely boils down to a couple of things: the foundation of mathematical conceptual understanding and societal perception. While students in the US are not expected to *like* or *get* math, in many other nations, students are expected not only to understand math but also to excel at it.

Changing the American view of math that leads to math anxiety is a monumental task. It requires changing the training of teachers nationwide, from kindergarten through high school, so that they learn to teach the *why* behind math and to combat the wrong math views that students may develop. It also involves changing the stigma associated with math, so that it is no longer viewed as unpleasant and incomprehensible. While these are necessary changes, they are challenging and will take time. But in the meantime, math anxiety is not irreversible—it can be faced and defeated, one person at a time.

False Beliefs

One reason math anxiety has taken such hold is that several false beliefs have been created and shared until they became widely accepted. Some of these unhelpful beliefs include the following:

There is only one way to solve a math problem. In the same way that you can choose from different driving routes and still arrive at the same house, you can solve a math problem using different methods and still find the correct answer. A person who understands the reasoning behind math calculations may be able to look at an unfamiliar concept and find the right answer, just by applying logic to the knowledge they already have. This approach may be different than what is taught in the classroom, but it is still valid. Unfortunately, even many teachers view math as a subject where the best course of action is to memorize the rule or process for each problem rather than as a place for students to exercise logic and creativity in finding a solution.

Many people don't have a mind for math. A person who has struggled due to poor teaching or math anxiety may falsely believe that he or she doesn't have the mental capacity to grasp mathematical concepts. Most of the time, this is false. Many people find that when they are relieved of their math anxiety, they have more than enough brainpower to understand math.

Men are naturally better at math than women. Even though research has shown this to be false, many young women still avoid math careers and classes because of their belief that their math abilities are inferior. Many girls have come to believe that math is a male skill and have given up trying to understand or enjoy it.

Counting aids are bad. Something like counting on your fingers or drawing out a problem to visualize it may be frowned on as childish or a crutch, but these devices can help you get a tangible understanding of a problem or a concept.

Sadly, many students buy into these ideologies at an early age. A young girl who enjoys math class may be conditioned to think that she doesn't actually have the brain for it because math is for boys, and may turn her energies to other pursuits, permanently closing the door on a wide range of opportunities. A child who finds the right answer but doesn't follow the teacher's method may believe that he is doing it wrong and isn't good at math. A student who never had a problem with math before may have a poor teacher and become confused, yet believe that the problem is because she doesn't have a mathematical mind.

Students who have bought into these erroneous beliefs quickly begin to add their own anxieties, adapting them to their own personal situations:

I'll never use this in real life. A huge number of people wrongly believe that math is irrelevant outside the classroom. By adopting this mindset, they are handicapping themselves for a life in a mathematical world, as well as limiting their career choices. When they are inevitably faced with real-world math, they are conditioning themselves to respond with anxiety.

I'm not quick enough. While timed tests and quizzes, or even simply comparing yourself with other students in the class, can lead to this belief, speed is not an indicator of skill level. A person can work very slowly yet understand at a deep level.

If I can understand it, it's too easy. People with a low view of their own abilities tend to think that if they are able to grasp a concept, it must be simple. They cannot accept the idea that they are capable of understanding math. This belief will make it harder to learn, no matter how intelligent they are.

I just can't learn this. An overwhelming number of people think this, from young children to adults, and much of the time it is simply not true. But this mindset can turn into a self-fulfilling prophecy that keeps you from exercising and growing your math ability.

The good news is, each of these myths can be debunked. For most people, they are based on emotion and psychology, NOT on actual ability! It will take time, effort, and the desire to change, but change is possible. Even if you have spent years thinking that you don't have the capability to understand math, it is not too late to uncover your true ability and find relief from the anxiety that surrounds math.

Math Strategies

It is important to have a plan of attack to combat math anxiety. There are many useful strategies for pinpointing the fears or myths and eradicating them:

Go back to the basics. For most people, math anxiety stems from a poor foundation. You may think that you have a complete understanding of addition and subtraction, or even decimals and percentages, but make absolutely sure. Learning math is different from learning other subjects. For example, when you learn history, you study various time periods and places and events. It may be important to memorize dates or find out about the lives of famous people. When you move from US history to world history, there will be some overlap, but a large amount of the information will be new. Mathematical concepts, on the other hand, are very closely linked and highly dependent on each other. It's like climbing a ladder – if a rung is missing from your understanding, it may be difficult or impossible for you to climb any higher, no matter how hard you try. So go back and make sure your math foundation is strong. This may mean taking a remedial math course, going to a tutor to work through the shaky concepts, or just going through your old homework to make sure you really understand it.

Speak the language. Math has a large vocabulary of terms and phrases unique to working problems. Sometimes these are completely new terms, and sometimes they are common words, but are used differently in a math setting. If you can't speak the language, it will be very difficult to get a thorough understanding of the concepts. It's common for students to think that they don't understand math when they simply don't understand the vocabulary. The good news is that this is fairly easy to fix. Brushing up on any terms you aren't quite sure of can help bring the rest of the concepts into focus.

Check your anxiety level. When you think about math, do you feel nervous or uncomfortable? Do you struggle with feelings of inadequacy, even on concepts that you know you've already learned? It's important to understand your specific math anxieties, and what triggers them. When you catch yourself falling back on a false belief, mentally replace it with the truth. Don't let yourself believe that you can't learn, or that struggling with a concept means you'll never understand it. Instead, remind yourself of how much you've already learned and dwell on that past success. Visualize grasping the new concept, linking it to your old knowledge, and moving on to the next challenge. Also, learn how to manage anxiety when it arises. There are many techniques for coping with the irrational fears that rise to the surface when you enter the math classroom. This may include controlled breathing, replacing negative thoughts with positive ones, or visualizing success. Anxiety interferes with your ability to concentrate and absorb information, which in turn contributes to greater anxiety. If you can learn how to regain control of your thinking, you will be better able to pay attention, make progress, and succeed!

Don't go it alone. Like any deeply ingrained belief, math anxiety is not easy to eradicate. And there is no need for you to wrestle through it on your own. It will take time, and many people find that speaking with a counselor or psychiatrist helps. They can help you develop strategies for responding to anxiety and overcoming old ideas. Additionally, it can be very helpful to take a short course or seek out a math tutor to help you find and fix the missing rungs on your ladder and make sure that you're ready to progress to the next level. You can also find a number of math aids online: courses that will teach you mental devices for figuring out problems, how to get the most out of your math classes, etc.

Check your math attitude. No matter how much you want to learn and overcome your anxiety, you'll have trouble if you still have a negative attitude toward math. If you think it's too hard, or just have general feelings of dread about math, it will be hard to learn and to break through the anxiety. Work on cultivating a positive math attitude. Remind yourself that math is not just a hurdle to be cleared, but a valuable asset. When you view math with a positive attitude, you'll be much more likely to understand and even enjoy it. This is something you must do for yourself. You may find it helpful to visit with a counselor. Your tutor, friends, and family may cheer you on in your endeavors. But your greatest asset is yourself. You are inside your own mind – tell yourself what you need to hear. Relive past victories. Remind yourself that you are capable of understanding math. Root out any false beliefs that linger and replace them with positive truths. Even if it doesn't feel true at first, it will begin to affect your thinking and pave the way for a positive, anxiety-free mindset.

Aside from these general strategies, there are a number of specific practical things you can do to begin your journey toward overcoming math anxiety. Something as simple as learning a new note-taking strategy can change the way you approach math and give you more confidence and understanding. New study techniques can also make a huge difference.

Math anxiety leads to bad habits. If it causes you to be afraid of answering a question in class, you may gravitate toward the back row. You may be embarrassed to ask for help. And you may procrastinate on assignments, which leads to rushing through them at the last moment when it's too late to get a better understanding. It's important to identify your negative behaviors and replace them with positive ones:

Prepare ahead of time. Read the lesson before you go to class. Being exposed to the topics that will be covered in class ahead of time, even if you don't understand them perfectly, is extremely helpful in increasing what you retain from the lecture. Do your homework and, if you're still shaky, go over some extra problems. The key to a solid understanding of math is practice.

Sit front and center. When you can easily see and hear, you'll understand more, and you'll avoid the distractions of other students if no one is in front of you. Plus, you're more likely to be sitting with students who are positive and engaged, rather than others with math anxiety. Let their positive math attitude rub off on you.

Ask questions in class and out. If you don't understand something, just ask. If you need a more in-depth explanation, the teacher may need to work with you outside of class, but often it's a simple concept you don't quite understand, and a single question may clear it up. If you wait, you may not be able to follow the rest of the day's lesson. For extra help, most professors have office hours outside of class when you can go over concepts one-on-one to clear up any uncertainties. Additionally, there may be a *math lab* or study session you can attend for homework help. Take advantage of this.

Review. Even if you feel that you've fully mastered a concept, review it periodically to reinforce it. Going over an old lesson has several benefits: solidifying your understanding, giving you a confidence boost, and even giving some new insights into material that you're currently learning! Don't let yourself get rusty. That can lead to problems with learning later concepts.

Teaching Tips

While the math student's mindset is the most crucial to overcoming math anxiety, it is also important for others to adjust their math attitudes. Teachers and parents have an enormous influence on how students relate to math. They can either contribute to math confidence or math anxiety.

As a parent or teacher, it is very important to convey a positive math attitude. Retelling horror stories of your own bad experience with math will contribute to a new generation of math anxiety. Even if you don't share your experiences, others will be able to sense your fears and may begin to believe them.

Even a careless comment can have a big impact, so watch for phrases like *He's not good at math* or *I never liked math*. You are a crucial role model, and your children or students will unconsciously adopt your mindset. Give them a positive example to follow. Rather than teaching them to fear the math world before they even know it, teach them about all its potential and excitement.

Work to present math as an integral, beautiful, and understandable part of life. Encourage creativity in solving problems. Watch for false beliefs and dispel them. Cross the lines between subjects: integrate history, English, and music with math. Show students how math is used every day, and how the entire world is based on mathematical principles, from the pull of gravity to the shape of seashells. Instead of letting students see math as a necessary evil, direct them to view it as an imaginative, beautiful art form – an art form that they are capable of mastering and using.

Don't give too narrow a view of math. It is more than just numbers. Yes, working problems and learning formulas is a large part of classroom math. But don't let the teaching stop there. Teach students about the everyday implications of math. Show them how nature works according to the laws of mathematics, and take them outside to make discoveries of their own. Expose them to math-related careers by inviting visiting speakers, asking students to do research and presentations, and learning students' interests and aptitudes on a personal level.

Demonstrate the importance of math. Many people see math as nothing more than a required stepping stone to their degree, a nuisance with no real usefulness. Teach students that algebra is used every day in managing their bank accounts, in following recipes, and in scheduling the day's events. Show them how learning to do geometric proofs helps them to develop logical thinking, an invaluable life skill. Let them see that math surrounds them and is integrally linked to their daily lives: that weather predictions are based on math, that math was used to design cars and other machines, etc. Most of all, give them the tools to use math to enrich their lives.

Make math as tangible as possible. Use visual aids and objects that can be touched. It is much easier to grasp a concept when you can hold it in your hands and manipulate it, rather than just listening to the lecture. Encourage math outside of the classroom. The real world is full of measuring, counting, and calculating, so let students participate in this. Keep your eyes open for numbers and patterns to discuss. Talk about how scores are calculated in sports games and how far apart plants are placed in a garden row for maximum growth. Build the mindset that math is a normal and interesting part of daily life.

Finally, find math resources that help to build a positive math attitude. There are a number of books that show math as fascinating and exciting while teaching important concepts, for example: *The Math Curse; A Wrinkle in Time; The Phantom Tollbooth;* and *Fractals, Googols and Other Mathematical Tales.* You can also find a number of online resources: math puzzles and games, videos that show math in nature, and communities of math enthusiasts. On a local level, students can compete in a variety of math competitions with other schools or join a math club.

The student who experiences math as exciting and interesting is unlikely to suffer from math anxiety. Going through life without this handicap is an immense advantage and opens many doors that others have closed through their fear.

Self-Check

Whether you suffer from math anxiety or not, chances are that you have been exposed to some of the false beliefs mentioned above. Now is the time to check yourself for any errors you may have accepted. Do you think you're not wired for math? Or that you don't need to understand it since you're not planning on a math career? Do you think math is just too difficult for the average person?

Find the errors you've taken to heart and replace them with positive thinking. Are you capable of learning math? Yes! Can you control your anxiety? Yes! These errors will resurface from time to time, so be watchful. Don't let others with math anxiety influence you or sway your confidence. If you're having trouble with a concept, find help. Don't let it discourage you!

Create a plan of attack for defeating math anxiety and sharpening your skills. Do some research and decide if it would help you to take a class, get a tutor, or find some online resources to fine-tune your knowledge. Make the effort to get good nutrition, hydration, and sleep so that you are operating at full capacity. Remind yourself daily that you are skilled and that anxiety does not control you. Your mind is capable of so much more than you know. Give it the tools it needs to grow and thrive.

Thank You

We at Mometrix would like to extend our heartfelt thanks to you, our friend and patron, for allowing us to play a part in your journey. It is a privilege to serve people from all walks of life who are unified in their commitment to building the best future they can for themselves.

The preparation you devote to these important testing milestones may be the most valuable educational opportunity you have for making a real difference in your life. We encourage you to put your heart into it—that feeling of succeeding, overcoming, and yes, conquering will be well worth the hours you've invested.

We want to hear your story, your struggles and your successes, and if you see any opportunities for us to improve our materials so we can help others even more effectively in the future, please share that with us as well. **The team at Mometrix would be absolutely thrilled to hear from you!** So please, send us an email (support@mometrix.com) and let's stay in touch.

> **If you'd like some additional help, check out these other resources we offer for your exam:**
> **http://MometrixFlashcards.com/SAT**

Additional Bonus Material

Due to our efforts to try to keep this book to a manageable length, we've created a link that will give you access to all of your additional bonus material.

Please visit http://www.mometrix.com/bonus948/sat to access the information.

Made in the USA
San Bernardino, CA
21 February 2020